Computer Graphics for Artists: An Introduction

Andrew Paquette

Computer Graphics for Artists:
An Introduction

 Springer

Andrew Paquette
School of Game Architecture and Design
Breda
The Netherlands

ISBN: 978-1-84800-140-4   e-ISBN: 978-1-84800-141-1
DOI: 10.1007/978-1-84800-141-1

British Library Cataloguing in Publication Data
A catalogue record for this book is available from the British Library

Library of Congress Control Number: 2008922190

All illustrations, unless stated otherwise, © 2007 Andrew Paquette

Cover Illustrations: Front cover: Heaven bound, © 2005 Andrew Paquette
Back cover: Nurbs motorcycle and render by Robert Joosten, freshman IGAD student

Printed on acid-free paper

9 8 7 6 5 4 3 2 1

Springer Science+Business Media
springer.com

Contents

List of Illustrations

Introduction

In 1435, the Italian scholar Leon Battista Alberti wrote a Latin treatise titled *De Pictura* (on painting). In 1436, it was translated into Italian and distributed. It is the first known publication on the subject of *linear perspective*, a subject very closely related to the very heart of modern computer graphics. The treatise was partly based on observations made by the great Florentine sculptor and architect Filippo Brunelleschi, though other artists from the same period were also experimenting with the technique. The Italian Renaissance in painting was to some considerable extent dependent on this major discovery.

Linear perspective demonstrated that a realistic representation of a 3D environment could be calculated based on rules that govern how our eyes see the world around us. Because these rules could be written down, and because they worked, innumerable artists were able to replicate the results Alberti described and linear perspective became a standard tool for most artists all the way up to the present day (Figs. 0.1 and 0.2).

 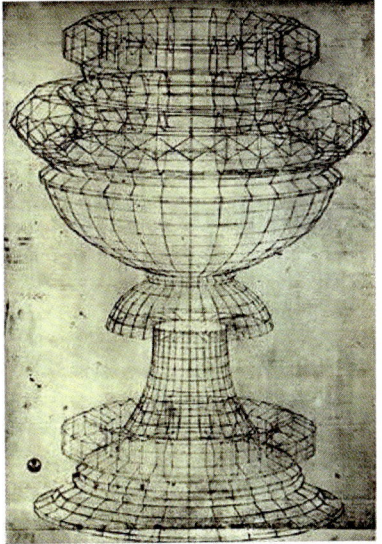

Fig 0.1
Piero Della Francesca, *Brera Altarpiece* 1472–1474
Fig 0.2
Paolo Uccello, *Chalice* 1450

With the invention of the computer, it was inevitable that this knowledge would be turned into software, and it was. When this happened, the modern era of 3D computer graphics, perhaps the most significant, advance in the visual arts since the discovery of perspective was made.

The work of other artists was also used as the basis for innovations in computer graphics. Leonardo Da Vinci's work on aerial perspective was incorporated into 3D rendering software, just as the work of Impressionist and Pointillist artists like Claude Monet and Georges Seurat became the basis for pixel-based representations of visual information (Fig. 0.3).

Fig 0.3
Georges Seurat, *Bridge of Courbevoie* 1886/1887

Without the observations of these artists, there would be no computer graphics. Computer graphics are possible only because there are people who looked at the world around them, and went to the trouble not only to describe what they saw, but also to understand what they saw.

Knowledge of a subject is what makes the difference between a novice and an expert. If I look under the hood of a car, I see a bunch of blackened metal objects. A mechanic sees an engine, gaskets, spark plugs, hoses, and many other things he can identify, knows the purpose of, and can assemble himself if necessary. For a computer graphics artist, the difference between a true expert and a novice who just sees a jumble of stuff under the hood is observation (Fig. 0.4).

Fig 0.4
Power tech engine block

Linear perspective stems from the *observation* that parallel lines seem to converge as they move farther away from our eye. The reason isn't that they are actually coming together, but that the human eye is nearly spherical in shape to accept visual information from all sides. The result is shapes that appear to converge the closer they are to the pupil (Fig. 0.5).

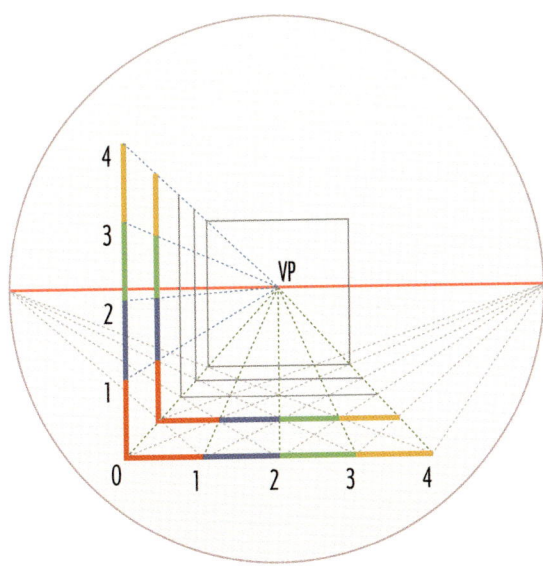

Fig 0.5
Linear perspective

The red line in this illustration is the horizon line, the point labeled "vp" is the vanishing point, the circle is the total field of view (fov), the vanishing points that connect with the fov are *diagonal* vanishing points, and the colored bars are for measurement.

To reproduce this on paper, artists would draw a straight horizontal line to represent the horizon, then a point in the center of the line to represent the *vanishing point* (this corresponds to the center one's pupil). Another horizontal line is then drawn either above or below the horizon line and subdivided equally, with evenly spaced lines drawn directly into the *vanishing point*. These lines represent parallel lines and may be used to measure height, width, or depth. These lines simulate how parallel lines as seen by the human eye converge in toward the pupil (Fig. 0.6).

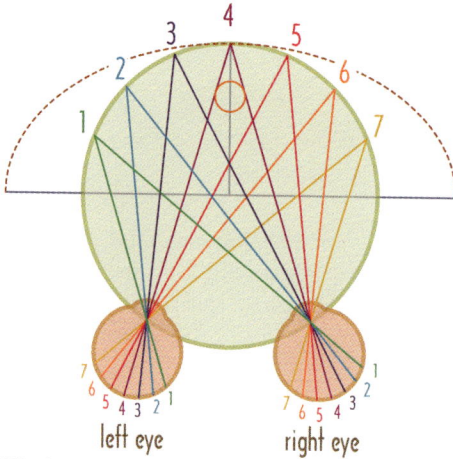

Fig 0.6
Stereovision

As the point of focus shifts to the right or left of center, the angle formed by the ray from each eye to the subject becomes more acute. This causes some distortion and an exaggerated impression of curvature.

The original form of linear perspective did not take into account lens curvature, so it was only an approximation of what a human eye sees. Nevertheless, it worked well enough that for 500 years, it was the basis for almost every great work of art made during that period. Later, engineers worked out engineering perspective and they did take *lens curvature* into account. With it, lens curvature could be represented accurately. It is this form of perspective that is now used for computer renderings (Fig. 0.7).

Fig 0.7
Lens curvature

Notice how the curvature of the reflective hemisphere affects the reflection cast upon it. This is the same thing that happens when visual information in three-dimensional space is projected onto your eye.

Leonardo's observation that colors become less distinct over distance became known as *aerial perspective*. He used this to more accurately describe observed details, most famously in the background of the painting *Mona Lisa*. Other artists used the technique as it became better known, and descriptions of it became commonplace in books about art. The phenomenon Leonardo saw, described, and went to some trouble to understand was caused by the fact that our atmosphere contains many tiny light-occluding particles such as dust and fog. At near distances, they do not affect our vision because there are not as many of these particles between our eye and the object we are observing as when we refocus our eyes on a distant object. In computer graphics, *aerial perspective* is known as *environmental fog*. The effect is used effectively to simulate great distances in computer renderings (Fig. 0.8).

Fig 0.8
Shadow in the Summer (© 2005 Stephan Martiniere)

This is an excellent modern example of atmospheric perspective in a painting. Notice how the color in the background is muted because it is flooded with the primary light color. In extreme distances, individual color differences are normally indistinguishable because of this effect.

Without the work of pointillist artists like George Seurat and Henri-Edmund-Cross, or their nearest inspiration, Claude Monet, we might never have seen what we now recognize as 3D computer graphics. What these artists discovered was that if they broke a color into its primary components, it would be seen as the original color. They expanded on this observation by making hundreds of paintings, each of which tested the limits of what came to be known as *pointillism*, a style of painting using nothing but brightly colored dots, or points. These paintings became the basis for pixel-based graphics. Without a method to make a two-dimensional image on a screen, no amount of knowledge regarding perspective would be of any use. With it however, linear perspective could be used to calculate what an image should look like on a 2D plane, and pointillism allows the computer to generate the image (Figs. 0.9 and 0.10).

 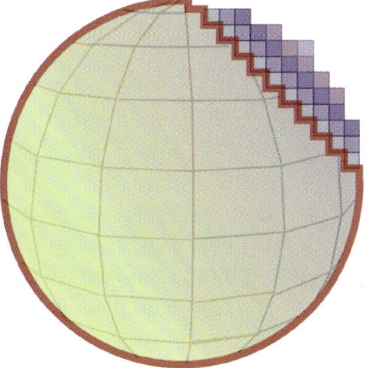

Figs 0.9 and 0.10
Pointillism and the pixel

These observations by artists led to key discoveries that had (and are still having) far-reaching results. By themselves, the observations would be of little use if the artist were unable to communicate what he had seen or what caused the effect. To be able to articulate, what one has seen is exactly what a computer graphics artist must do. This is the primary skill and it falters if that artist's observation skills are weak.

Today, computer animation software has pointillism, aerial perspective, linear perspective, lens curvature, and many other observations built into the program. Now, the software will perform the mechanical calculations for you, just as a calculator will add numbers. The trick is that you need to be able to input the right numbers. In computer graphics, this means you have to be able to see, understand,

and describe your subject to your software in a language it understands. If you do your job properly, you will receive in return a beautifully rendered image.

Knowledge of a computer animation program will not by itself make anyone into a competent professional animator. They may learn the buttons, they may learn the language of the application, but without well-described *observations*, the raw data needed to create a computer rendering, this knowledge is insufficient to be a truly successful computer artist. To be a successful computer artist, you also need to understand how to look at the world around you, or imagine the one within, with great clarity. You must be able to see detail that others miss, understand why it is there, what it is for, how to distinguish it from its neighbors, and describe it to your application.

The skills just described are the basis for this book. They are application independent and are true of every 3D application currently made. As 3D professionals, you will discover that 3D applications change on a nearly annual basis and that every few years the most popular application will have changed to something new. When this happens, artists who understand computer graphics for what it is, a way to place their real-world observations into an application capable of generating a rendering (even if it is a real-time game engine), will never be out of a job. The reason is that the applications are much easier to learn than these other skills, and their employers know that.

This book is about computer graphics; it is not about computer graphics applications. In this book, you will learn the meaning and usage of computer graphics tools and terminology, but more importantly, the basic observation skills needed to do something great with that knowledge.

The information contained herein is meant to comprise the first portion of a university-level introduction to Computer Graphics course. The layout of the book follows the class structure of my first two modeling classes for freshman students (they are staggered with two animation classes). Although a great deal may be learned by simply reading the text, it is highly recommended that any serious student also performs every exercise offered here.

The first part of the book, 3D1, focuses on fundamental principles of how 3D space is represented in a computer, user interface, basic polygonal modeling tools, and other information essential to getting started as a 3D artist. The second part of the book, 3D2, introduces the more complicated subjects of surfaces, topology, and optimization. Each of these has their own importance, and all help inform the student to make better creative and technical choices with his work.

Andrew Paquette

Part I: 3D1: Introduction to 3D Modeling

Modeling is where all 3D projects must begin, because without a model, there is nothing to animate or render. Studying modeling is also an excellent means of familiarizing an artist with basic concepts of Computer Graphics. By understanding modeling, an artist will also be more comfortable with the software he uses, finding errors in his work, and avoiding problems he might otherwise encounter.

This section is designed to provide a student with a solid foundation in polygon-based modeling and animation applications.

Chapter 1: 3D: What Is It?

Imagine American astronaut Neil Armstrong when he first landed on the moon. Soon after this historic event, he ventured outside the moon lander and planted an American flag in the dusty gray soil of the moon. Now, imagine the intersection of that flagpole and the moon's surface as the center of the universe. In computer graphics, that would make that point the *world origin*, and it would be the point against which every other distance is measured. With that point known, the distance from the world origin to Armstrong's hand may be measured, the exact location of earth may be found, and Bluebeard's treasure may be located. Without it, at least as far as your computer is concerned, all these things are floating aimlessly and invisibly through space (Fig. 1.1).

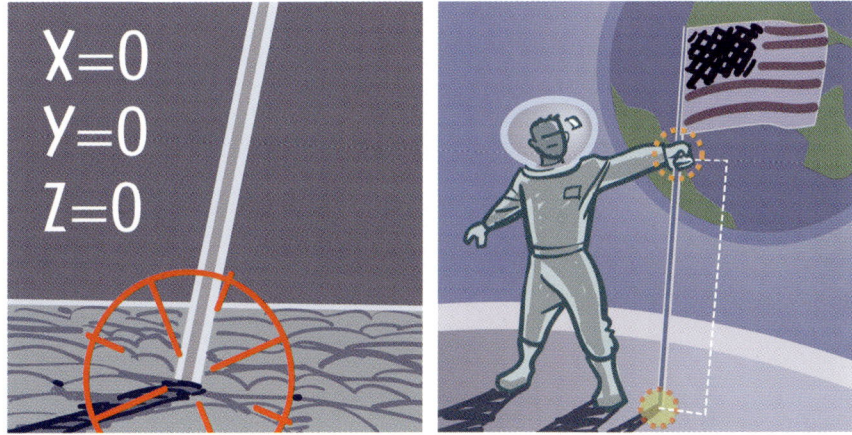

Fig 1.1
On the left is the location of zero, on the right, a measurement based on zero

The origin doesn't have to be on the moon, it can be anywhere. You can draw an "x" in a notebook and make that the world origin. It doesn't matter *where* it is, but it does matter *that it is there*. Without a world origin, there is no universe, at least as far as your 3D application is concerned. It needs to be given an origin, or a starting point, so that it knows where things belong. The reason is that in computer graphics, all 3D data are stored as *X*, *Y*, and *Z* coordinates. These coordinates are meaningless without a zero point to measure them against.

In surveying, it is called a *station point*. Usually, it is an iron bar painted with even divisions on it and planted into the ground, just like Armstrong's flag. It is then sighted with surveying instruments, and all distances are calculated from it. That is exactly what a world origin is for. It is also the first thing the software needs to know before it can do anything. In your case, you don't *have* to know this fact to start making objects in 3D any more than you have to understand linear perspective either. In both cases, the software has this information built in and it does the work for you. However, not knowing this information can cause a great deal of frustration later, because it affects how tools behave. These concepts are how your application sees the world, and you have to understand that if you are to smoothly interact with a 3D application.

You can add numbers with a calculator by pushing buttons, but if you don't understand the concept of adding, the calculator is of no use to you because you won't know what the results represent. In the same way, a 3D application will perform many functions invisibly, but if you don't know what it is doing, you won't know what to expect, or how to work out a problem. The first thing you need to remember then is that the *global origin* is a *station point* against which all dimensions are measured. It is used as a way to locate the center of *world space*, a term that describes your working environment.

The world origin is usually represented on screen with a 3D icon of some kind, to show the three major *axes*. They are known as the *X*, *Y*, and *Z axes* and represent the three perpendicular vectors used to define space within your program. Pointing in the opposite direction are the *negative X*, *Y*, *Z* axes, for a total of six primary vectors (Fig. 1.2).

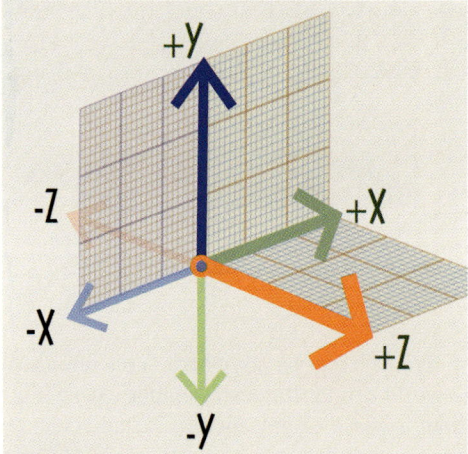

Fig 1.2
World coordinates

These are very much like the *X*, *Y* grids you may have drawn in Math class to plot the location of a point. They are used in much the same way in 3D applications as well, but with an additional axis to represent the *depth*. This is the *Z-axis*, also known as the *depth axis* (Fig. 1.3).

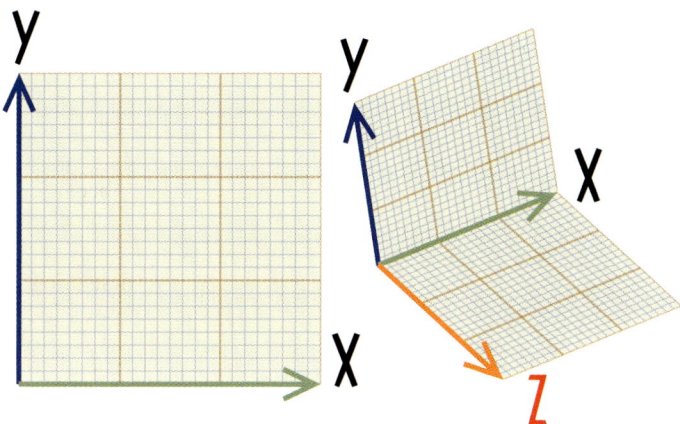

Fig 1.3
2D and 3D coordinate systems

In 3D, some applications used Z as the *up-axis* and others used the Y-axis. Another difference is known as either the *right-hand rule* or the *left-hand rule*. Today, most application developers have mostly settled on using the Y-up, left-hand rule standard, so you are unlikely to see the old-fashioned Z-up, right-hand rule world space used most often in the 1980s. This book uses the left-hand rule convention (Fig. 1.4).

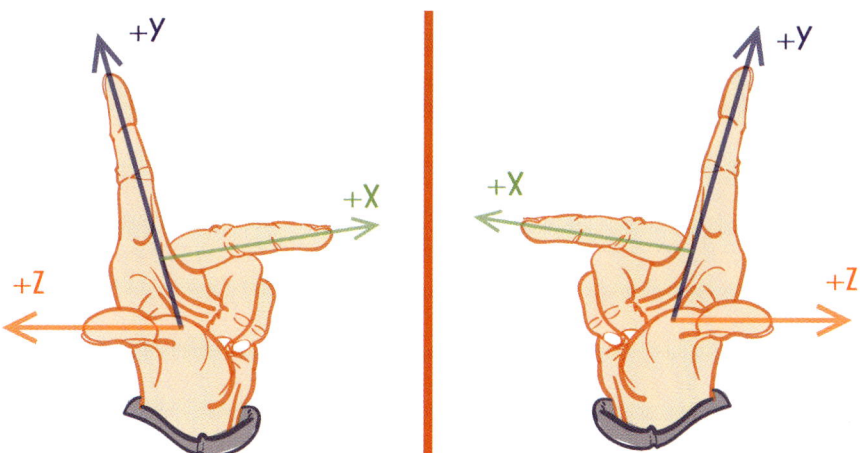

Fig 1.4
X-axis is reversed depending on which rule you use

In addition to defining the Y-axis as *up* and the Z-axis as *depth*, the X-axis is used to define *width*. In this way, the location of a coordinate may be described with a group of three numbers, each of which represents a measurement along one of the three major axes, a given distance from the world origin.

To locate a point in space then, your software needs a *global origin*, to be used as a *station point*. It then needs to have a group of numbers to identify where on each of three axes the point lies. To your application, this is what such a coordinate looks like:

2 3 1

And this is what it looks like to you (Fig. 1.5).

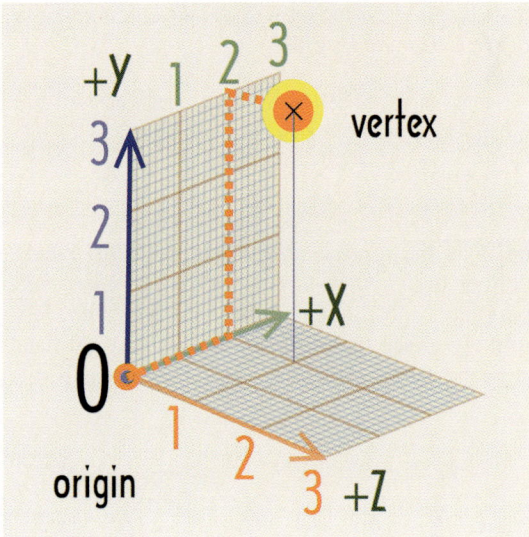

Fig 1.5
A vertex

In this case, the coordinates given identify a point located two units away from zero, extending in positive X, three units up in positive Y, and one unit from the global origin in Z.

Believe it or not, that is the basis of all computer graphics. World space, combined with the ability to define coordinates, allows you to create characters, worlds, animations, and many other things. If you are a modeler, your job is to put the points where they belong and connect them properly. If you are a texture artist, you need to affix your textures to 3D objects. If you are a *lighter*, you must define the location of your lights and their aimpoints. As an *animator*, you will define where things move to, all using X, Y, Z *coordinates*.

Computer graphics, or *CG*, has borrowed a number of mathematical terms to describe the various elements used in 3D applications. Many of the terms are recognizable from the study of Geometry. This fact is the probable origin of the use of the word *Geometry* to refer to 3D models. If someone complains to an animator that "the geometry is messed up," the animator might respond, "tell it to the modeler, he's the one who made it."

The model is where most files begin, and to understand it a little better, its elements should be defined.

A *vertex* is a single coordinate for a *point* in world space. It has no dimension and very few properties by itself. To make it into an *edge*, it requires another point. This only defines a line, and as such, still cannot be rendered. To render it, a third point must be defined, to create a *triangle*, also known as a *face* or a *polygon*. Most often, it is called either a *poly* or a *triangle* (Fig. 1.6).

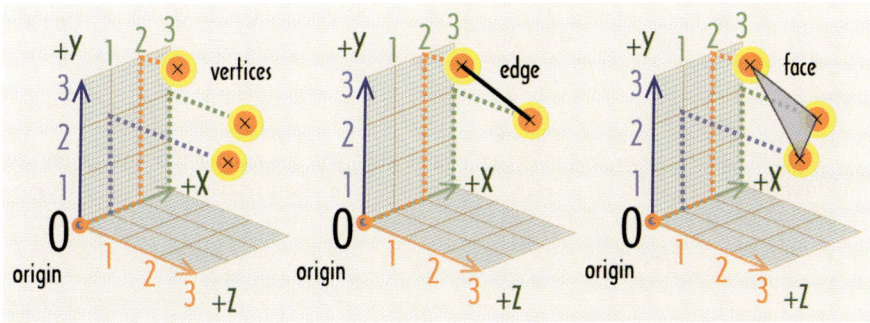

Fig 1.6
Vertices, an edge, and a face

Take a pencil and a piece of paper. Draw a dot on the paper. That is a "vertex," a location in space, identified by your pencil mark. Move the piece of paper. You are now animating the vertex.

To know the location of your pencil dot, you simply need to know how far from the global origin it is in each of the three major axes. This is just like plotting a point in Math class, except now you have an extra dimension to work with. Instead of following the *X*-axis horizontally for four units, then heading up another five, you now also have to travel *in* three units. In CG, a vertex in this location would be written something like this, depending on the format:

V 4 5 3

Now that you know where your dot is, you can do quite a lot with it. You can attach attributes to it or animate it, but you cannot render it. A vertex does not have any light reflective surfaces and cannot be rendered.

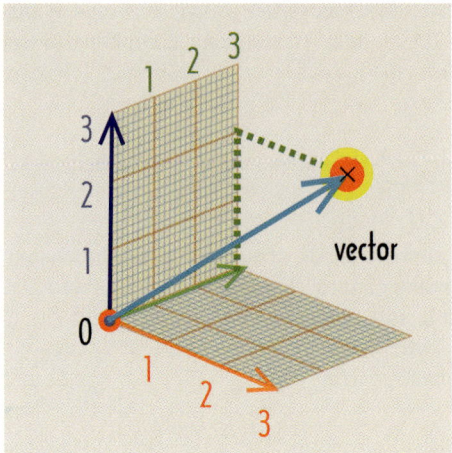

Fig 1.7
A vector

At the moment, your file is pretty sparse, but you do have a few things so far. In addition to the items already mentioned, you now have a *vector*. This is different from the axis vector mentioned earlier. Here, your vertex creates a *direction*, or a *vector*, away from the origin. This may not seem important now, but vectors can be very important, even if they are invisible (Fig. 1.7).

Now draw another dot. In CG, a pair of vertices is written like this:

V 2 3 1
V 3 2 2

The actual numbers don't matter, just that the first column tells you it is a vertex, the second column is the *X*-axis, the third column is the *Y*-axis, and the fourth column is the *Z*-axis. The *order* of the "vertices" (plural of vertex) is also important. Some programs will number vertices to help identify them. Other programs use the vertex order in the file to identify the vertex. In this case, the first vertex in the list is number 1, and the next vertex is number 2, and so on.

An ASCII format file of your scene would now look something like this:

V 2 3 1
V 3 2 2
V 1 2 3
F 1 2 3
G default

This tells you that you have three vertices, a face made out of the three vertices, and a default name for the object. Now you have something to render. Light can bounce off of a face and that quality is required for a rendering to be made (Fig. 1.8).

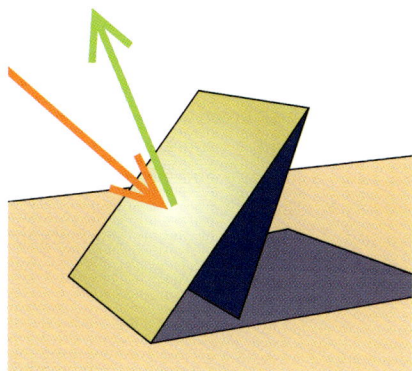

Fig 1.8
A light ray

There are several ways to modify the *components* of this face. Regardless of the tool you use, the end result is a modification to the coordinate value of individual vertices. This is accomplished with a *transformation matrix* (Fig. 1.9).

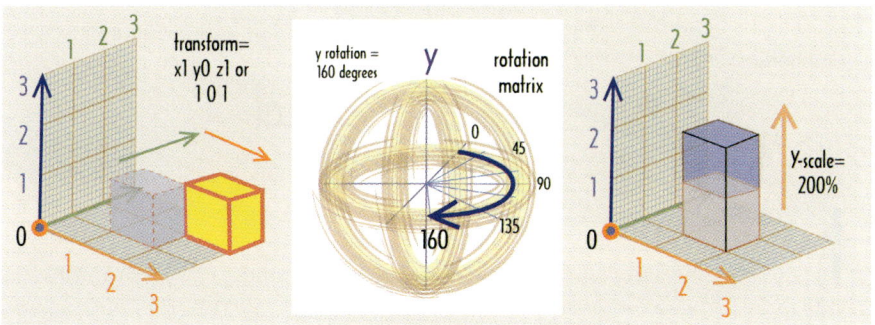

Fig 1.9
Transform, rotation, scale translation types

A transformation matrix is attached to a *node* on your object. A *node* is like a luggage tag for your suitcases. It tells you what is inside the bag and where it belongs. The transformation matrix has nine primary attributes. They are:

Transform X, Y, Z
Rotate X, Y, Z
Scale X, Y, Z

They also have one minor attribute, visibility, which can be set to on or off (default is on). With these ten values, you can do just about anything you can think of to your object. For animation, a state of the matrix is stored for each frame of animation, and is used to modify the position, size, and rotation values of an object over time.

A transformation matrix wouldn't work without a *local axis* for your object. A local axis looks a lot like the group of three axes displayed at the global origin, but instead, it is located in the middle of your object. Most programs allow you to move the local axis anywhere you like, but the important thing is that you have one. For a rotation animation for instance, the rotation values stored in the transform matrix would be based on the location of the object's *local origin* instead of the global origin. This is a good thing, because otherwise your object might wildly rotate around the wrong pivot point. Set it to the corner of your triangle, and it will rotate around that corner instead (Fig. 1.10).

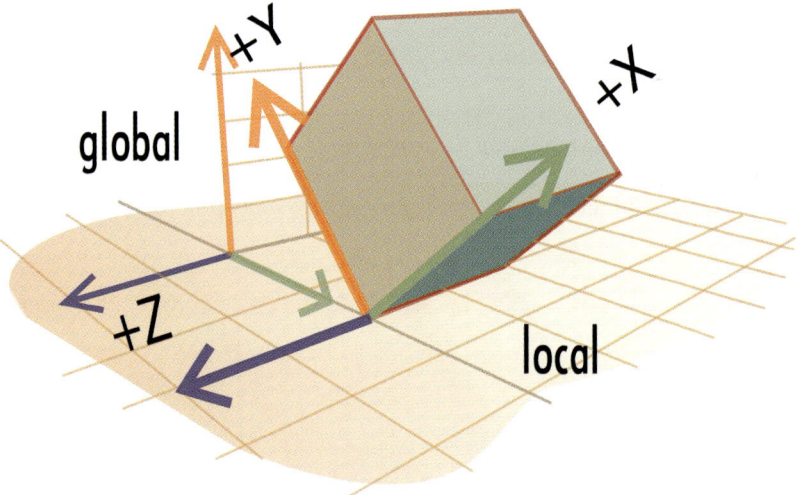

Fig 1.10
Local axis

The difference between a *world origin* and a *local origin* can prevent you from being able to move an object the way you would like, or from animating something properly.

You might not think a triangle is all that much fun to look at. Draw a happy face on it. That makes it more interesting, doesn't it? Color it in. Now you have a *texture map*. A texture map is used to add detail to a CG object, in this case, color detail. Texture maps are kept in separate files from geometry, called *image files*. These files can be in almost any format or size, just so long as it is a format compatible with the renderer being used (Fig. 1.11).

Fig 1.11
Polygon, texmap, and mapped polygon

A texture map is attached to a triangle, also called a *polygon*, or *poly*, by using *texture coordinates*, more commonly called *UVs*. UVs are like vertices, except they are positioned over a texmap, to identify which part of the map will be rendered under which UV. The UVs are also attached to the vertices of your object, to identify which parts of the map are attached to which vertices. If you liked to build kites, but weren't very good at it, you might use tacks instead of glue to pin your kite paper to its wooden struts. The UVs are like the tacks and the texture map is like the kite paper. The struts are the wireframe of your model (Fig. 1.12).

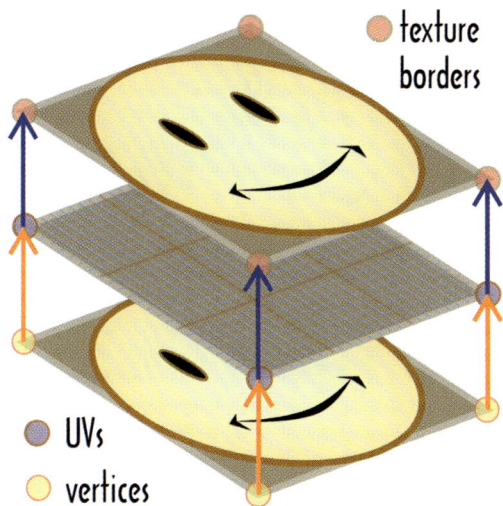

Fig 1.12
How a texture map is attached to a polygon

In the triangle example, you will have one UV for each of the three vertices of your object. These UVs will be connected by edges that correspond to the edges of your polygon, and the connection pattern between its vertices. The UVs can be adjusted in a *texture editor*, to modify which part of a texture map is rendered within their borders. If done properly, your happy face will show up where it is supposed to; not upside down, backward, or distorted like a funhouse mirror. Done right, it will look fine, i.e., if you had any lights.

Turn on the lights in your room. You can see much better now. In CG, it's even worse than in real life. In CG, if you don't have any lights, it's not just dim, it is black. You can't see anything, because every pixel is set to 0 0 0, *black*.

A CG light is a lot like your first two vertices and an edge. That would be enough to define a *directional light*, which is just a vector and some other values. A *spotlight* is a bit more complicated, because it also has values for cone radius and penumbra. A *point light* is just a single vertex for a location. With each of these lights, and others, light is projected along vectors. If the light collides with your object, it bounces off and becomes a nonblack pixel in your rendering (Fig. 1.13).

Fig 1.13
Necessity of light

There is one last component required for all of these things to work properly, a *normal*. A normal is a vector, usually perpendicular to the surface of each triangle. These are automatically generated for you, but some programs allow you to modify them. To draw a normal, you only need to make a locator, in this case one that determines the second vertex of a vector. The first "vertex" is the center of your polygon. Edges and vertices inherit normals from the face they belong to. For faces that share an edge, normals are averaged between the values for either face (Fig. 1.14).

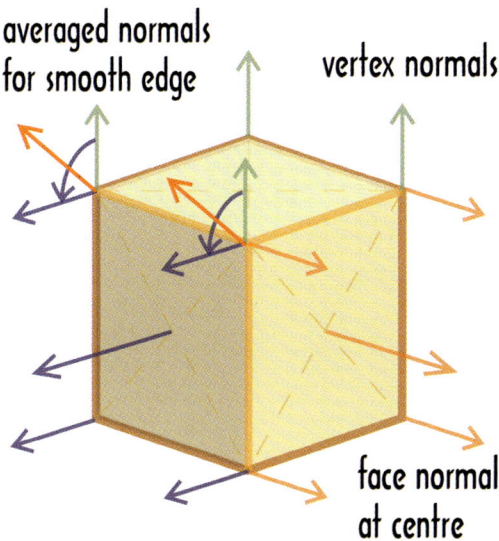

averaged normals
for smooth edge

vertex normals

face normal
at centre

Fig 1.14
Normals and averaged normals

The normal is used to calculate how a ray of light affects your object. Does it skim off to the side? Or does it hit it straight on, causing a dazzling brightness? This affects the rendering calculation dramatically, so it is important for these to be set correctly (Fig. 1.15).

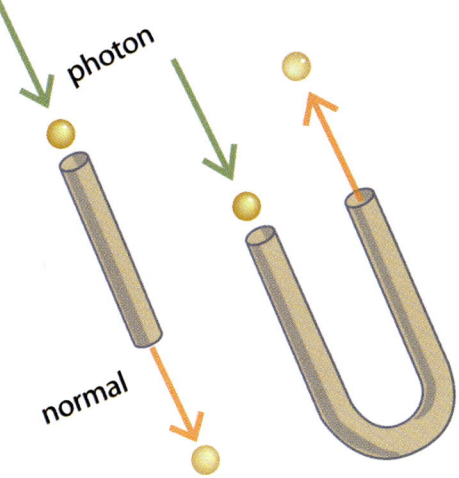

photon

normal

Fig 1.15
Incorrect normal on left, correct on right

An incorrect normal will cause light to pass through a polygon, like a ball through a straight pipe, without returning a color value to the camera. The result is that *back-facing polygons*, polygons that should face away from the camera, instead face toward it and are rendered instead of polygons in front that should block them. The effect is like looking at the inside of a mold used to cast another object (Fig. 1.16).

Fig 1.16
Reversed normals, as seen in mirror

These are the seven basic physical elements of CG (Fig. 1.17):

1. Vertices
2. Edges
3. Faces
4. UVs
5. Textures
6. Lights
7. Normals

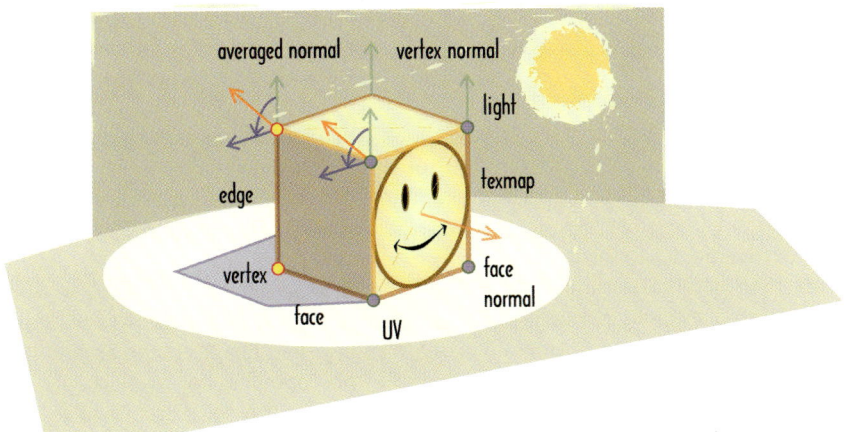

Fig 1.17
The seven basic elements of CG

These are the five basic conceptual elements of CG:

1.   Global coordinates
2.   Local coordinates
3.   Vectors
4.   Transformation matrix
5.   Light

All computer renderings are built out of the elements just described, or varia-tions of them. Learn what they are and what they can do, and you will understand how your software sees the world.

Basic Tools: Your Interface

Animation applications vary considerably in some respects, but they also have much in common. Some take pains to be compatible with other applications; others go to great lengths to avoid compatibility, even with previous versions of themselves. Despite these variations, all animation applications do pretty much the same thing; they allow a user to create a 3D file through a *graphical user interface*, also known as a *GUI*. Therefore, the two things that a user needs to know to make a 3D object for a CG animation are the basics of 3D and the GUI.

Some programs have specific commands that are not a part of any other program, but most programs have the same basic tools. They also have very similar methods of watching what is going on inside their virtual 3D workspace.

When you first open a 3D application, you will see a window, also called a *viewport* that has a representation of *world space* drawn within it. *World space* is literally the global origin and everything around it, all the way to infinity. Of course, no computer really goes to infinity because the numbers would be too big. Instead, they are cut off and rounded, usually between six and ten decimal points.

On the screen, world space usually looks like an origin icon plus a grid. Depending on which viewport you are looking at, *orthographic* or *perspective*, you may be looking at a flat grid made of perpendicular angles, or a grid made out of convergent lines that can be twirled around in 3D. An *orthographic grid* is drawn perpendicular to the *orthographic camera* and the *perspective grid* is drawn to vanishing points determined by the position of the *perspective camera*. If you look carefully, you may notice that the convergent lines in the perspective window are curved. This is because camera lenses are convex and images curve around the surface of the lens. This effect is noticeable in photographs, but most people do not notice it when looking around them because they are so accustomed to the effect on their own eyes (Fig. 1.18).

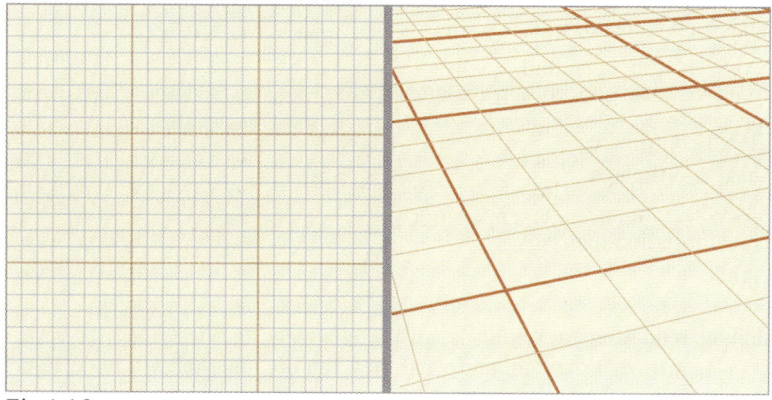

Fig 1.18
Orthographic and perspective grids

If you go to your perspective viewport and expand it, you will find that there are three primary ways to interact with it. You can *pan*, *tumble*, and *zoom*. This is what each of these does:

- Pan – moves the camera within a camera plane as defined by the current viewport
- Tumble – rotates the camera in three axes around a fixed point, usually a selected object or component (your choice)
- Zoom – moves the camera closer or farther away from an object, following a vector perpendicular to the viewport

Once you have become acquainted with your applications' camera and viewport tools, you can view most anything you want, from any angle or zoom factor you like. This is the first step of using a 3D package.

The second step is to make a vertex, or a face, or maybe a *geometric primitive*. A geometric primitive is a simple object like a cube, sphere, or cylinder. There are other types of primitives, but these are the most common (Fig. 1.19).

Fig 1.19
Cube, sphere, and cylinder

In your application, look for a tool or a button that will allow you to create a cube. Invoke the command and a cube will appear on your screen, drawn in *wireframe*. Wireframe is a way to represent an object in line only. It draws vertices and then connects them with straight lines. Some programs allow you to turn *back facing* on or off. This option allows you to turn off the display of faces that go behind other faces. The result is that the back of your object is blocked, making it less confusing to look at (Fig. 1.20).

Fig 1.20
Wireframe display mode, with backfacing polys off on the left, all polys displayed on the right

Now turn *shading* on. With shading on, you will see your cube as a solid object, as lit by a default light. It isn't a very attractive light, but it renders fast and works for most purposes. You will find yourself shifting from wireframe to shaded mode often while you work, so make sure you remember how to do it (Fig. 1.21).

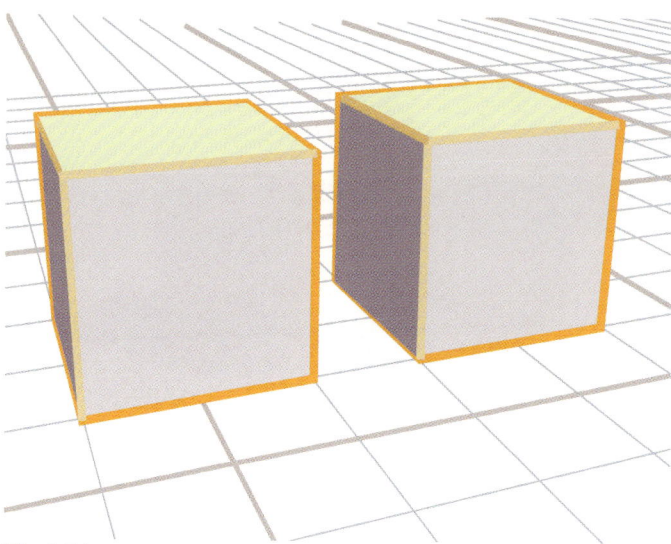

Fig 1.21
Shaded display mode

There are other display options and it is worth your while to go through them. You can turn display of different elements on or off (like lights, vertices, faces, edges, nurbs, cameras, etc.). It is a long list and you can have some fun exploring it yourself. In practical reality, you will not use more than about 10% of the options for about 99% of your career in CG, depending on your specialty, so you don't have to become an expert at everything but it isn't a bad idea to know what is inside your tool chest.

The last two things you need to know before you can get to work on the first exercise are how to select an object and how to manipulate the transformation matrix. Find your selection tool and practice with it. This tool will allow you to select whole *objects*, but also *components*, or parts of an object, like individual vertices, faces, or edges. Next, look for your *transform*, or *move* tool, and move your object. Do the same with scale and rotate. In each case, pay attention to whether your object is *transforming* relative to the global origin, its own center, or somewhere else. This tells you where the object's *pivot* is located. You will need to move the pivot often when you work, so check your manual to find out how to move your object's pivot in addition to the object itself (Fig. 1.22).

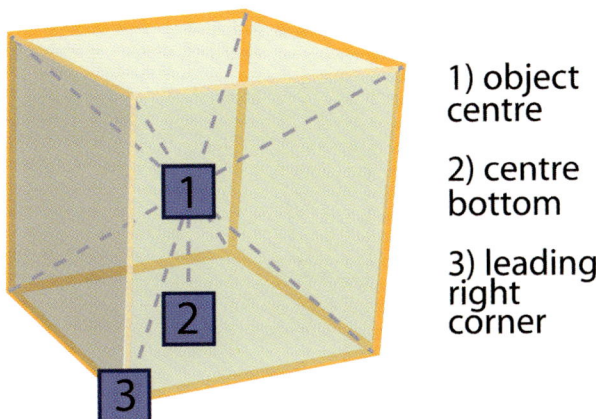

1) object centre

2) centre bottom

3) leading right corner

Fig 1.22
The three most popular locations for object pivots

Most applications usually have hotkeys associated with the three primary transformation commands because they are so frequently used. Look up the hotkey shortcuts and practice using them. Using hotkeys will save you a great deal of time. Another time saver is *direct entry*; this allows you to type in a transformation, like 50 units, instead of doing it visually. This is especially useful when you need your modifications to be exact.

If you want to select only a part of your object, or a *component*, you will have to select by component. This usually means using a separate component menu. Component selection is one of the most important concepts in 3D modeling. Without it, many editing tools would not work and it would be much more difficult to make certain models. Component selection also allows a CG artist to have much greater control over an object than if left reliant on global- or object-level editing tools alone. Most objects require some amount of component-level editing (Figs. 1.23–1.25).

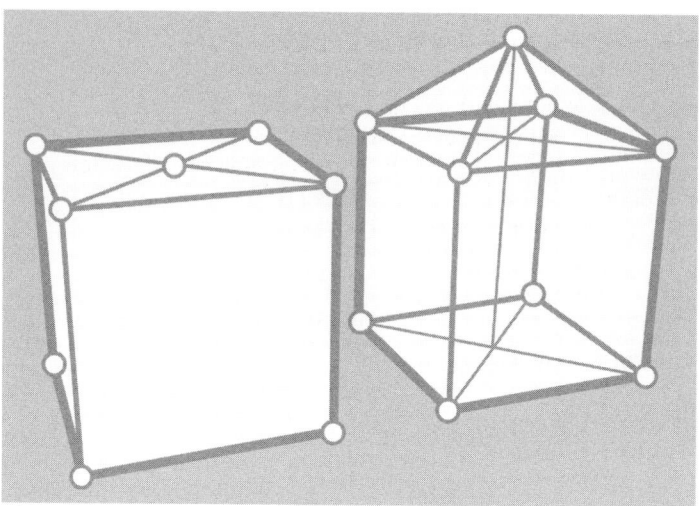

Fig 1.23
Vertex translation

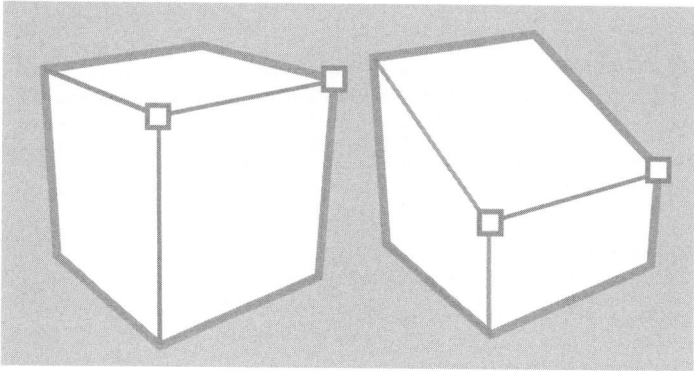

Fig 1.24
Edge translation

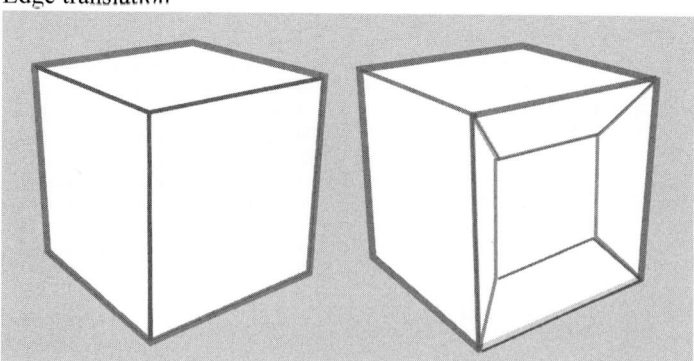

Fig 1.25
Face extrusion and scale

Just as you can modify an object by selecting its components and transforming them, you may create an object out of raw components.

If you want your shape aligned with the grid, you should use *grid snap*. *Snaps* are tools that allow you to position objects and components accurately relative to the position of something else in the scene. The most common snapping tools are:

- Grid snap – snaps to grid
- Curve snap – snaps to a curve
- Vertex snap – snaps to a vertex

Some less common snaps are these:

- Edge snap – snaps to edge center
- Face snap – snaps to face center
- Object snap – snaps to object center

In the early years of computer graphics, UVs were not automatically generated for you as they are today. Instead, they had to be *projected*. It can be done with the press of a button today, but make sure you press the right one. Projecting UVs is done in very much the way a movie projector casts an image on a screen. If someone walks in front of the light, part of the movie will be projected on that person. Some parts of the image will be stretched or distorted, because the rolling contours of the person's body aren't aligned at a flat perpendicular angle to the *projection plane*, which in this case is the movie screen. Distortion is not good in CG, so you want to pick the projection type that is least likely to cause this error with your object (Figs. 1.26 and 1.27).

Fig 1.26
UVs projected correctly

Fig 1.27
UVs projected incorrectly

A triangle's vertices all lie in the same plane, and are therefore *planar*. Because they are planar, a planar projection is most appropriate, as in the illustration above.

Basic Transforms and CG Elements Exercise: Folding Carton

Now that you have been introduced to some of the basics involved in 3D, it is time to see what can be done with it. The following example is designed to illustrate the following:

- How a simple polygonal object is constructed
- Component-level editing
- Transformation tools
- User interface
- The difference between *clean* and *messy* geometry
- The relationship between 2D and 3D space

How it is made:

1. Find a folding carton. This can be a food take-out box from a restaurant, a snack food box, a milk carton, or any other kind of flat die-cut box that is folded into a 3D shape (Fig. 1.28). Video games are sold in these, perfume bottles, light bulbs, and many other common items.
    - For extra difficulty, pick a box that has tapered edges instead of rectangles at fold lines.
    - For a lot of extra difficulty, pick a box with *curved* fold lines.

Fig 1.28
A take-out food container, meant for nonliquid contents

2. Unfold the box.
3. Scan the box. If it is too large to fit on your scanner, scan it in parts,
    then stitch them together in an image-editing program like *Photoshop*.
    Be careful to crop the image, so that there are no borders around the
    carton itself, not even a single pixel wide.
    •   If you don't have a scanner, measure the box with a ruler and then
        make a drawing based on those measurements.
4. Import your image into your 3D program.
5. Trace the outline of the object to make a large multisided polygon
    (Fig. 1.29).
6. Draw the fold and cut lines into the object by cutting it into smaller
    sections (Fig. 1.30).

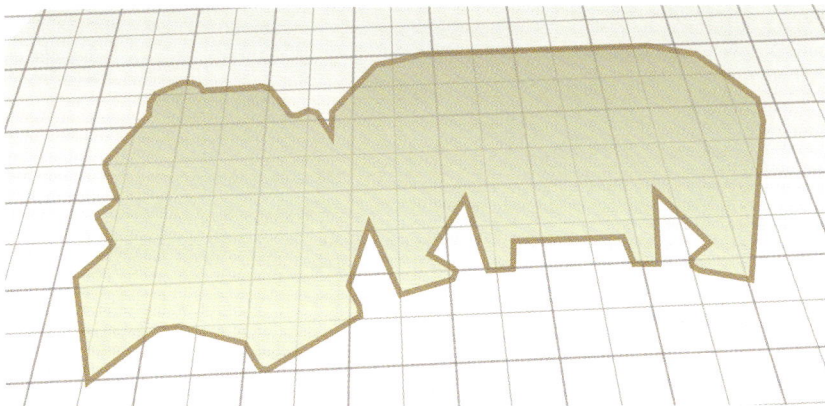

Fig 1.29
Traced carton pattern as open polygon

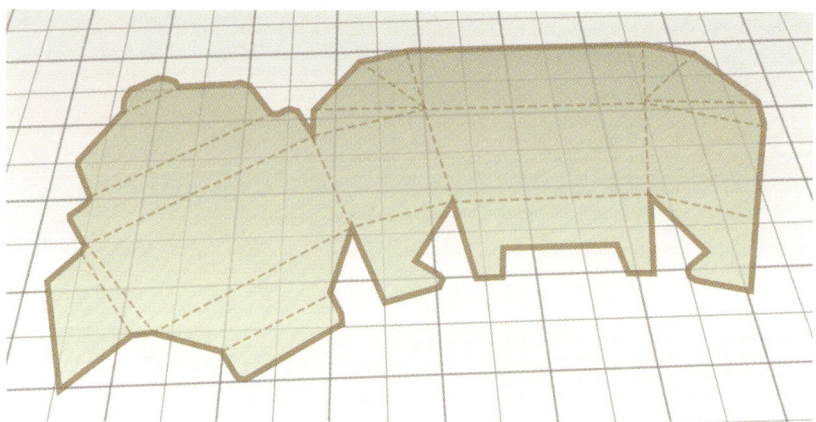

Fig 1.30
Carton pattern, subdivided along fold edges

- For extra difficulty, *extrude* the box to give it a little extra depth.
7. Project UVs on the box using a planar projection tool. In this case, you want it oriented *Y*-up, so be careful to do that in your application.
8. Create a material, or *shader*, by going to your materials editor. Use the scanned image of your flat carton for the color channel of the shader.
9. Assign your shader to your carton (Fig. 1.31).

Fig 1.31
Carton pattern with texture applied

10. Make a duplicate of your carton.
11. Fold the duplicate (Fig. 1.32).

Fig 1.32
The folded carton

The finished file will include a flat carton pattern and a folded carton made from the pattern. The reason a duplicate is made is to compare it with the original object and also as backup in case of mistakes.

Project Overview

To build the folding carton, a number of things must be done. If done properly, an attractive carton will be the result. Most students make errors along the way. The project is not as easy as it may sound at first. The goal is less about making a perfect carton (though that is a welcome result) and more about practicing with the primary elements of the interface. In some cases, it will be about doing pitched battle with the interface.

Fighting your software happens when you don't understand how to communicate your wishes to the application. If you want your vertex to move along the X-axis, but it moves along the Y-axis instead, you have a problem. It isn't an uncommon problem, even for professionals. In this example, it could be because you've switched from global to local space (or vice versa) and forgotten to switch it back. This project should expose you to a number of errors like this, so that you can be comfortable with your interface later on. You do not want to deal with simple interface errors when you are working on critical models and have a deadline hanging over your head. The interface is how you communicate to your application and you need to be very sure of yourself when using it.

The directions require a folding carton. This is the *subject*. It may also be called a *target*, because the goal is to aim for it, and match its appearance as closely as possible. To the extent this is not accomplished, the target has been missed.

The folding carton was chosen as a target for highly specific reasons. This is done partly because this type of object has characteristics important to the *seeing* part of the lesson, and also to remind you that when you are working, you are not always able to select your subject and must be able to make any subject you are asked to build.

Selecting the target object is an important part of the exercise. Some cartons are easier to build than others. For reasons that are evident later, a carton built exclusively out of parallel edges will be much easier to construct than a carton that has tapered fold lines (Figs. 1.33 and 1.34).

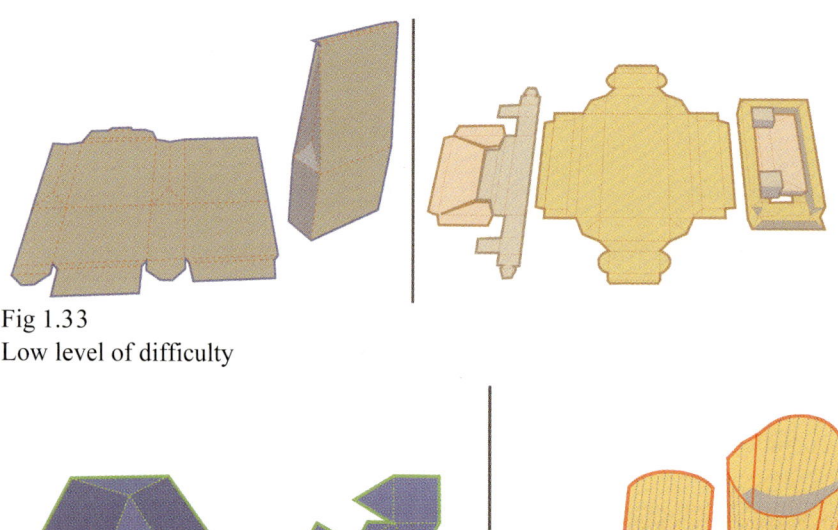

Fig 1.33
Low level of difficulty

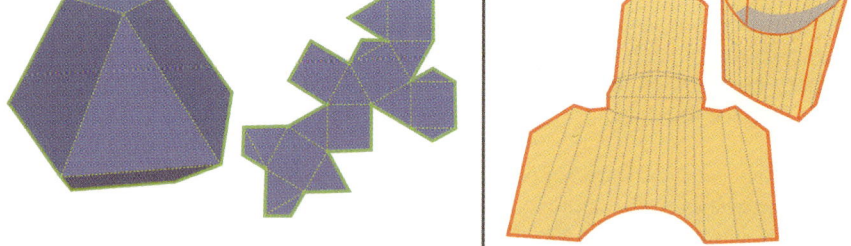

Fig 1.34
High level of difficulty

The level of difficulty may be increased if the carton is built with depth instead of as a flat, *two-sided* polygon.[1] If you do this, you must follow these steps or risk error:

First, make the flattened version of the box, complete with projected UV coordinates. If you have followed the instructions properly, this will work the first time, without any need for editing.

Extrude the face to create depth. You may cut your fold lines into the polygon before or after the extrude operation. Some applications will create new faces around every edge in your polygon. With those applications, it is best to subdivide the model after the extrude operation. If your application allows you to extrude multiple faces at once without creating new faces on either side of every edge, you may divide your polygon before extruding (Figs. 1.35 and 1.36).

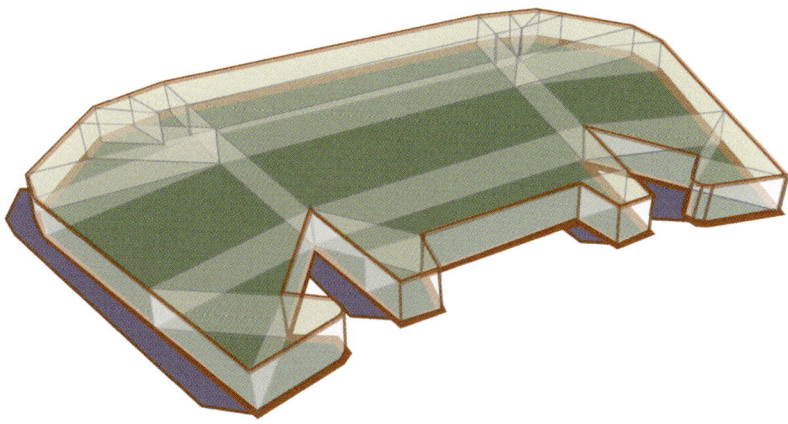

Fig 1.35
Incorrect extrusion (notice extra faces within object)

---

[1] A *two-sided* object is one where the renderer has been instructed to render both sides of a face. This is not used for objects that will never be seen from both sides because it increases render time for the object. It is sometimes used to save render time, because a two-sided polygon can be used in place of a larger polyset, required to define the depth of an object correctly. For a sheet of paper for instance, it may be a two-sided quadrilateral, or it may be six quads, one quad for top, bottom, sides, back, and front. If it is built with sides, the object will be made out of one-sided polygons where only the side with the normal facing out is rendered.

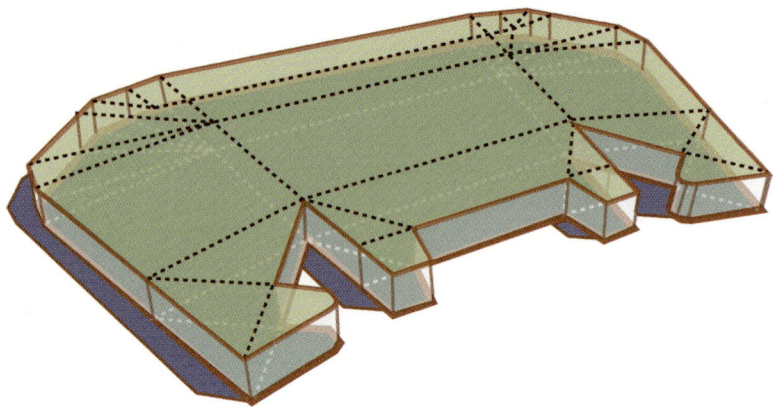

Fig 1.36
Correct extrusion (there are no extraneous interior faces)

Under no circumstances should you edit your UVs after projecting them. If you do, you have either made an error or will miss part of the point of this exercise.

You will need to unfold your carton if it isn't unfolded to begin with. This means that you will have to empty it of any contents first, to prevent unwanted spills.

Scan one or both sides, depending on whether you have decided to make the interior in addition to the exterior. Making the interior adds to the level of difficulty. There is a special problem you will have to solve if you intend to do this. The answer is at the end of the chapter; see if you can figure it out.

If your carton is too large to fit on your scanner, and this is likely, cut it along its fold lines and scan each piece separately. When you have scanned them all, reassemble them in your photo-editing software. Be very careful to crop the final image, so that the edges are flush with the edges of your object. Any border at all will cause you some problems.

If you want to see the error a border will cause, make two maps, one cropped properly and the other not. Later on, you can apply them both and you'll see a big difference.

If you do not have access to a scanner, you may make a drawing of the carton. If you do it this way, you should measure it carefully and make the drawing to scale. Remember that in CG, a model is nothing more than a bunch of *measurements*. If you make a mistake, it will affect the appearance of your model.

This is an important concept to understand, because to some, the importance of measurements to 3D art is not clear. As an example, here is a description of a real discussion that once took place between the author and an MIT graduate who is very prominent in the CG industry. The subject was a simulation project we were both working on, one where a decision had been made to use inaccurate dimensions for an environment to save our engineers the trouble of modifying their engine to recognize accurate, and different, door widths and so on.

If the project had merely been a game, this might not have been a problem, but as a simulation, it was a problem. The reason is that changing the dimensions, or measurements of the objects, also changed their shape, and changing their shape also changed how they behaved. In our case, it meant that three soldiers abreast could simultaneously enter any door instead of only one. The MIT graduate didn't see this, instead, he said, "If it looks okay, we don't have a problem." What he didn't understand was that the measurements affected what it looked like, and because the way it looked was based on its dimensions, it also affected behavior within the simulation. He was accustomed to faking the results he expected using 2D effects because his primary area of expertise was in film, where the end product is a 2D image. For our simulation, our job ended with an uneditable 3D object. The difference is not insignificant.

Unlike a paint program like Photoshop, where pixels are the raw material from which everything is built, in 3D, it is measurements. Get them wrong and many other things may go wrong as well. In the situation described above, the 3D elements for our project would be rendered in real time on a game console. This meant that there would be no opportunity to modify the "images" to "look okay." It would look exactly the way it had to look based on whatever its dimensions are (Fig. 1.37).

Fig 1.37
The difference between a humanoid face and a fish face is the distance between the eyes, a measurement

If you make a drawing, you will not have a texture map for your object, but you will be able to build it in 3D. If you have an image-editing program, you should construct a texture map that imitates the appearance of your flattened carton. You will need this to evaluate how well you achieve project goals.

Once you have your *reference* for the project, you will need to open your 3D application and build it. When you do, your goals are these:

Do not make too many polygons. Use your own judgment to determine what is and what is not "too many." Your answer to this question will be analyzed when you have finished.

Build the flat version of the carton and apply its texture *before* you fold it. This is very important. If you apply the texture afterward, you will have to edit it heavily to get the same result as if you had done it correctly to begin with.

Fold your carton into shape using your application's transformation tools. Do not cheat by creating a carton in its folded state to begin with. If you do, you will miss some of the learning opportunities present in this exercise.

Folding the carton will require you to properly set the *fold axis* for each fold. Whenever this axis corresponds to any of the six major axes of world space, your job will be fairly easy. If the folds are not aligned to these major axes, it will be more difficult because you will have to define the axis yourself (Fig. 1.38).

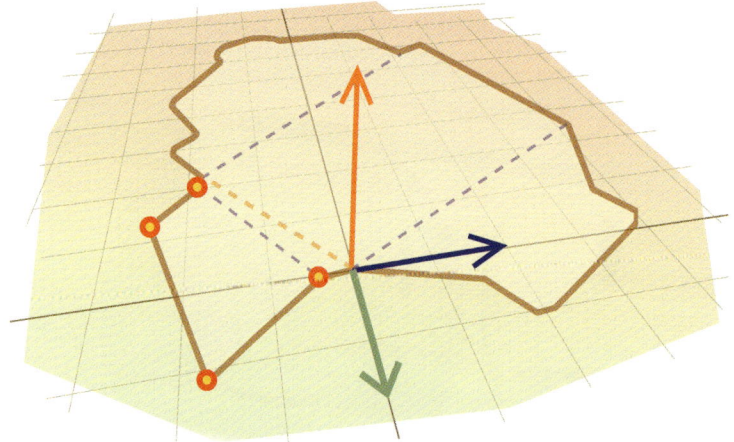

Fig 1.38
How do you fold the highlighted vertices along the orange highlighted edge?

Usually, this is done by selecting either a pair of vertices or an edge and identifying it as a transformation axis. This is why tapered shapes are less easy to fold. The tapered edges mean that the object has at least some folds that are not aligned with the major axes of world space. You can also reset your local axis to match an edge, or simply rotate the entire object to align the desired transformation axis with the global coordinate system (Fig. 1.39).

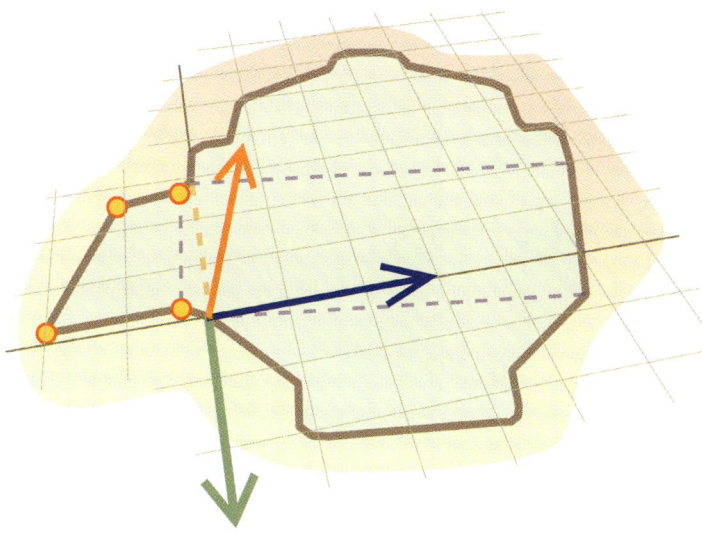

Fig 1.39
An otherwise difficult fold is made possible by rotating the model so that the desired fold axis is aligned with the global axis

You want the end result to be *clean*. This means that you do not want unnecessary vertices, overlapping edges, or crazy quilt cuts marring your polygons. Edges that are straight in your target should be straight in your finished polygonal model. If they are parallel, you should make them exactly parallel. Measurements should match. For this reason, it is a good idea to measure the object. You can do this from the scan instead of the original if you like, because scanners retain dimension information.

You want to practice using your viewports, transformation tools, and poly creation tools. Do not shy away from them, but use them as much as you can. That is part of what this exercise is about.

When you need to move, rotate, or scale something, try doing it to *components* like vertices, edges, and faces instead of the entire object. In this project, you will probably need to move many groups of vertices or faces to fold the individual flaps of your carton.

Applying your scanned image to the object is an important part of the project. It must, and should, fit your carton pattern perfectly. This will require you to *project UVs*, or *texture coordinates*. For this project, all you need is a simple *planar projection*. It may be rotated the wrong way. If so, rotate it in 90° increments until it is correct. See your applications' documentation for instructions how to do this.

UV coordinates editing (Fig. 1.40):

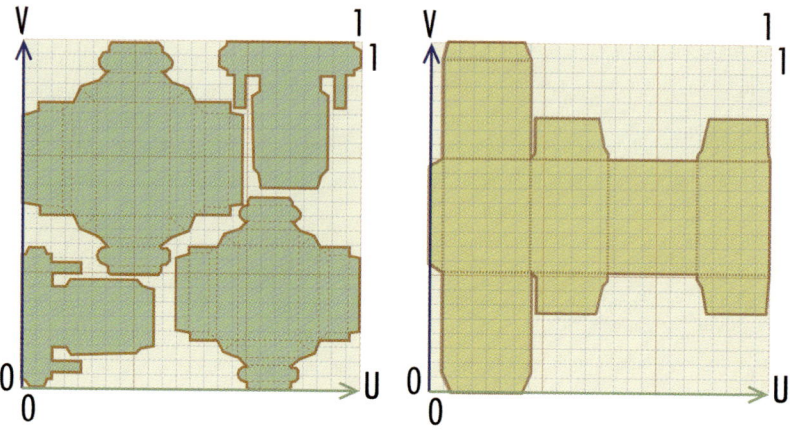

Fig 1.40

Two examples of a finished UV layout. The example on the left is for the inside and outside of a two-piece carton. The example on the right is for a one-sided one-piece carton

Both examples are correct, but the mapping technique utilized on the left requires some prior experience. The example on the right is more in the spirit of the project, which is in part designed to demonstrate how easy UV mapping can be if the artist starts with an unfolded version of the model.

Time. If done properly, it should take you the following amount of time for each stage of the project:

1.   Reference scanning and adjustment; no more than an hour
2.   Tracing of image, depending on complexity; up to half an hour
3.   Subdivision along fold lines; from a few minutes to an hour, depending on complexity
4.   UV projection; less than a minute
5.   UV editing; none to about 15 min if you elect to do this
6.   Folding; this is where you will spend most of your time. A simple carton can be folded in 15 min. A complicated one can take several hours

If you spend more time than mentioned here, then you are doing something wrong.

Chapter 2: Clean Geometry

Think of the litter in a cobweb covered, insect-infested, soaking wet moldy basement buried in refuse. If this is your target subject, you can build it using *clean geometry* or messy geometry (Fig. 2.1). The difference is that if the geometry is not clean, you will not be able to easily navigate this file, and when you try to render it, it will likely produce errors.

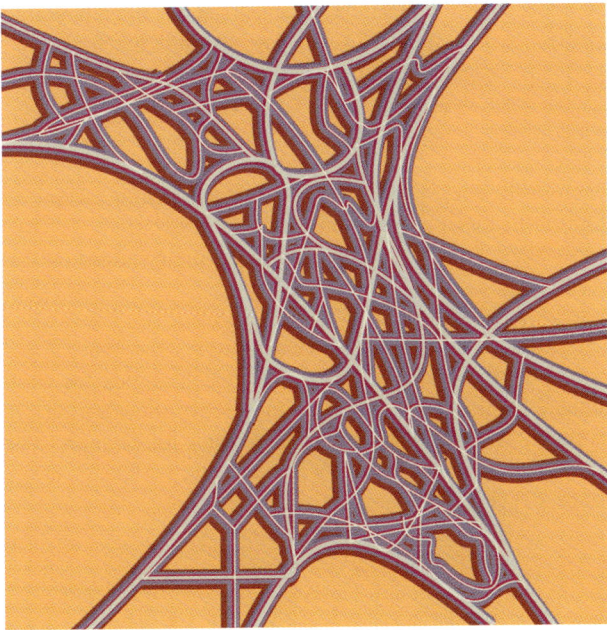

Fig 2.1
A cobweb

A filthy cobweb may be defined with the same clarity and strength as a newly built suspension bridge on a sunny day, and *it should be* if it is to be rendered properly. In the same way, a simple white cardboard box can be constructed so sloppily that it is impossible to import into a game engine, or render for a single frame of animation.

No matter what it is you make; it must be clear, accurate, and well organized.

The term *clean geometry* refers exclusively to the contents of a 3D file when those contents are free of technical errors, well organized, and a good likeness of the subject. The goal of this chapter is to explain what *clean geometry* is, provide a project that will teach you how to make a clean file, and then some feedback at the end to help you analyze your own work to determine how successful you have been.

There are many things that can go wrong in the modeling process to corrupt your geometry. These are *technical errors*. Sometimes, you will be forced to take intermediate steps during construction of an object, like setting up wooden frames before pouring a concrete foundation. If you forget to take down the frames after the concrete has set, you've made a *construction error*.

If you do not take the time to figure out what every single item in your scene is, and how you intend to find it again once it is built, you will have *organizational errors*. An example of this is naming. If everything in your scene is given a default name, you will have hundreds or thousands of objects with indecipherable names. You may remember that *P10289736* is the sewing machine and *P10279736* is the fungus on the carpet, but most people don't remember things that well. The three types of error described here, *technical, construction,* and *organizational* are the most common causes of sloppy geometry.

Here are examples of each of these error types, using various folding cartons as examples. Pay careful attention to these descriptions and the illustrations. If your file contains any of these mistakes, you do not have clean geometry and must fix your object.

Triangle count. You should have no more than two triangles for every four-sided face. If your object has depth, you may have up to ten triangles for each four-sided flap (i.e., 12 minus 2 for the edge connected to the rest of the carton). If your object has rounded corners, you may add up to two vertices for each arc. For die-cut shapes, you may have two vertices for every arc and one vertex for every angular deviation in excess of $30°$ (Fig. 2.2).

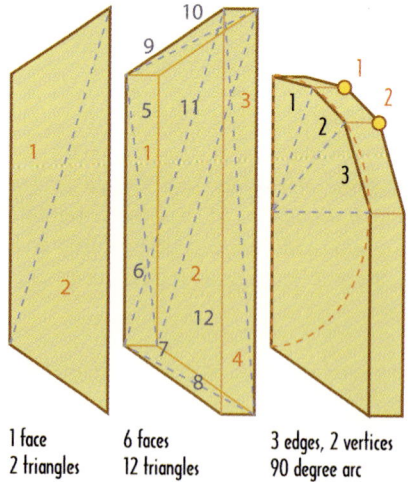

1 face   6 faces   3 edges, 2 vertices
2 triangles   12 triangles   90 degree arc

Fig 2.2
Triangle count

Coincident/overlapping vertices. This is when two or more vertices of the same polyset share identical *XYZ* coordinate values. Sometimes, if the values are not the same, but are within a very close tolerance (like 0.001 of a unit), they are also considered to be *coincident.*

These frequently occur when an artist accidentally cuts an edge so near to a vertex that it is difficult to see that it has happened. They also happen when an artist is using a vertex snap to move one or more vertices, and accidentally puts them in the wrong place. If you have overlapping vertices, they should be welded together. If they haven't been, this is considered sloppy because the extra vertices can interfere with texturing, animation, and lighting as well as creating extra memory demands on your renderer (Fig. 2.3).

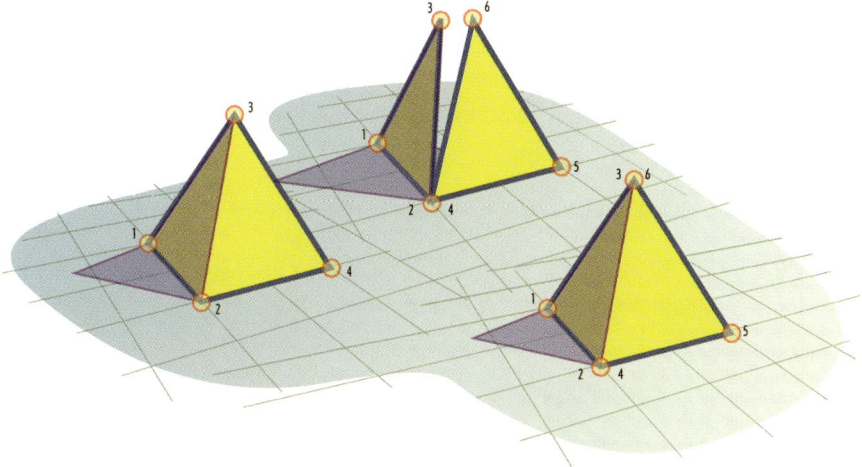

Fig 2.3
Shared vertices across edges, nonshared vertices, and coincident unshared vertices

If you have unmerged coincident vertices in your model, determine how many you have, then use a calculator to find the percentage of unneeded vertices in your model. You should not have any, and anything over 2% of the total is a serious blunder.

Spikes. Spikes usually occur when you move a single vertex while intending to move another one. This is the result of sloppy selection habits. Usually, an artist should verify his selections before moving them to prevent this kind of error. A spike is a vertex that has been pulled away from the main body of the model, without detaching it (Fig. 2.4).

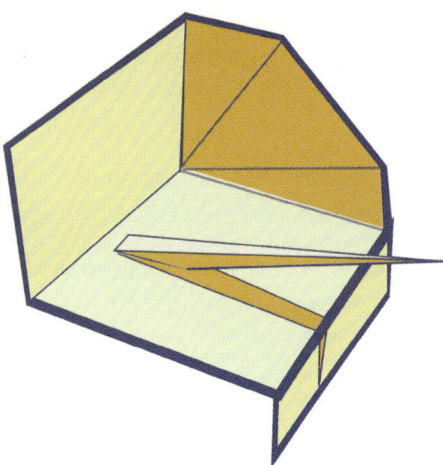

Fig 2.4
A spike. Most often, spikes are less obvious than this

You should not have any spikes in your object. If you have even one, your model cannot be used as is and must be fixed before delivery.

Bow-tie faces. An *n*-sided face (usually a quad) that has been twisted so that its normals, if triangulated, would be facing almost 180° away from each other (Fig. 2.5).

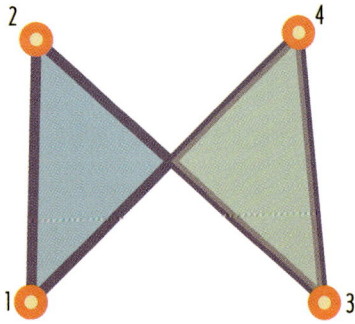

Fig 2.5
A bow-tie face

The easiest way to picture this is to imagine a square of cloth stitched to two rods on either side. If one of the rods were rotated 180°, it would create a bow-tie shape, where the top and bottom edges cross each other. This is the same as a bow-tie polygon.

Bow-tie faces can be difficult to find if they are quite small or are stretched into an obscure cavity of your model. Normally, these are made accidentally, due to improper vertex selection followed by a translate operation. Bow-tie faces are always *nonplanar*, so if your application has a nonplanar highlight function, they may be located by its use.

To fix a face of this type, it is often easiest to delete it and then rebuild the face as it should be built. The only exception is if the vertices of the bow tie are not represented elsewhere in the model and it would be difficult to reposition new vertices in those locations. If this is true of your model, then you should trace over the existing polygon with a new one before deleting the bow-tie face.

You should not have any bow-tie faces in your model. You should check for these and eliminate any you find before delivery.

Smoothing errors. Split normals when they should be united, or united where they should be split adversely affect render quality (Fig. 2.6).

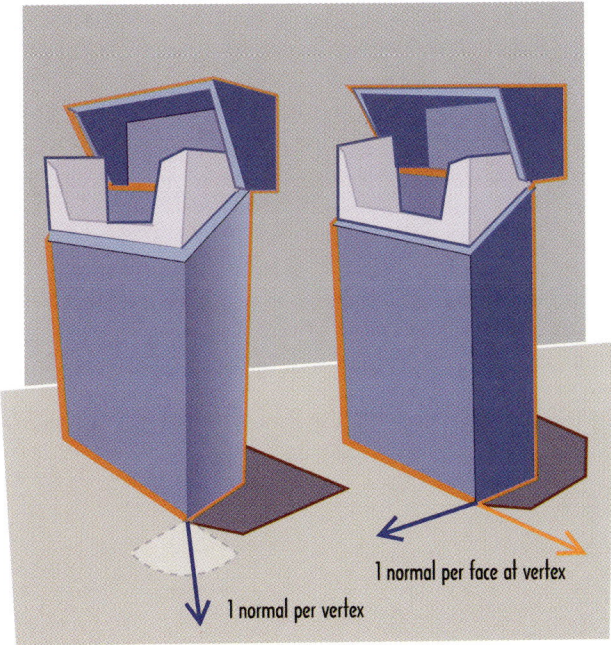

Fig 2.6
Averaged normal on leading edge of box (*left*), split normal on *right*; "smooth" and "hard," respectively

Renderers may render either a hard edge where adjacent faces meet at an edge, or it may use *smooth shading* across the edge. Depending on the type of object and edge, either might be correct. Most objects have edges that fall into both categories, and the more complicated an object is, the more likely it is that it will not be all hard, or all soft, edges.

To render a *smooth edge*, your object will have a single *averaged normal* between two adjacent faces. What this means is that the value for the normal of each face is averaged and a median value found. This causes the *smoothing* effect on the edge. For a hard edge, the normals are *split*, so that the edge has two or more normals at every vertex. Each normal is identical to the normal of each of the faces that meets at that vertex. This causes *hard shading*.

Hard shading would typically be used to define the sharp corners of a table. Smooth shading would be used on every edge of a ball, to prevent a faceted appearance.

Improper smoothing causes shading anomalies when rendered. These resemble out-of-place streaks of dirt or unexpected shadows. Depending on textures, the effect may not be prominent, but often it disrupts the surface of an object enough that it is undesirable.

If the smoothing attributes of your object have not been properly set, you will get shadows where they do not belong on your object. On your carton, you may also get edges that should appear sharp, but do not because this has been ignored or set improperly.

Smoothing errors significantly degrade the quality of rendered output. Therefore, it is best to check your model for this type of error and fix any examples of it that you find before moving on.[2]

Floating faces. One or more faces that belong to a polyset but are not physically connected to the main body of the polyset (Fig. 2.7).

---

[2] Many older video games, primarily those made before Microsoft's first Xbox, have significant numbers of smoothing errors. This is because older console systems were not able to distinguish between hard and soft edges within an object. Instead, the entire object had to be either hard or soft.

Fig 2.7
Floating faces can be very difficult to find because they are often quite small.
Even their shadows are tiny

These are a problem when the floating faces become lost in a file, usually because either they are very distant from the main polyset or they are so small they
are difficult to find.

The most common causes of this problem are automatic and/or globally performed operations that can delete connections between polygons in the same
polyset. Merging vertices with a very high tolerance can cause this, as can any of a
number of automatic polygon reduction tools that use edge length or distance between vertices to determine whether it will merge or delete vertices. If the setting
is too large, whole faces can be destroyed, leaving orphaned triangles floating
around in your scene.

One way to check for the presence of floating faces is to select your object and
then try zooming on it. If you zoom out farther than you expect, you may have
unwanted polys floating around. Another way to check is to select every face in
a very large area. If you see any suspicious highlighted points where they don't
belong, you may have one or more floating faces.

Floating faces cannot be tolerated in any project.

Separated faces. This happens when you build each flap as a separate part or you accidentally *explode* your model. For certain fold operations, this is a cheat that allows folding without distorting the shape of the polygon, but it is cheating in the context of the carton assignment, and if the end result is not brought back together into one polyset, it creates serious geometry errors (Fig. 2.8).

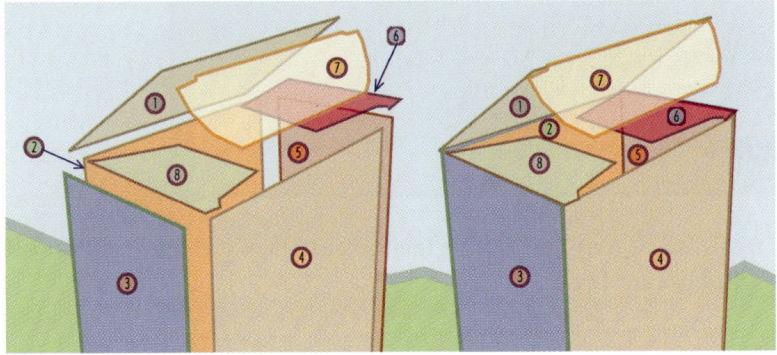

Fig 2.8
The model on the *right* is incorrect because each of its faces is a separate object, as shown in the illustration on the *left*

This particular error is generally considered to be extremely sloppy, as opposed to a simple oversight, like some of the others already mentioned. This is the type of mistake that should be quite apparent even to a novice while working on a model. Do not allow this to happen to your work.

Self-penetration. One of two things, or both, causes this. If your object was not traced accurately, the sides will not match when the carton is folded. The other cause is improper rotation. Most often, both are seen together because the artist will try to over or under transform a flap into position to make up for a measurement error when building the object (Fig. 2.9).

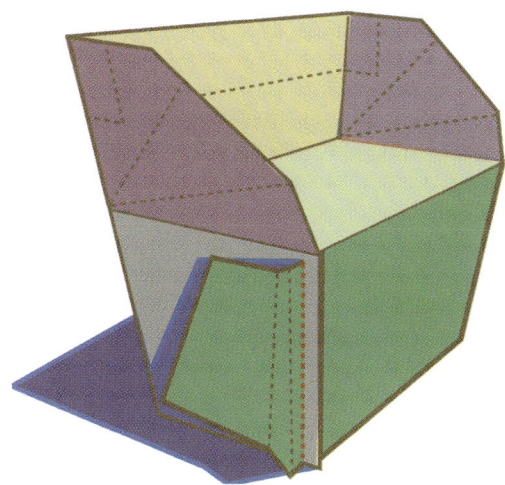

Fig 2.9
Notice how the green flap penetrates the gray side of the carton. This is not allowed

Origin offset. During the folding process, you are quite likely to move the carton away from the global origin. You should move the object back to the global origin when you are done. If you do not, it is considered sloppy work. An accepted industry standard is to have the front of your object facing positive *Z* and to have its center or bottom center located on the global origin (Fig. 2.10).

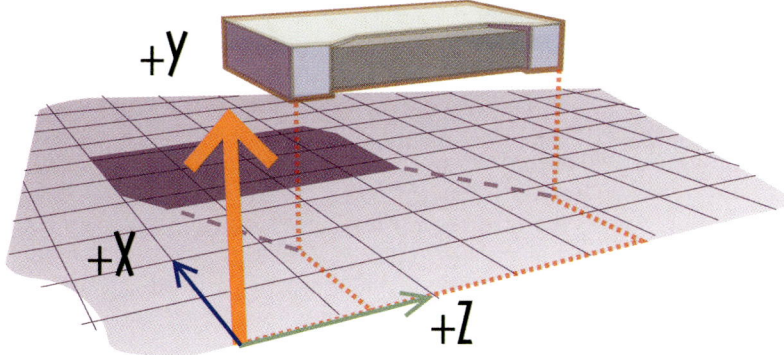

Fig 2.10
Origin offset

This error is not uncommon for inexperienced artists, but it can be very irritating, especially for animators because their animation depends on a correct, untranslated start position.

Nonplanar faces. Faces with four or more sides where one or more vertices do not lie within the same plane as any group of three vertices from the same face.

Nonplanar faces are renderable in most renderers, but can cause unpredictable results. The greater the distance a nonplanar vertex is from the primary plane of the face, the greater the distortion is likely to be. The reason is that the renderer triangulates all nonplanar faces.

If the renderer triangulates a face, it must first decide which way to cut the polygon. Depending on how far from being in the same plane the vertices are, the result can be anything from invisible to a serious fault (Fig. 2.11).

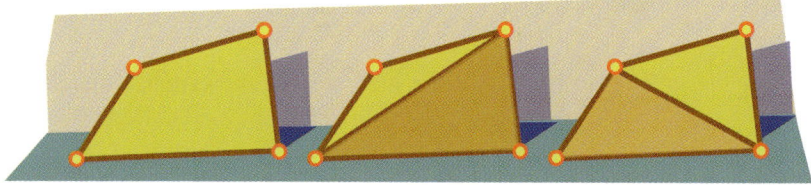

Fig 2.11
The polygon on the far *left* is a nonplanar quad. To the *right* are the two possible outcomes of triangulating the polygon

This is an extremely common mistake, even among professionals. The most common solution is to disguise the problem by subdividing the object globally to increase the polycount. This does not eliminate the error, but reduces its prominence to a level that in most cases is difficult to detect. When working on projects where polycount is an important factor (that would be almost anything), it is better to modify this by hand, without recourse to global subdivision.

Distortion. Some cartons have flaps that, when folded, pull adjacent flaps with them because they are not cut along their edges. With objects like this, it is likely that some distortion will occur during the folding process. There are other causes for distortion, the most common of which is inattention during the pattern layout stage of the project (Fig. 2.12).

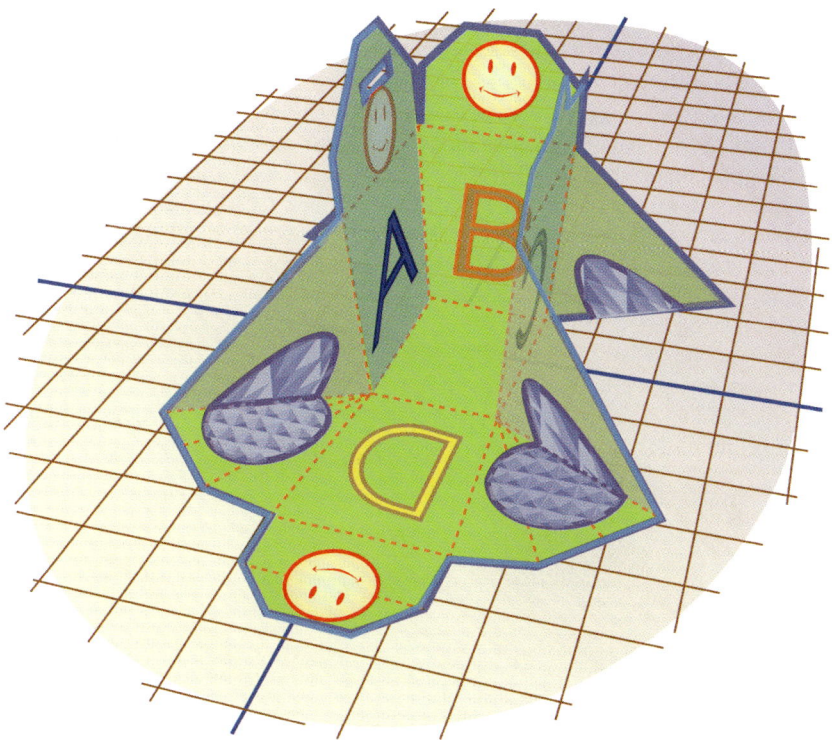

Fig 2.12
In this polyset, triangles connected to flaps *A*, *B*, and *C* have been severely distorted during a rotation operation

Distortion is allowed in certain situations, such as during an animation when it is thought that the movement of the object or camera blur will disguise any distortion. In other situations, especially in close-up shots for theatrical effects, this is not allowed and should be eliminated if present.

Wrong-way normals. A polygonal face where the normal vector is pointing 180° away from the front of the object has wrong-way normals.[3]

Some artists fold one direction; others do the opposite. Depending on which direction you fold your carton, you may or may not have reversed normals.

---

[3] It is possible, though rare, to change a face normal so that it renders as if it is reversed, but the angle of difference is not 180° from the correct orientation.

A face with a reversed normal will appear to be invisible until you turn the camera to the reverse side of the object, where the face will suddenly reappear. Whenever you think you are missing a face, the most likely answer is that it has a *reversed normal*; these are very easy to check for and simple to fix. They are a problem only if you have been incautious with your technique and have manufactured a great many of them. Then, you must search every face of your entire model, flipping normals one by one until they all face the right direction. Some programs allow you to *unify* an object's normals, to make them all point inside or outside, but it doesn't always work. If you use such a tool, you should be prepared to check the result (Fig. 2.13).

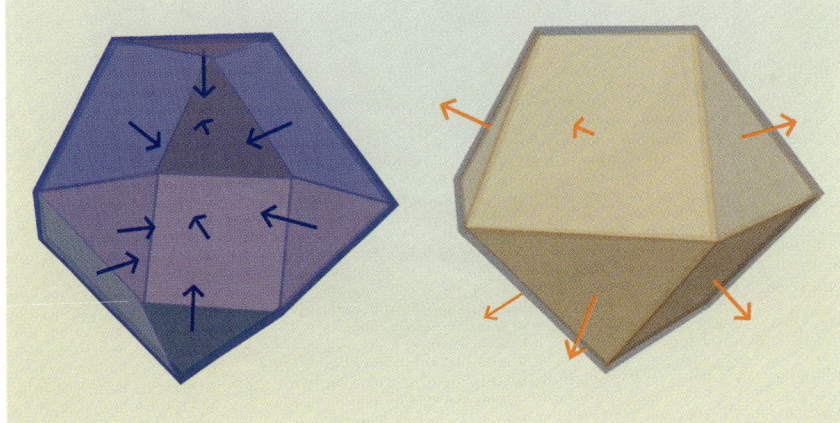

Fig 2.13
Incorrect normals on the *left*, correct on the *right*

Incorrect normals are an extremely serious error and must be fixed wherever they are found. Unfortunately, it is very easy to create this error and you should expect that any model you make would contain at least some reversed normals.

Extremely high polycount. If you have faces that do not contribute to the shape of your object and don't affect the manner in which it is textured, you have completely unnecessary polygons in your model (Fig. 2.14).

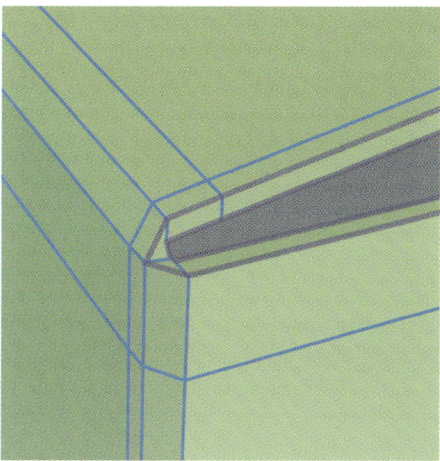

Fig 2.14
Three extra rows of vertices are clearly visible on this model from the carton project

It is generally accepted that exceeding a polycount budget by as much as 10% is not an error if the added polygons contribute to the model. If they do not, it is an error, even if the polycount budget is met exactly.

Misaligned texture. This happens when your texture map is not properly projected and edited (Fig. 2.15).

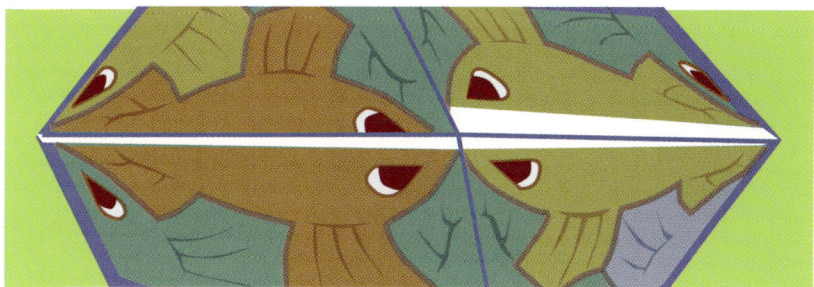

Fig 2.15
Note the whitespace along the seams. In this example, the error was caused by improper UV manipulation

For the carton project, it can only happen if one or both of two things is true:

- You have whitespace around your map.
- You edited the UVs after projecting them.

Depending on the reason this error appears on your model, it can be a more or less serious error. If the mistake is due to whitespace in your texture border, it is easy to fix in an image-editing program by cropping the texture map. If it is due to incorrect texture coordinates, it is more difficult to fix, especially if you've already folded the carton. If this happened with your project, rather than fixing the UVs on the folded carton, it is better to go back to the original unfolded state, reproject the texture coordinates, and then fold the carton all over again.

N-sided polygons, also known as n-gons. With the exception of certain custom-built specialty renderers, most renderers render triangles only. This means that if your object is not built of triangles, the renderer will triangulate your object before it is rendered. If you have a nurbs object,[4] it converts the object into polygons, then triangulates it before rendering. The reason is that normals for a triangle have an absolute value, but for four or more sides, they must be averaged. If the object is *planar*, or all of its vertices lie within the same plane, the normal for the polygon will be the same as for any triangle within it. Many game engines and commercial renderers will not render a polygon with more than four sides. Some will render the polygon, but there is a serious possibility it will not render properly.

N-gons are frequently, but not always, nonplanar. A nonplanar polygon usually does not render as expected and should be reduced to either *quads* (four-sided faces) or triangles. Planar quadrilaterals and triangles only are legal (Fig. 2.16).

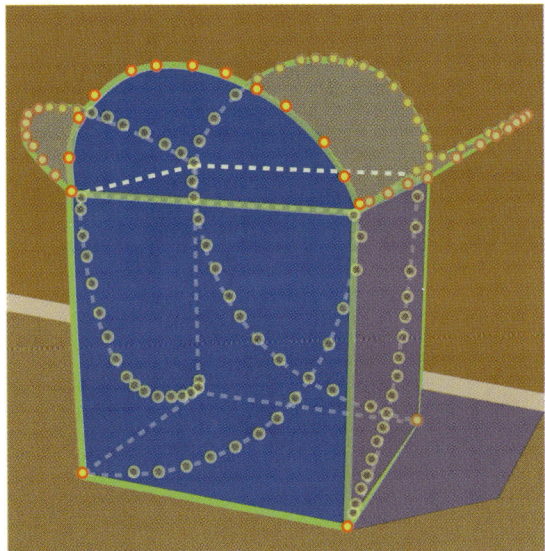

Fig 2.16
Note the number of vertices along a single edge. Whenever you have only two edges on either side of a vertex, you have a polygon that needs to be further subdivided or risk creation of an illegal *n*-gon

---

[4] More on these later.

n-gons cannot be tolerated in a model, but are a very common by-product of the modeling process. Most professionals will create these unintentionally while building an object, and then carefully check the model when they are done and eliminate any *n*-gons they find. A very fast solution to this is to simply triangulate or quadrangulate the object using a global function. The drawback to this method is that it may cut polygons in unexpected ways. Usually, an artist will check a model for all the more prominent locations an error might reside, fix them by hand, and then triangulate the model to catch any small examples he missed.

Unattached (free) faces. This error is usually the result of a conscious decision made to solve a problem, but it is, nevertheless, an error. For the carton project, it happens when an artist isn't sure how to fold a polygon that is attached to other polygons that must move with it. This "solution" requires the removal of the offending faces. The type of carton most likely to create this situation (as in the example given here) is one designed to hold fluids, like a milk carton. The reason is that cartons of this type cannot have open seams or they will leak. To fold it in 3D will cause distortions unless handled properly (Fig. 2.17).

Fig 2.17
The two triangles in this image are connected to the carton on only one edge instead of all three

Solution 1: Detach faces of this type and rotate them individually, then add them back into the polyset and weld the vertices on common edges.

Solution 2: Add a skeletal system to the carton so that when one flap is rotated, connected flaps move with it in an appropriate manner.

If this error is present in your model, it is incomplete and must be fixed.

Extrude error. This occurs when an artist adds depth to the carton after folding it. It can also occur prior to folding, but in that case the effect is of a number of unwanted interior faces as demonstrated earlier. With this type of error, the corners of the object are split along fold lines. This is literally inaccurate and unacceptable for this project (Fig. 2.18).

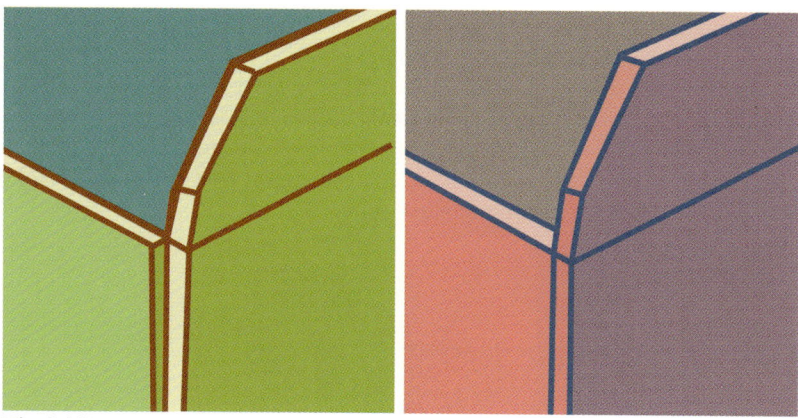

Fig 2.18
Incorrect on the *left*, correct on the *right*

Abnormally large, or abnormally small, face aspect ratio. An *aspect ratio* is the height to width ratio of any given object. If an object's height is 3 and its width is 1.5, then it has an *aspect ratio* of 2. If it is the other way around, with a height of 1.5 and a width of 3, the AR = 0.5.

A large AR for a polygon is any number above 4. Depending on the object, it may be as high as 8 without a problem, but much larger than that and you will have long skinny triangles that do not render well.

A small AR is the same as the long number, but in reverse, so 0.25 is acceptable, and even 0.125 in some circumstances, but below that you should consider modifying your triangulation pattern to increase the AR, so that the triangle isn't too distorted.

An ideal AR for rendering purposes is 1.0 (Fig. 2.19).

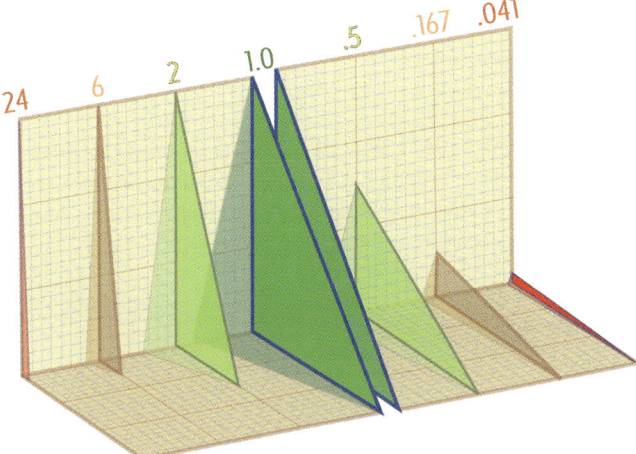

Fig 2.19
Eight triangles, with aspect ratios ranging from 24 to 0.041

Use the *shortest edge-length rule* here to help you determine how to triangulate an object by hand, so that you keep your polygon aspect ratios as close to a value of 1.0 as possible.

Triangulation patterns. It is useful to get in the habit of triangulating your polysets, so that they light evenly and are easy to understand. When looking at complex polysets, triangulation pattern errors can cause serious object recognition problems (Fig. 2.20).

Fig 2.20
Edge layout

Both circular polysets have the same number of vertices and triangles. The edges of the yellow polyset are distributed more evenly than the green polyset. This makes the object easier to understand at first glance and will result in a smoother render.

Lamina faces. When two or more faces share all of the same edges, a *lamina face* is created. This is different from a coincident vertices problem, because with lamina faces there are usually no coincident vertices, despite the presence of more than one face between whatever vertices are present (Fig. 2.21).

Fig 2.21

Polygon 1 has a lamina face. When rotated, it will *flicker* as the software attempts to determine which of two coincident faces is in front of the other. Face 2 is not a lamina face and displays properly

Most artists will not make these intentionally, but there are tools that will cause this error to occur. The best clue that a lamina face is present is if, in shaded mode, a *flickering* is noted when rotating the camera around the face. If this is present, or if the shading on the face appears wrong, you should do a face count to determine how many faces are present. If there is more than one and there should be only one, you probably have lamina faces. Another test is to turn on the normals for the object. Sometimes you will see normals pointing in opposite directions on what appears to be the same face.

Duplicate edges. Two or more edges that occupy the same space will cause rendering problems that resemble smoothing errors.

These edges are frequently the result of vertex merging; automatic cleanup and automatic polycount reduction operations. Sometimes, they occur during manual editing, but are more often a product of the automatic tools.

Duplicate edges can be very difficult to find if you aren't looking for them. The easiest way to know they exist is if you try to cut a face, but cannot. This sometimes means that the edge you see and want to cut is not the only edge present. In this case, another edge might not be properly connected to the rest of the face, and so your cut attempt is impossible because you are unintentionally selecting edges that do not belong to the same face (Figs. 2.22 and 2.23).

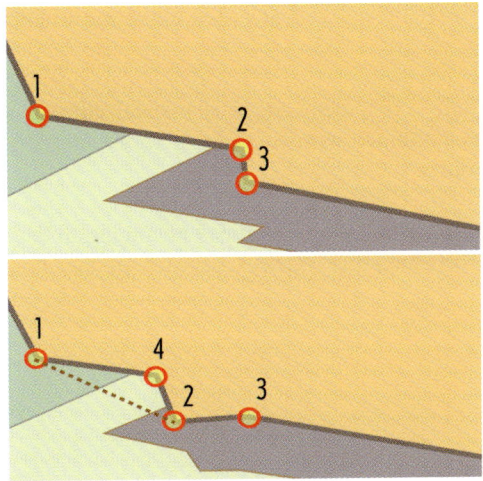

Fig 2.22
In this image, hidden edge 1|4 is exposed when vertex 2 is moved

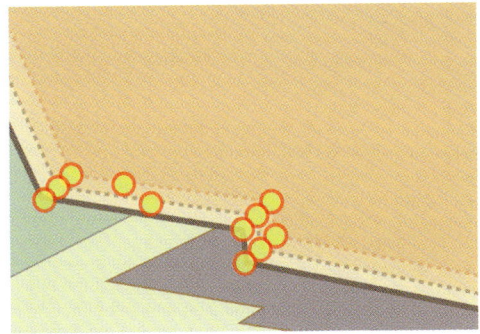

Fig 2.23
This image represents a face with duplicate edges *after* they have been discovered and pulled away from the face. Prior to discovery, these edges, and the extra vertices that define them, are invisible

In the top image, three vertices are visible. Only when vertex 2 is translated, as shown in the lower frame, the existence of vertex 4 is known. If the extra edge directly connected between vertices 1 and 2, then vertex 4 would only be visible from the opposite side of this polygon.

A *partially coincident edge* is easier to detect than a *coincident edge* because you may select an edge and see that its length is not correct. It either terminates before reaching a visible vertex, or extends straight through and beyond a visible vertex. In either case, this observation indicates the presence of two or more edges where you expect to see one. With partially coincident edges, there are usually three or more.

The most common cause of partially coincident edges is manual editing of polygons that have five or more sides combined with later use of vertex merging, face deletion, or other optimization efforts.

Coincident faces. Two or more faces where all of the vertices belonging to each face have identical *XYZ* values as corresponding vertices on each of the other faces (Fig. 2.24).

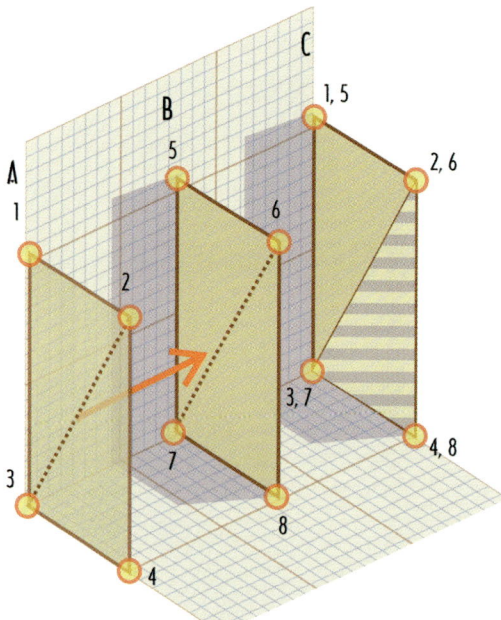

Fig 2.24

When face *A* is made coincident with face *B*, the polyset *C* is the result. Polyset *C* contains individually selectable faces *A* and *B* as well as all of their components. Polyset *C* will not render properly, but can be fixed if faces *A* and *B* are separated

The most common cause of this error is the use of polygonal extrusion tools, then canceling the operation after the extrusion is made, but before the new faces have been moved into position. Another common cause is duplicating an object without moving it to a new location. This is especially common when the object copy function is mapped to a hotkey and then it is accidentally pressed.

Coincident faces may be found when there is *flicker*[5] during camera rotation in shaded mode. Another indication of *coincident faces* is when you attempt to edit a face, but you cannot. Sometimes, it is because you select a face that cannot display properly because it is drawn underneath the one you can see, so the results of your editing are not visible.

Cracks, or gaps, within a polyset. An opening in a polyset where the polyset is supposed to be closed creates an unwanted gap (Fig. 2.25).

Fig 2.25
A typical geometry gap in what should be a closed pair of rectangles

A *false gap* is when a polygon has a *reversed normal* and appears to be missing, but is not. When you think you have a gap, you should always check to see if it is a *false gap* before you fill it, or risk creating *coincident faces* or even *lamina faces*.

---

[5] *Flicker* is caused when the renderer is forced to decide which of two coincident faces is in front of the other. Because they are *coincident*, it cannot determine

This error is most often caused by translation or rotation errors. Another common cause is when two or more pieces are brought together into the same polyset, but edges that should be adjacent are not sealed.

Frequently, unless great care is taken during the design process, shared edges between different components of an object have a different number of vertices. For a polyset to be free of gaps, either side of a common edge must have the same number of vertices. The most practical solution is usually to either add or subtract vertices from one side or the other, then to snap the vertices together and merge them when done.

Holes. A *hole* is a polygon with two or more complete borders, one inner and one outer, made of adjacent edges that form two or more unbroken loops (Fig. 2.26).

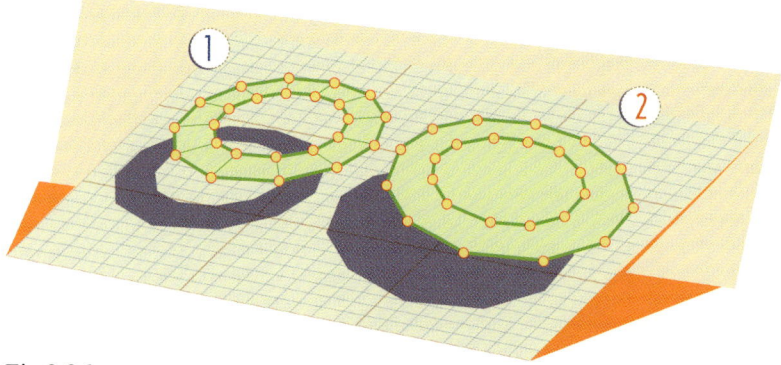

Fig 2.26
The polygon on the *right* does not have the inner ring of vertices connected to the outer ring by edges, as on the *left*. This creates a *hole* error

Some applications will render a polygon with a hole, but they may not render it correctly. Depending on your renderer, the result could be like either of the two examples illustrated above. Unless you have a specific reason for building a hole, you may want to clean up any that you have built.

Unlike a nonhole polygon, a polygon with a hole does not have an easily defined start and endpoint for triangulation purposes. This can cause some geometry-editing functions fail.

that either is truly in front of the other. The renderer will then either try to draw both at the same time or it will switch from one to the other and back again. Either way, you will see an obvious flickering as the renderer tries to solve this problem.

A face with a hole must be an *n*-gon or the hole would be impossible. This increases the risk of the *n*-gon also being nonplanar. Combined with loss of editing functionality, it is usually best to triangulate a hole and then edit any remaining problems afterward.

The most common source of this error is when an artist first makes an object like the example on the left in the illustration, and then deletes the edge connections.

Nonmanifold geometry. Like hole geometry, it is not literally an error to make nonmanifold geometry, but it can interfere with some editing functions, so it is good to know what it looks like. Nonmanifold geometry describes polygons that cannot be unfolded flat without overlap due to a convergence of three or more edges at a single vertex (Fig. 2.27).

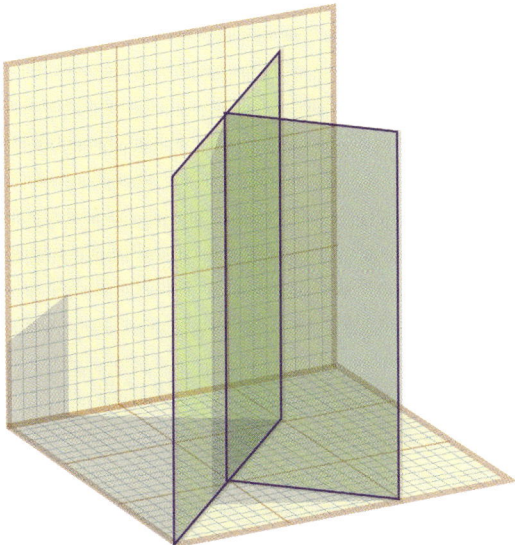

Fig 2.27
Nonmanifold geometry. If unfolded, the polygon on the *right* would have to either overlap the polygon on the *left* or be cut free to have nonoverlapping texture coordinates

Excessively dense vertex groupings. A polyset where the number of vertices per linear unit is much greater in one location than in another creates this problem.

The shape of an object sometimes requires this, but if it does not, care should be taken to avoid this result. First, it indicates a higher level of polygonal resolution in one area than in another. If this is the case, the smoother portion of the object will unflatteringly draw attention to the less smooth part. Secondly, this indicates an incomplete state of any *de-rez* process that may have been started, where the resolution of an object is reduced to a designated polycount (Fig. 2.28).

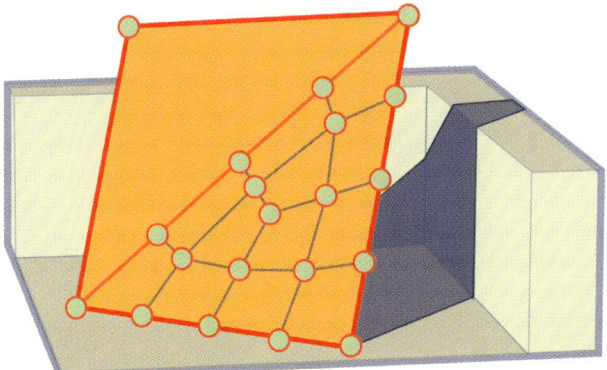

Fig 2.28

The orange object should have only four vertices. Because the mesh has been subdivided on one side, it has a much higher number of vertices in one half of the object than the other. Because they are the same size and there are no other benefits to the extra vertices, this is a waste of vertices

Ragged polyset borders. An edge shared by two polysets where the edge travels across the logical border between the two parts and back again without regard for the logical division between the two.

This happens when an inexperienced artist, concerned only with the overall shape of an object, disregards logical internal boundaries within an object (Fig. 2.29).

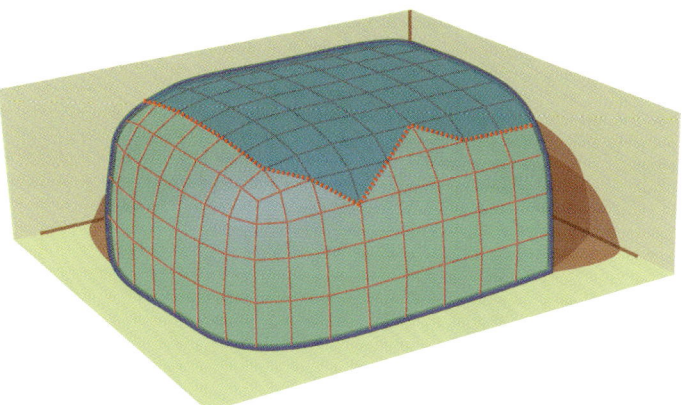

Fig 2.29
In this object, the *dotted red line* represents the border between two polysets. Unless your object requires a jagged edge for a specific reason, they are considered undesirable. They usually result from inattention during editing polyset face members

Isolated vertices. Any vertex that is connected to no more than two other vertices by edges is an isolated vertex (Fig. 2.30).

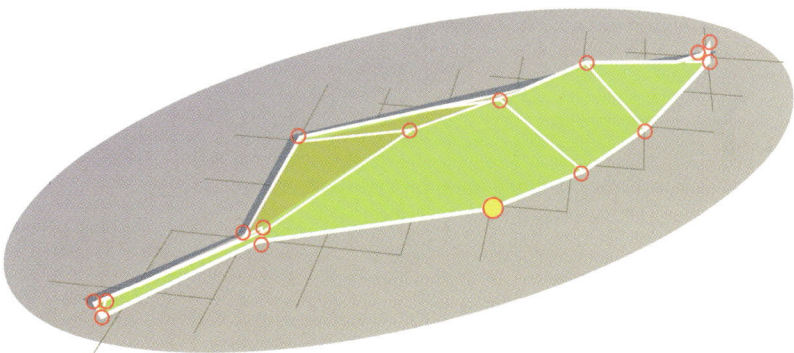

Fig 2.30
In this example, the highlighted vertex is an *isolated vertex* because it has fewer than three edge connections

Vertices of this type contribute nothing to a model and must be deleted. They are very common and may be created in many ways. All major applications have tools built to find and eliminate these pesky remnants of the modeling process, but sometimes it is best to simply select them and delete.

If you use the select and delete solution, be careful to avoid selecting corners of flat planes because these are technically isolated vertices even though you want to keep them.

Locked normals. An object with locked normals often renders nearly black, with very faint highlights, despite having a strong light (Fig. 2.31).

Fig 2.31
In this example, the floor does not have locked normals, so it receives a shadow from the character. The character's normals are locked, so it renders as a silhouette

You will know this has happened if your object does not seem to receive light when lights are brought into your scene. It will receive light, but so faintly that it will barely be detectable. The reason is that it will only accept light from the same position as the lights from the scene it was in when the normals were locked.

Most applications have a button that will allow you to unlock normals. If this does not work, you should be able to recalculate them by reimporting your object.

This error is increasingly rare. You may only encounter it occasionally, but it is disturbing if you don't know what it is (Fig. 2.32).

Fig 2.32
Here, a character model has had its vertices reordered. This causes edges to
connect to the wrong vertices, with the result seen here

Offset vertex order. This usually happens during corrupted save operations
and is not evident until reopening the file. It is one of the few errors that is impossible to miss. It causes your vertices to be connected improperly. The resulting shape
usually looks like a number of jagged triangles, with a faint resemblance to your
model only evident in its size and silhouette. Depending on how serious the error
is, it may be possible to fix by creating a script to renumber the vertices in your file.

Zero edge-length faces. A face whose edges are each zero units in length (Fig. 2.33).

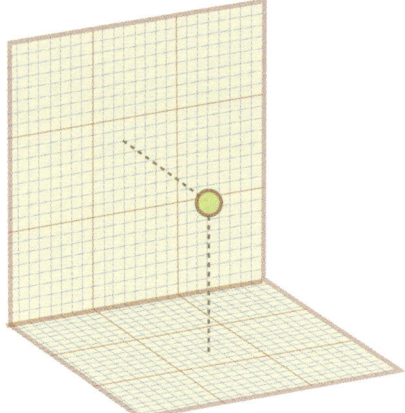

Fig 2.33
A zero edge-length face can be selected, but will not be visible as more than a single highlighted pixel

These faces occur during merge vertex and other de-rezing operations. They can be very difficult to delete because their zero edge-length condition makes them illegal in a way that makes it difficult to perform many editing operations on them, including deletion. For instance, they are literally *faces*, but because they have no physical dimension, they are not treated as faces. Deleting them is often not possible, nor can their component edges and vertices be deleted because doing so would delete the face as well. Sometimes, the only way to delete these is to use a global operation on your object that selectively truncates an entire side of it, and make sure it is the side containing the zero edge-length faces.

If you have a cleanup tool that can find these, use it. Faces of this type are highly illegal and can cause crashes in game engines and renderers. Some renderers will ignore them, but others may behave unpredictably.

Hidden challenges in the carton project. Putting a skeleton into a carton, especially the type that contains fluids can eliminate certain types of translation distortion.

Texture coordinates on the inside of the box will be reversed unless you manually reverse them. This is only true of cartons where thickness is added.

If you first attempted a very simple object, you should next attempt a more complicated carton before moving on, to give you the opportunity to solve some of the more complicated transformation problems that will be present. The skills taught in this exercise are essential to working in any 3D program. If your object contained a large number of errors, you should make another carton before moving on.

Organization

Organizing a file can be like trying to find your grandparent's tax returns from 50 years ago. You don't know where they are, what they look like, how they might be labeled, or whether they have been destroyed or lost. The principal challenge, when organizing a CG file then, is to make sure this doesn't happen. You want to be able to find any element of your scene quickly. You want to be able to give your file to someone else, and without any instruction that person should be able to navigate your file just as well as you can. You don't want any of the parts you labored over to get lost, or connections between related objects to be broken like so many war orphans and their lost parents (Fig. 2.34).

Fig 2.34
If your file is well organized, you won't need to be a detective to find anything

Your file should be so well organized that when other artists open your file, they will be impressed by how neat it is. They will be fascinated to such a degree that they will check and recheck the file to make sure they haven't missed anything, but they won't have because your file will contain no litter.

Accomplishing this is not difficult if you know how, but it does require some patience. Failure to properly organize your file can lead to serious consequences. It is one of the primary causes of professional discourtesy between artists. If one artist cannot locate or use a needed element due to improper organization, disagreements will arise. The larger a file is, the more elements it has, and the more likely it is that this will happen. In your work, you need to develop good organizational habits immediately. The sooner you start, the better off you will be.

The two primary methods of organizing a 3D file are through *naming* and *grouping*.

Naming simply means to think up and assign a unique name for every element in your file. Depending on your file, this could mean naming a small group of element types or a very large group. For a simple model, you may only have to name the object itself. If there is only one object of that type in your scene, it is even easier. If it represents a suitcase, the name could simply be *suitcase*. Here are some tips for naming objects:

Use *padded numbers*. These are numbers used as suffixes at the end of a name for your object. The *padding* consists of leading zeroes at the beginning of the number. These cause the numbers to sort properly in a computer. Failing to do this will result in the number "2" coming after the number "002" or "19." If you *expect* to need less than a hundred numbers, use a two-space pad or ##. If you need less than a thousand but more than a hundred, use a three number pad, ###, and so on.

Lowercase/uppercase. Capital letters sort ahead of lowercase letters. Keep this in mind when you decide how you will name objects in your file. Some programs use capital letters as hotkeys. To avoid accidentally invoking hotkeys, and to keep their object organization nice and neat, many artists name objects in their scene starting with a lowercase letter. If it requires more than one word, the second and each successive word are capitalized. Here is an example: suitcase-LeatherRed02.

Use a *naming convention*. A naming convention is most often used for files that belong to a common database, but is also used to name components within a file. A famous naming convention that is no longer commonly used is the *8.3 convention*, forced on PC users by the MS-DOS operating system. This convention required users to provide no more than eight characters for a file's primary name, then three characters or less for a *suffix*, with a dot in between.

In computer graphics, *descriptive names* are usually preferred because they are easier to understand by team members. Here are some examples of different conventions:

1.   Suitcase.obj (8.3)
2.   sc01.obj (initials, padded, 8.3)
3.   suitCase (lowercase/uppercase, descriptive)
4.   suitCase01 (lowercase/uppercase, descriptive, padded)

Whatever convention you decide to use, you must consistently apply it or it will be of little value.

Grouping is an operation that combines objects under a common node (Fig. 2.35).

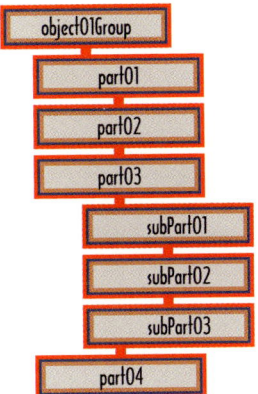

Fig 2.35
Hierarchy example

If an object is grouped to itself, a new node will be created and the original object grouped under it. If two or more objects are selected, they will be grouped under a new node. In some applications, it is possible to group an object to another object. When that is done, no new node is created. If you do this, keep in mind that the top-level object will not be individually selectable unless its subordinate objects are removed from the group.

Grouping is an excellent way to organize different elements of a scene and to create *hierarchies* of objects. For instance, if you are building a hairbrush out of several parts, you will want to group all of the subordinate parts under a name like *hairbrush*. If the hairbrush rests on a table littered with other props, you may want to group all of these items under the group *desk props*. This in turn might be grouped to *desk*, which is a member of the group *furniture*, and that is part of the group *living room*, etc. Ultimately, you want your scene grouped in an ascending hierarchy that allows you to select different elements of the scene easily, and at differing levels of detail.

If your hierarchy is not logical, your file may be confusing to others. Worse, it may not animate or render properly. Grouping affects animation because animation is applied to individual nodes. If those nodes are part of a group, then all nodes subordinate to the animated node will be affected by the animation of well. If you have the tires on the right side of a car grouped together, for instance, they will rotate together, even if their opposites on both axles remain motionless.

If you move a subordinate node from its position below an animated node, it will immediately cease to be animated by that node. In the same way, if an animated node is added to a group, all of its new subordinates will inherit its animation. For this reason, objects that will be animated independently of other scene elements are kept independent at the group level as well.

From now on, you should get in the habit of naming and grouping everything you make. This is one of the easiest skills you can possibly pick up, yet the value it returns is well worth the effort it takes because many people (including professionals) are not willing to make the extra effort to do this properly. The result is that people who do name and group their scene objects properly are generally more highly regarded than those who don't.

Most 3D applications have *layers*, a method of sorting selected items under arbitrarily named separation barriers. Often layers have several attribute flags that may be set for all objects within them. The most common are visibility and *sensitivity*.[6] If the sensitivity flag is off, objects on that layer cannot be selected, but they will be drawn to the screen as long as the visibility flag is set to on.

Layers are useful for creating temporary working space as you construct an object or a scene. With them, you can store stray objects that are either unfinished, in the way, or temporary save objects just before you execute a risky modeling operation.

Material assignments are another way to organize data in a 3D file. With these, you may create several different *materials* for your scene, like wood, stone, and glass, and then assign individual polygons, groups of polygons, or polysets to them. Once this is done, most applications will allow you to select objects based on material assignment.

Organization is very easily described and executed. It takes a little patience but pays off disproportionately to your effort, and in your favor. Whenever you go through the tedious work that naming is sometimes considered to be, remember that you are saving yourself from future disagreements with colleagues and will simultaneously earn a reputation for being a considerate modeler.

---

[6] Like other terms of this type, the actual name of the function will vary depending on which application you are using.

Chapter 3: Measurements

In the first project, you didn't have to worry about measurements unless you weren't able to scan your carton reference. Even though most of you didn't overtly take any measurements, your actions caused measurements to be taken. When you scanned the carton, the scanner used a consistent pixel to linear dimension ratio, commonly known as *dots per inch*, or DPI. By doing this, the exact dimensions of your scanned carton become embedded in the resulting image. If it was scanned at 150 dpi for instance, and one edge was 750 pixels in length, then that edge is 5-in. long (Fig. 3.1).

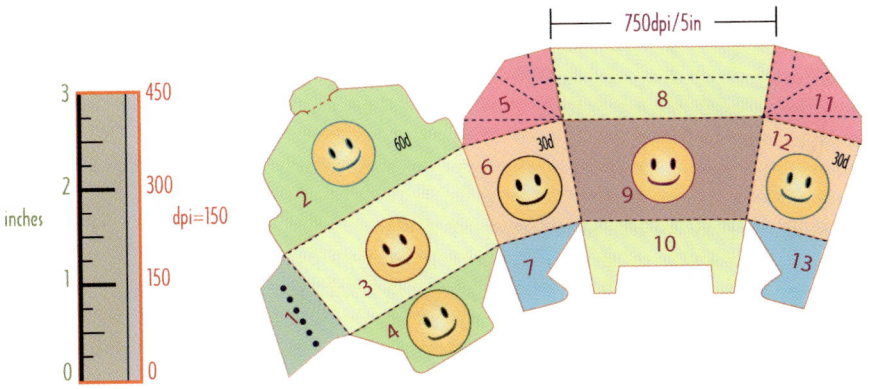

Fig 3.1
Correspondence of linear and pixel measurement units

In some ways, modeling is all about measurements, and without them, there would be no such thing as 3D graphics.

When you built your carton, that 5-in. side could have been almost any length, because there are many ways to import an image into a 3D program and some applications will import an image without regard for the DPI setting. This didn't matter for the carton exercise, because your goal was more about getting familiar with your applications' interface, transformation tools, component editing, and the relationship between a design and the finished object. Now it will matter, because for target objects that cannot simply be scanned in flat like a take-out carton, you will have to acquire the measurements yourself.

All things in a CG environment rely on measurements for their depiction. Models are constructed entirely of measurements of the distance from a three-dimensional station point to another three-dimensional location, or vertex. Textures are located on objects based on two-dimensional measurements within X, Y

object space. Lights are located based on measurements; their intensity is a measurement, as are all of their other variables.

Modeling, then, is measuring. The quality of the measurements used in a CG scene will determine the quality of the scene itself. Ask yourself this: what is the difference between 2 and 3 mm? In the context of this discussion, the difference is 150%. Imagine what that means. Robert Pershing Wadlow, the tallest man to have his height authenticated by the Guinness book of world records, was 8'11.1" (2.72 m) at his death. At this height, he was 150% as tall as someone who was 5'11" (1.81 m). Here is an illustration of Mr. Wadlow standing beside his brother as an example of the difference 50% makes to a measurement (Fig. 3.2).

Fig 3.2
Robert Wadlow and brother, the difference 150% makes

Despite the enormous difference between the height of Mr. Wadlow and his brother, and all other things that are 150% the size of something else, CG artists frequently mismeasure their subject by much more than 50%. This is especially true of newer artists, who have not developed sensitivity to accurate measurements yet.

Measurements, whether accurate or not, are called *dimensions* in the field of Computer Graphics (as well as in Architecture and Engineering). Dimensions are very important to the computer artist because they are the only tools by which the structure of a three-dimensional object may be described to any CG animation or CAD application.

So far, we have only discussed height. Height is only one measurement, and it is meaningless if depth and width measurements are inaccurate. If they do not match; if the bridge of the nose is longer than a finger and the finger is shorter than an ear, then you have internally inconsistent dimensions that will require a great deal of editing to fix.

This is why it is important to always have a fixed standard against which you may test your measurements. One way to do this is to simply decide that all of your measurements will be in millimeters (for small objects), centimeters (for human-scale objects), and meters (for larger structures). Once you have made this decision, you can measure your target object against the dimension units you have elected to use for that object class. The result will be accurate dimensions that you may easily use to construct an accurate replica of your target object. If instead you simply make things bigger or smaller than each other based on an estimate of their dimensions, you will have problems.

Measuring different types of objects presents different problems for an artist. This is why some objects are known to be more difficult than others to represent. This is as true of computer graphics as it was for artists who painted or sculpted their works hundreds of years ago. They too were measuring their objects, though in their case they rarely used measuring tools. Instead, they trained their eyes to recognize proportional differences between objects and then used this as a fixed standard against which they could test their dimension observations.

When Giovanni Bellini painted his famous masterpiece *St Francis*, the realism of the painting is largely a reflection of the accuracy of his observations regarding the dimensions of the elements in the painting, as well as their colors (another measurement). In this painting, Bellini painted several object classes that are very difficult to measure accurately in three dimensions. The figure of *St Francis*, for example, and his donkey are both characters and are made of many complex surfaces. The trees, grass, and other landscape elements are at least as complicated as the figures and in some cases, even more so (Fig. 3.3).

Fig 3.3
Giovanni Bellini, *St Francis in the Desert* 1480

This is because some things cannot easily be measured with a simple ruler or yardstick. There are many different types of measurements, and many ways to take these measurements. The primary types are these (Fig. 3.4):

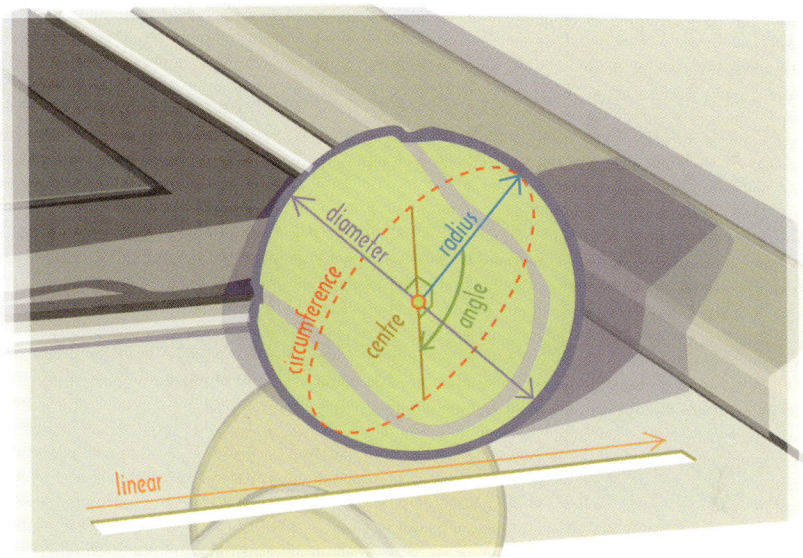

Fig 3.4
Measurement types

1. Linear
A dimension defined exclusively as the distance between one point and another. This can be the distance from a station point to a location on a given object,
or the distance between two points on the same or two different objects. Linear
measurements are the easiest to make. Most commonly, these are found in architectural subjects.

2. Radius
The distance from the center of a circle to any point on the circle. This is the
most common method of describing a circle in computer graphics.

It is often not possible to measure from the physical center of an object to its
surface to determine its radius. To determine this measurement, it is more common to first measure the diameter of a circular object and then divide the number
by 2.

3. Diameter
The length of a straight line that passes through the center of a circular object
and terminates at either end where it intersects the surface of the object. This
measurement type is not used in CG, but may be used to determine radius.

This measurement is usually fairly easily acquired by using a device known as a *caliper*.

   4.   Angle

The measure of deviation of two points from a common location.

This type of measurement is easily accomplished for planar surfaces by using a *protractor* or by *calculation* based on information contained in your target object.

Most often, angle measurements are of use in architectural and industrial design subjects. These are more easily ascertained than for characters or organic subjects, where angular measurements are rarely feasible due to surface complexity.

For nonplanar or three-dimensional subjects, angular measurements may be very difficult to obtain with any degree of accuracy. For extremely complex objects, these measurements are best taken after digitizing the object with a 3D scanner or digitizer.

   5.   Surface curvature

The angle of inclination of a tangent at a location on a surface combined with arc length.

Although all things have surface curvature, in CG, this term is not ordinarily applied to polygons or planar nurbs surfaces. Instead, it is used when describing surfaces that have a regular modification of tangent direction and value along the surface of an object. A car hood, the blade of a propeller, a leaf from a tree, or any form of human or animal anatomy are all examples of objects that have these types of surfaces.

Most often, surfaces described this way are known as *organic*.

Measuring surface curvature of an object is very difficult to accomplish accurately without using a laser scanner or a digitizer.

For objects with a high degree of surface curvature, a number of techniques are available to describe them. For engineering subjects, nurbs geometry is most commonly used. For characters and other complex organic subjects, either digitized geometry is used or drawings made of the subject.

In the case of drawings, they are approximations, and rely heavily on the skill of the artist who makes them and the ability of the modeler to interpret them.

6.   Geometric

This type of measuring has been in use for thousands of years and relies heavily on *proportions*, or the relative size or magnitude of any two items to each other, or of any part of an item to itself. To determine proportions accurately, Math or Geometry is used to divide circles and squares into parts that can then be recombined with other shapes to create new objects that are all based on a common network of measurements.

In this way, many of the world's greatest temples, mosques, and palaces were designed (Fig. 3.5).

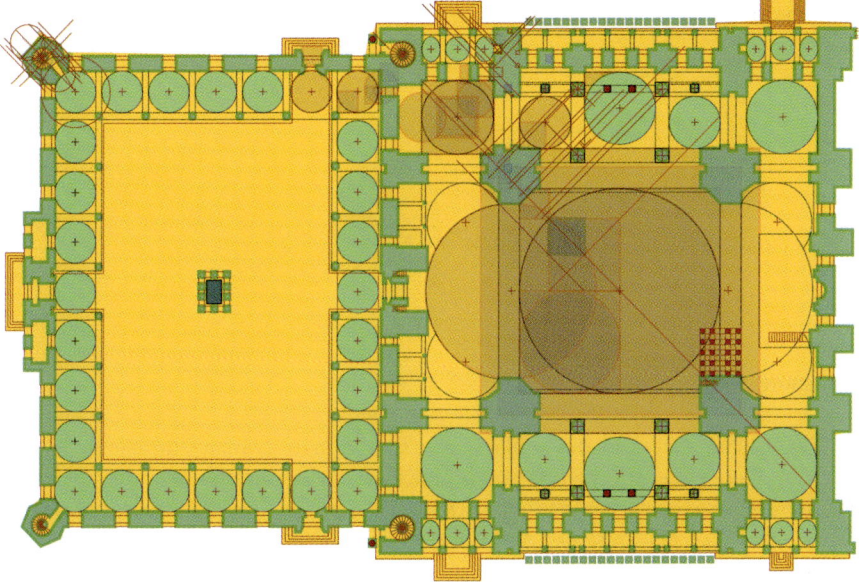

Fig 3.5
Floor plan of the Suleymaniye Mosque, Istanbul, Turkey

For many architectural subjects, a geometric analysis combined with a single linear dimension (usually total height or width of a structure) is enough to generate an accurate CG facsimile of the original.

You may wonder now if you are supposed to go out to a museum and digitize a suit of armor the next time you want to build a knight, or travel to India and measure the Taj Majal with a ruler to build a copy of that building. This is not usually practical, and most often is too time consuming for a typical CG project. What you should do, however, is to develop a sensitivity to dimensions and respect their value in any project. Therefore, before building something, you should always make an effort to obtain as many reliable dimensions as you can before you start. Here are some of the most common methods of achieving this (Fig. 3.6).

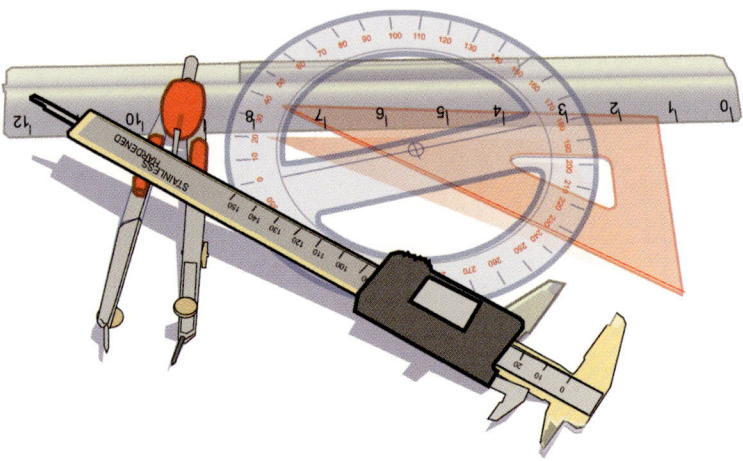

Fig 3.6
Measuring tools

If you have access to the subject, you should take as many measurements as you can. Depending on the object, you may use a ruler, protractor, tape measure, micrometer, yardstick, or any other measurement device, as appropriate. You should also take photographs. Your photos should capture all of the information needed to build your object. At a minimum, you should photograph the subject from several different *orthographic* angles:

- *Orthographic*. Aligned at 90° to the picture plane. For symmetrical objects, a side, front, and top view are usually sufficient. Asymmetrical details will require additional photographs.

The longer your lens is, the more orthographic the resulting image will be. The most common lens lengths (35–50 mm) will produce noticeable *fisheye* distortion when photographing large subjects from near distances. A 200-mm lens will give you a fairly good result, but you will have to be farther away from your object to photograph it properly. In enclosed spaces, this will not work (Fig. 3.7).

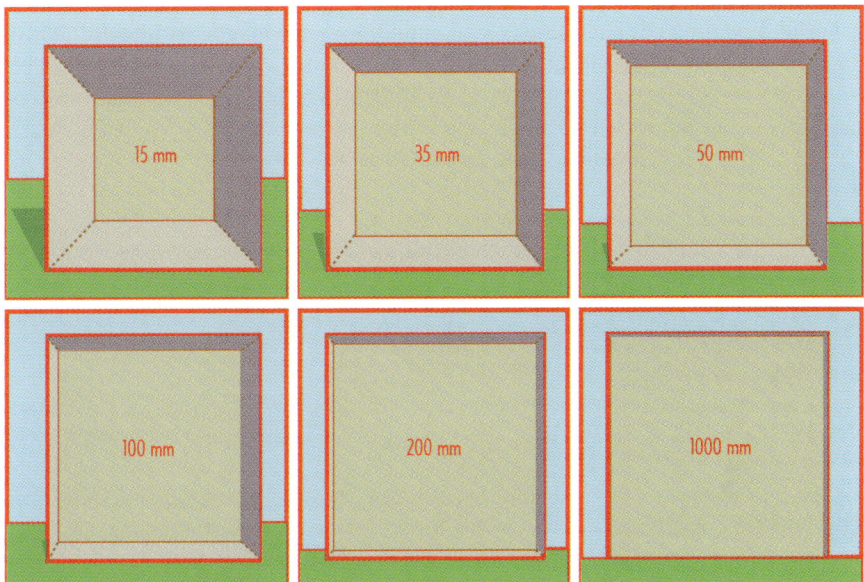

Fig 3.7
The same cube, viewed with six different lenses. The longer the lens, the more distortion is reduced, with the view becoming nearly orthographic, or without distortion, at 1,000 mm

If you do not have direct access to your subject, you will have to rely on whatever you can find through research. In a best-case scenario, you will find dimensioned drawings of your subject. This is most likely with architectural and industrial design objects, whose plans are often a matter of public record.[7] If you cannot find dimensioned drawings, and quite often this will be true, the next best thing is a group of orthographic photographs, particularly if combined with a known measurement of something in the scene.

Sometimes, you will find drawings of your subject, but no photographs. These may be better than photos, because they usually contain structural information that would otherwise be obscured by a photo.

A drawing, if it is not dimensioned, or if it is not drawn to scale, is always subject to interpretation. If you must work from this sort of reference, the degree to which you are sensitive to dimensions will determine your success.

_____

[7] Check out the US patent office website for online plans of many interesting objects from the simple to the extremely complex.

How do you improve your sensitivity to dimensions? By measuring things, this is the only way. At some point in your life, you learned how to identify colors because someone indicated to you which color names corresponded to which colors. In the same way, you can learn dimensions by measuring the objects around you and remembering the results. How tall is the average seat of a chair? Think about it for a moment. How tall could it be? How short is it? What is its absolute height, in feet or meters? Write down what you think the answer is, then take a ruler and measure a nearby chair and see if you got it right. Do the same thing for the width of a door, the height of a refrigerator, or any other group of common objects in your home.

If you are like most people, your answers were incorrect. People who have a professional knowledge of dimensions can accurately estimate them to within a single percentage point, but most people are off by at least 150%, or the difference between the height of the world's tallest man Robert Wadlow and his brother.

One reason for this is the difference between *absolute* and *relative* dimensions. Absolute dimensions are measurements made against a fixed standard, such as an inch or a centimeter as represented on a measuring device. Comparing one thing to another makes a relative measurement. In CG, a relative measurement can be just as accurate as an absolute measurement, because within a CG environment, all measurements are based on a fixed standard imposed by the software.

Outside of a computer, many people use a different type of standard for relative measurements. For them, things are "big," "small," or "average." Robert Wadlow, then, is not 8'11.2", an *absolute dimension*, instead, he is "big." The result of measuring in this way is that gross exaggerations take place. If something is "big" it is made too big. If it is "small" it is too small. If it is "average" and the real dimension of "average" is unknown, it could be just about anything. This is why Lara Croft's bed in the original *Tomb Raider* game for the PSX game console is large enough to accommodate an entire cavalry regiment and the horses they rode in on. The makers of the game wanted her to have a "big" bed, but gave her something that would have required special engineering to support and had no practical value outside of an even "bigger" bedroom, which she also had.

The *cascading effect* of inaccurate dimension estimates is that each inaccurate dimension will be compared relative to every other inaccurate dimension as new objects are added to a scene, and their sizes adjusted to suit. This can result in a building being far too big because a room is too big because a bed is too big because a "big" bed was desired. When the character meant to sleep in that bed is the right height (because most people know their own height), then everything else becomes wrong in comparison.

This also happens within objects. Most people are sensitive to certain gross measurements, such as that the upper leg is longer than the upper arm. Without training, however, they do not ordinarily recognize that the top view contour of their jaw is a truncated acute triangle. The angle is quite severe compared to most artist's expectations and is frequently distorted into either a square or a circular shape (Fig. 3.8).

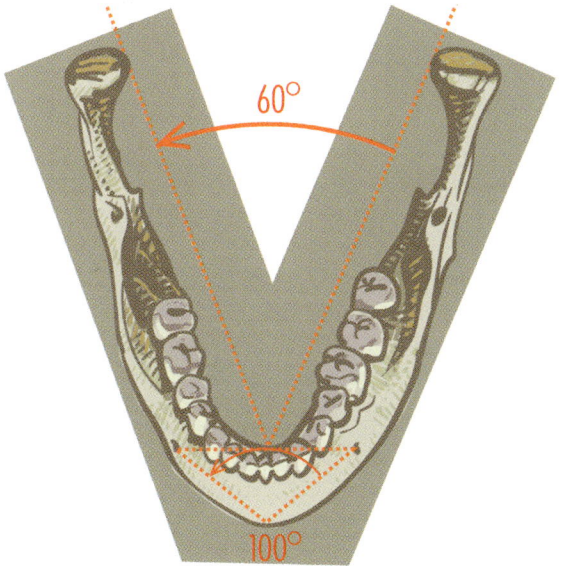

Fig 3.8
A human mandible, as seen from above. Note the severe 60° angle of the two sides of the bone. At its widest point, at the chin, it is 100°

With measurements, it is best not to guess. If you have a way to check, you should get in the habit of doing so, at least until you are familiar enough with dimensions that you can estimate them with reasonable accuracy (Fig. 3.9).

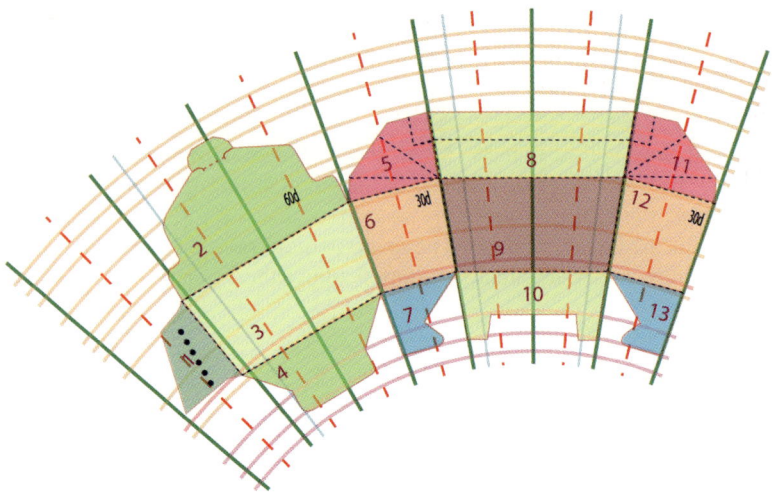

Fig 3.9
No guessing here. This carton has been built out of 2.5° sections, with 5° sections highlighted

In his book *Chaos*, author James Gleick asks his readers to estimate the length of the Atlantic American coastline. Like most people, your answer would probably be a few thousand miles long. According to Gleick, this answer is both right and wrong. The reason is that the answer assumes a *minimum measurement length* that would result in this answer. For this example, the minimum measurement that would result in an answer of several thousand miles would be between half a mile and a mile. Gleick rightly points out that if the minimum measurement were a meter, or a foot, or an inch, or a millimeter, the length of the Atlantic American coastline would be much larger. This is because of the fractal complexity of certain types of objects.

Using a mile as a minimum unit size results in much detail being skipped in the measuring process. If the detail were traced from point to point with a minimum unit size of a centimeter, the complexity of the coastline's contour could result in a measurement in the millions of miles long.

For this reason, it is always good to set a *resolution limit* when measuring your subject, so that unnecessary detail does not bog you down. If you are building a vacuum cleaner meant to be rendered at film resolution as seen from the perspective of a mouse, you will probably have to build details as small as a single millimeter in length. If it will be rendered as some room clutter in a video game, you will want to construct only much larger structures. You may include smaller measurements like the radius of the handle, but only because it is a part of the handle, which is the longest dimension in the object.

When you build a 3D model, remember the importance of accurate dimensions because they will to a large extent determine whether your object is credible to your audience. Even if you want to exaggerate a dimension, you are starting from a real dimension. If you are inventing a new object, you do so relative to known objects with known dimensions. No matter how you decide to do it, when you make a model, you are entering dimensions into your file. Most artists like to have control of this and all of the best artists can control it.

Chapter 4: Design and Reference

Almost every person over the age of 6 knows how to hold a pencil, how to use it to make marks, and how to erase marks previously made. Very few people are able to create a convincingly realistic drawing with that same pencil. The difference is less a matter of hand–eye coordination, tool use, or any other mechanical skill, but one of observation skills and understanding of the subject. When a skilled artist picks up a pencil to make a drawing of a model, he knows what kind of marks to make because the combination of his understanding of figure drawing and his own on-the-spot observations tells him what to do. Holding the pencil is incidental to his observation skills and his knowledge of how to translate a three-dimensional scene into a two-dimensional image (Fig. 4.1).[8]

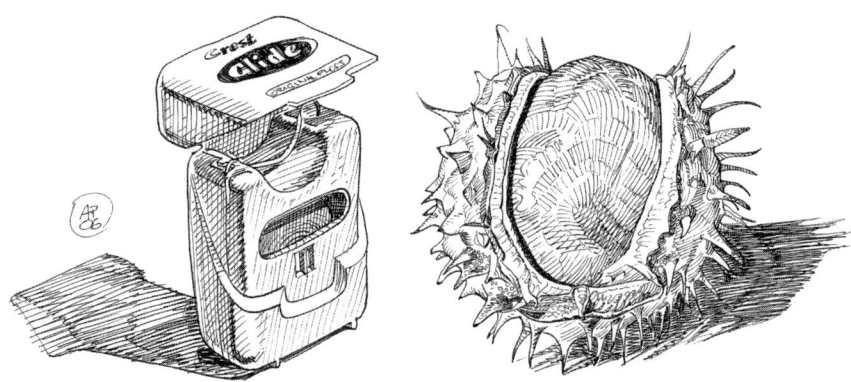

Fig 4.1
Floss container and horse chestnut. Two objects, one is far more complicated than it looks at first, the other, much simpler

In the same way for a CG artist, your observation skills are more important than your knowledge of tools. If you don't know what the object you wish to build is supposed to look like, how then should you expect to be successful? This means that you have to be able to describe, as well as recognize, your subject. There is a large difference between these two things. What makes a 1999 Buick LeSabre different from the previous year's model? When you build something in 3D, you should be able to make the kind of observations necessary to define that sort of difference between two similar objects. Now that you have an idea what CG tools you have at your disposal and the technology they are built from, it is time to consider your *target object*. The object you want to build is your *target* (Fig. 4.2).

---

[8] This is exactly what a *renderer*, software in a CG application used to *draw* your 3D scene to the screen, does.

Fig 4.2

In this drawing of several dolls, they are each separately distinguishable from each other. This is because observable characteristics that define differences between these objects have been recorded in the drawing. For instance, one doll has dark hair, another has lighter hair, and a third has barely any hair. One has a distinctive dot pattern on its clothing, one wears a dress with a ruffled collar, and the third wears a simple jumper style dress. All of these are structural details that are essential to communicating the unique visual character of each of the several targets in this drawing

Let's say you are asked to build a CG version of an ancient Etruscan vase. Some artists would immediately hollow out a cylinder and call it an "Etruscan vase." These artists would not last long in the CG industry. To execute a convincing CG version of this object, the artist must first find out what it is supposed to look like. This is the reference-gathering phase of a project. Some consider it to be the most important part of any project.

One of the fastest ways to find out what an Etruscan vase is supposed to look like is to use the Internet. A quick search of the term "Etruscan vase" brings up over 500 images on www.google.com. Most, however, were different enough from each other that a modeler would have to exercise his own judgment in selecting which one he wants to build (Fig. 4.3).

Fig 4.3
Three Etruscan vases

The exercise of choice in this illustration is the exercise of a *design choice*. This is a responsibility modelers are frequently given, if for no better reason but that their supervisors don't have the time to track down what every object is supposed to look like. Although some art directors will give you specific instructions for your projects, you will have to learn how to fend for yourself for all those other occasions when they don't. Design is a skill that the best modelers must have to at least some extent.

Design is usually more than simply selecting which object to make, though that is the first step of the design process: know your target. Going back to our example, if you look at these images, you will see that in addition to being quite different from one another, each image is incomplete.

Some of the vases clearly have a nonrepeating pattern running around its circumference, others have a repeating pattern. In both cases, they are incomplete. This is because none of these images contain a graphic description of the interior of these vases, or its bottom, or the other side of the object. In addition to that, some of them are insufficiently detailed to correctly reproduce their patterns.

If this was all the reference you had to choose from, and all of it was incomplete, then you become a designer again because you now have to somehow create the missing information. This is a very common problem in most commercial art projects, including CG. For an Etruscan vase, if it doesn't have to photorealistic, or accurate, or it will only be viewed from one angle (and the angle contains little more information than can be obtained from your sole reference image), then your solution can be simple. You can repeat whatever information you see on the front, so that it covers the back as well. You could guess at the color and shape of the interior as well as the bottom of the object, secure in the knowledge that hardly anyone is likely to notice this design sleight of hand.

What if the object doesn't have to be accurate but the pattern on it had to be recognizably Etruscan and it couldn't repeat even once as it wraps around the vase? If you don't have reference for it, then you will have to extend the image yourself, and that might require some drawing skill. This is a common situation in CG, and most modelers and texture artists will encounter some form of it regularly throughout their careers.

Another possibility is that the pattern can repeat, but the structure of the interior of the vase must be representative of what might be expected for an object of this type, even if its exact appearance is unknown. In this case, you would have to try and find out more about these types of objects, to learn how it would be made, or even better, to find photos or drawings of other vases of the same period that contain the missing information. With this information, you can add it to your model to fill in the blanks. Again, that is an example of a CG artist working as a designer, even though the task is to model an object.

Reference information is almost always incomplete in some way, whether provided to an artist or acquired by the artist. What if you are asked to make an "old-looking" vase for a video game? In this case, it doesn't have to be any specific kind of old vase, it just has to look "old." Now, you can either just grab any old vase you like or can get good reference of, or you can design it completely from scratch. If you do this, you will have completely designed your object instead of simply using design skills to fill in missing information.

But how would you do it? What do you know of old vases? If you aren't an expert in the field, you will probably have to do some research on the subject. The Internet is a good place to start your research, and if you get lucky, you may find everything you need there. As a rule, you can expect that the more general your requirements are, the more likely you are to acquire what you need on the Internet. The more specific your requirements are, the less likely you are to find what you want.

For designing something from scratch, if you want it to be interesting and convincing, you should look for similar objects to see how they are made, how they are painted, and how they are used, to give you a better idea of what your object should look like. The problem is, if you don't know anything about designing things, it will be difficult for you to do it. One of the best ways to learn how to design things is to first copy existing objects or use designs made by others. If you do not do this, your own designs are likely to reflect your inexperience.

The best reference of an existing object you could possibly get is access to the object itself. If you want to model an Etruscan vase and someone gives you first-hand access to one, you can't do much better than that. Or can you? Do you know what information you need to take from the object and communicate to your 3D modeling software? Almost all objects contain a large amount of visual information, and sorting through it to find what is, and what is not, important can be difficult unless you know what you are looking for.

Let's say you have a vase in front of you. What do you do with it? Do you just let it sit there beside your computer and take observations by eye as you work in your CAD application? What if it was a car, or an elephant? What then? Just because you have access, it doesn't mean that the job of reference gathering is over. In reality, it has only just started. And if you don't have access to the object, you have to know what information you need to extract to replicate the object in your computer.

An artist's ability to acquire legible, accurate reference is often a reliable indicator of the potential success of his project. This point is not to be underestimated. If you cannot find, acquire, and understand good reference, your ability to produce a satisfactory result will be severely crippled.

For the feature film *Spider-Man*, digital sets were made of New York City. This is because Spider-Man had to convincingly swing through canyons made of these buildings, and it was felt that using CG buildings would give the filmmakers more control of the shots.

Before any CG artist was given the task of making models of the buildings, a team of photographers was sent to New York City to photograph preselected buildings for reference. Hundreds of rolls of film were shot. Special permission had to be obtained from building owners and tenants to photograph buildings from every floor, as well as the rooftops. This trip was not inexpensive, but it was money well spent because of the valuable data it produced for the special effects team.

In addition to the custom photography for the project (and all the work of developing, sorting, scanning, and organizing the results), blueprints were obtained whenever possible. The success of these buildings in the film is largely a product of the effort that was made to obtain good reference.

Here are some examples of similar reference-gathering efforts for an independent project (Figs. 4.4–4.6).

Fig 4.4

This photo collage was made from dozens of photographs culled from over a thousand photos that were shot of this building. Despite the high number of photographs, significant portions of the building were not photographed (due to location difficulties and carelessness), as indicated by the *color green* in this image.

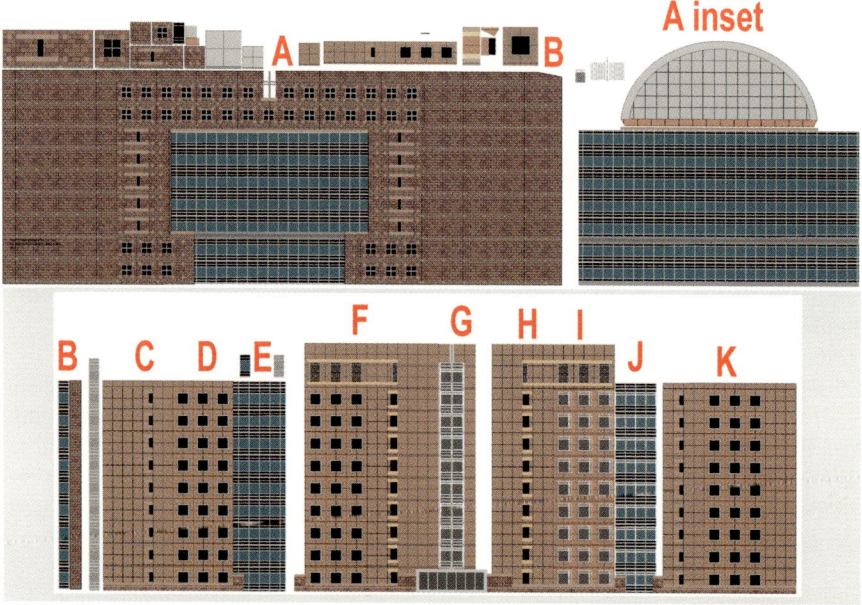

Fig 4.5

This is a schematic view of the entire exterior of this building, along with a row of tilable sections located at the upper left. This drawing was generated based on data contained in reference photos taken at the site, including the assembled collage reproduced above

Fig 4.6
The most difficult piece of information to get for this building was a photo from above. The CG version of the building originally contained several mistakes because of this missing data, but Google Earth came to the rescue with an excellent satellite photo and the building was finished

When looking for reference, you must be careful to keep in mind what you need and how you will be using it. For film effects work, a detailed master design document is normally made as a guide for any 3D objects that need to be made for a project. Depending on the skill of the artist responsible for making the document, they can be very useful, or not useful at all. In video games, these documents are only infrequently made, and then only for the most prominently featured objects in the game.

The biggest problem with these design documents is that artists who have no knowledge of how CG objects are built can be assigned to make them. For this reason, the CG artist himself has to fill in the blanks. On a perfect project, this is what you would want as reference for a project:

1. Several perspective views of your object, the total group of which adequately illustrates all pertinent structural information and how all of your objects' parts are related to each other (Figs. 4.7 and 4.8)

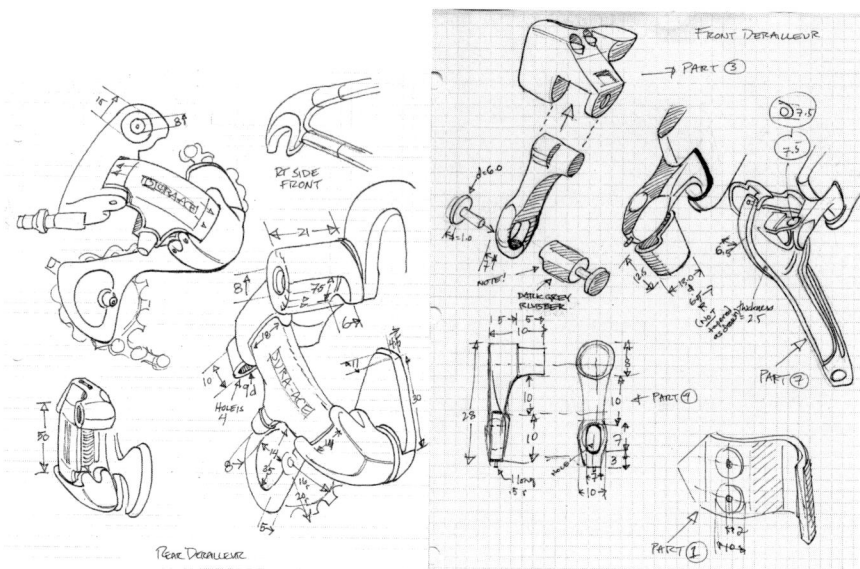

Figs 4.7 and 4.8

Perspective views, Rear and front derailleur, Y-foil. Take note that dimension information is provided in this drawing (in millimeters)

2. Several *orthographic views* of each of your objects' parts (also known as *schematic views*), all drawn to scale (Figs. 4.9 and 4.10)

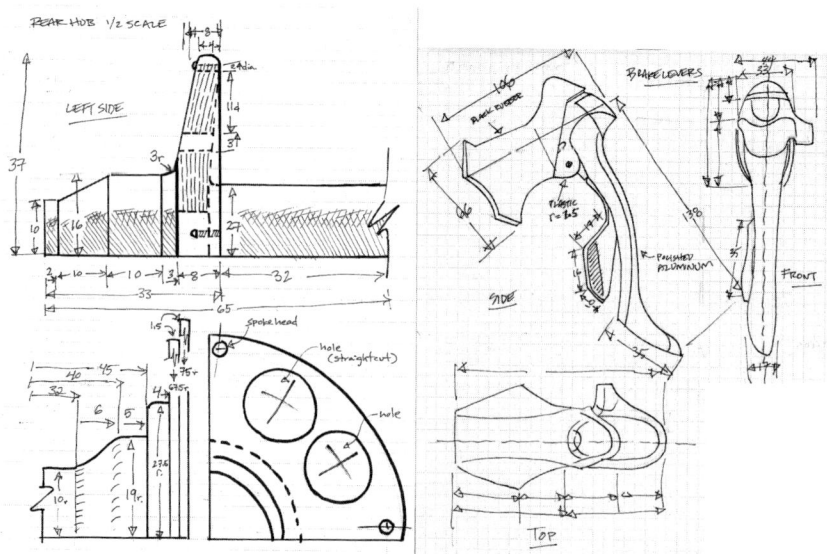

Figs 4.9 and 4.10

Schematic views, Rear hub and brake lever, Y-foil

3.   Color and texture images (Fig. 4.11)

Fig 4.11
Decals for model of Y-foil. A separate drawing would designate where each label belongs. Note that the labels are scaled correctly relative to each other

4.   A *material schedule*, or description of every type of material used for your object (Fig. 4.12)

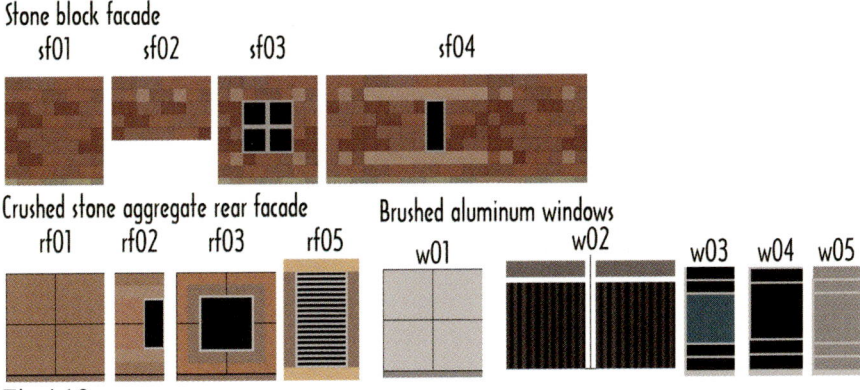

Fig 4.12
Material schedule for *courthouse* building model

5.   Correct names for your object and all of its parts, using a naming convention if applicable on your project
6.   Accurate measurements

7.   Photographs of the subject, to show how it looks in different lighting
     conditions

It is extremely unlikely that you will find all of this from secondary sources, but
you can make it yourself. Sometimes, your task is to make something so simple
that you don't need to go to a lot of trouble to make it, in such a case you can get
by with a simple photo from the Internet. If you want to make something that is
truly convincing, however, it is best if you acquire the information listed above.

Any old reference, however, will not do. Here is another example from the film
industry: On the movie *X-Men 2*, one of the CG artists was asked to texture the
CG double of a character in the movie. A highly paid production designer gave
him a drawing as reference. The problem was that, although every person responsible for approving the drawing had liked it and approved it, none of them realized
that it was entirely insufficient for the CG artist (Fig. 4.13).

Fig 4.13
This drawing is similar to the example described. It is a professional drawing, but
it raises many questions for any artist asked to build a model from it

The drawing showed the character from the front, or rather, it showed the right half of his torso, from the front. The artist had been told that characters could be mirrored right to left, so he didn't bother showing both sides of the body. He figured that he was just a guy in jeans, so he didn't need to bother showing the legs. Everyone has the same back muscles, so he didn't show the back. The drawing had what appeared to be stylized chest anatomy, but from the way it was drawn, it was unclear whether it was stylized chest anatomy, or the artist simply didn't know his chest anatomy very well. Either way, because it didn't represent real human anatomy, it made the CG artist wonder what he was supposed to do with the character's back. Should he stylize it also? He didn't know. To top it all off, the artist used dramatic lighting in the drawing, with heavy shadows and bright highlights that concealed structural detail. The drawing did look nice as a drawing, but as something to model from, it raised more questions than it answered.

The CG artist then asked for more drawings to clarify his questions, but the original artist had by then moved on to another project. In the end, the CG artist had to spend several months redesigning the character in such a way that a 3D model could be made that resembled the sketch, but that could be built in 3D without any obvious faults.

To do this, he had to answer every design question he had about the drawing. He found a group of anatomy books and some comic books, to show what the character looked like in the comic, which was nothing like the movie, and what human anatomy looked like. He had to determine the shape and size of the character's legs, the creases in his trousers, the anatomy of his back muscles, various sides of his arms, the back of his head, hairstyle, and anatomical details obscured by the lighting in his reference drawing. By the time he was done, he'd made a very nice model that looked great in the film, but he had put more design effort into it than the original designer (Fig. 4.14).

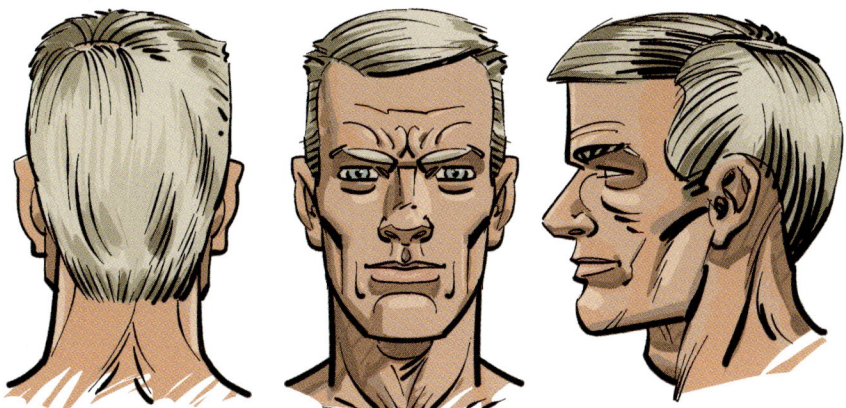

Fig 4.14
This drawing of a character's head does answer most questions a modeler might have about the intended structure of the target object

The type of problems he encountered with the reference drawing is typical. Even the *Spider-Man* team, with all their reference photos and blueprints, had problems. Their reference was about as good as could be hoped, but even so, it wasn't perfect. Because the buildings were so tall and so close together, they couldn't get a good undistorted view of the front of any building. They did try, but the resulting photographs show the top of the buildings quickly receding almost to a point at the top, just like a pair of train tracks in a perspective drawing.

To get around this problem, the crew took photos from different floors of adjacent buildings opposite the target building. They then assembled all of these photographs into a huge digital collage to represent the full face of the building. But, these weren't right either. The photos couldn't help but be taken at different times of day, so shadows were pointing all over the place, sometimes obscuring this detail, sometimes another. Other things got in the way too: pigeons on a ledge, pedestrians, cars, street signs, even the building itself. Some buildings had projecting sculptural detail that blocked the photographers' view of whatever was on the other side of it.

So, even when you get as much great reference as you can, you still have to make some of it up. This is where it is handy to have some drawing skills. What you will have to do in a situation like this is to make some drawings that make sense of the information you do have, and make a credible attempt to fill in the data you are missing.

The most common type of source material artists work from when working in 3D is drawings. The drawings can be made by any of several different people. Sometimes, they are made by a *production designer*, sometimes by the *art director*. Depending on the project, your reference may be made by a *concept artist*. Sometimes, you make it.

Each of these job titles denotes a different type of skill and level of experience. People who work under any of these designations will usually approach the project slightly differently. The differences can be quite meaningful to the person who works from their drawings.

Concept artist. Usually, but not always the least experienced of the three job types mentioned above. A concept artist is generally not required to make highly finished drawings. Instead, they tend to make many fast sketches, usually of single objects in a camera-like perspective view. Rarely, they will also generate *orthographic projections* of the subject. These are very valuable to the 3D artist if made correctly.

Production designer. In film, a production designer can have a very strong effect on the look of a film. These artists are sometimes highly skilled render artists who do not know how to design anything or how to make any kind of useful orthographic breakdown of their designs. The better production designers can make highly detailed drawings of everything they design, with nothing left to chance. They will show each object from multiple views; orthographic and perspective, as structural outlines and with color (texture), with all parts named, and they may even include some drawings of the object as it is meant to be used or animated.

Art director. An art director from the film or television industry will usually have either an architectural, interior design, or industrial design background. These creative professionals are almost always able to make excellent reference material for 3D model making. If the art director is from the game industry, they are most likely to have an advanced level of concept design skills, but without the specific real-world construction experience commonly found among their colleagues in filmed entertainment. For this reason, their work frequently suffers from lack of accuracy and insufficient structural detail.

You. You will be called on to draw your way out of 3D design problems from time to time. These will be imposed on you in drawings made by other people. If the drawings do not answer all of your modeling questions, you will likely have to answer those questions yourself by modifying or recreating the concept with your own drawings.

This is not a desirable situation, but it is quite common within the industry. Because designers frequently do not understand the needs of 3D artists, they make mistakes. Here are some of the most common errors you are likely to encounter:

1. A single perspective drawing, without orthographic breakdowns, errors in the perspective that make all attempts at measurement hopeless, and missing detail.
2. A highly finished and attractive rendering of the target object. Artists who are skilled at making these presentation drawings are not aware that the effort they put into making the drawing appealing as a drawing actually introduces elements that are problematic for modelers. Shadows, reflections, and motion lines are among the unnecessary artifacts included in these drawings that the CG artist must learn to ignore.
3. Mechanically impossible objects. This is a problem if the object will be animated in a manner that is inconsistent with the design.

When making design documents, pay attention to the checklist below as you work. It will improve the results.

To make usable reference:

1. Identify your target object.
2. Acquire reference:
   - The object itself
   - Photos
   - Drawings
   - Measurements
3. Analyze your reference for missing design information. It is unusual for any single reference source to be complete, so whatever you have is likely to be incomplete. Expect this, and you will more quickly discover what is missing.
4. Make notes on the missing data and answer any open modeling questions to the best of your ability. Examples:
   - Is this line closed or open?
   - Is the object symmetrical or not?
   - Is this board meant to be in front of that one, or is it the other way around?
   - Are these supposed to be regular or irregular divisions between windows?
5. Identify and locate common features in multiple reference sources.
6. Construct your own plan views based on source reference and your analysis of it.
   - You do not have to be an accomplished draughtsman to execute this step. Working with measurements is what makes this easy. As long as you work to scale, all you need to be able to do is convert full-scale measurements into a smaller scale for your drawing.
7. All parts and groups must be named in your design documents. Take care to spell all parts correctly, to find out the proper name of each part, and to create correct *grouping hierarchies*.

- A *grouping hierarchy* is how a number of elements are grouped to-gether. For instance, you wouldn't group a left ear on a character with its right hand because they would never be animated together. You would, however, group a hand under a wrist, the wrist under the elbow, and the elbow below the shoulder, because each of these parts depends on the preceding element of the grouping hierarchy for physical support.

As you should see by now, design is dependent on reference and reference is dependent on measurements. If your measurements are wrong, your model will also be wrong. If your design is poor, your model will be also. If you have insufficient reference, your model will be incomplete. Learn how to acquire or create these three things to be the best CG artist you are capable of being.

Chapter 5: Basic Modeling Tools

Most CG animation and CAD applications come equipped with a basic set of very similar tools. Each application usually has their own special tools that no one else has, but the basic set is the same from application to application. This chapter explains what these common tools are and how they work (Fig. 5.1).

Fig 5.1
Simple tools are often the best, and the most used

There are several different ways to generate a polygon in CG. The most common are:

1. Geometric *primitives*
    - These are predefined common shapes. All packages offer cubes, cylinders, spheres, cones, and planes. Other types of primitives you may find are stars, toruses, decahedrons, dodecahedrons, octagons, pyramids, geodesic spheres, and others.
2. Direct input
    - This is what was used to make the carton in Chap. 1. Each point was clicked into existence as the exterior border of the carton was traced.
3. Spline controls
    - Otherwise known as building from curves. With this method, a curve shape is defined and then used as the basis for the shape of some polygonal geometry. Numerous tools work with these to define how the spline will be used.

4.   Conversion
    • Conversion is used to *convert* a nonpolygonal format to polygons. This is useful when normal polygon tools are not able to quickly describe the target shape. These will be discussed in the second half of the book.

The purpose of these tools is to quickly arrive at certain types of shapes that would be difficult to describe without them. You could literally start with a cube or a plane and, by adding vertices, as they are needed, transform each point until the final model looks like anything you want it to be. In this way, a cube can become a computer, a tiger, a house, a rock, or anything at all. The problem is that for certain types of shapes, it is difficult to position each point exactly correctly. If you wanted to make a sphere out a cube for instance, by simply adding and repositioning points, although it could be done, it would be very difficult to build the model without making dents or small bumps all over its surface. This is why you would use a sphere geometric primitive to make a sphere instead of building it out of something else.

Most objects are a product of a number of different types of shapes mixed together. A pen for instance; a pen is not really a simple cylinder, but it is very similar to a cylinder. Some CG artists might build a pen out of a cylinder primitive for this reason. They would start with the cylinder, then add points and modify them until it looked right. Even more likely, an artist would use a *revolution* tool. This type of tool will take a profile shape, turn it a specified number of times around a specified axis, and create faces to connect each of the segments. With this tool, a model of most pens could be made very quickly and accurately. For those that have some asymmetrical detail, or a detail that cannot be built as part of the revolution operation, another object may be attached, like a pen clip, if the pen has one.

Some objects are *simple objects*, meaning that they can be built in a single operation, without editing. Other objects are *complex objects*, meaning that they require either a combination of polygon creation tools, or editing, or both. Most objects in CG are complex. Some forms of dinner plates, or a saucer from a cup and saucer pair, are excellent examples of simple objects. These types of objects are built from a single profile curve rotated 360° around an axis. A more complex object is a fork or a spoon. In both cases, there is a difference between the shape of the handle and the business end of either instrument that requires more than one tool to create. You should learn to recognize the difference between simple and complex objects, but to help you do that, you should have an idea what the various common tools do and how they are used (Fig. 5.2).

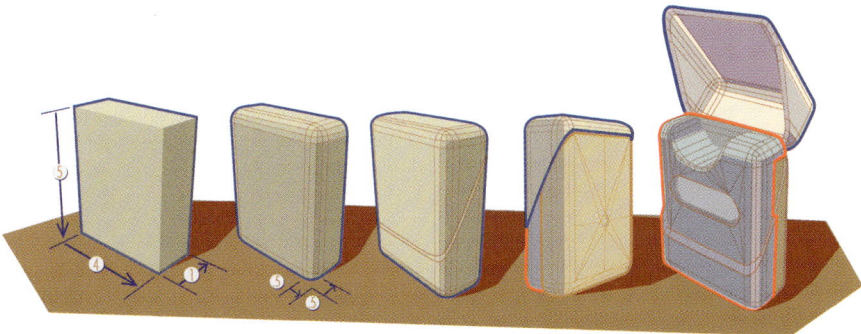

Fig 5.2
A floss container is easy to build from a primitive. First, make a cube that matches the dimensions of the floss container. Then, bevel your object. Cut the lid into the container, carve in any incised detail, then split into separate parts and modify as needed

If you are using the primitive modeling method, then the commands you are most likely to invoke are all component-editing tools. What these allow you to do is add or remove vertices, or to move those vertices in predefined ways.

Adding vertices (Fig. 5.3):

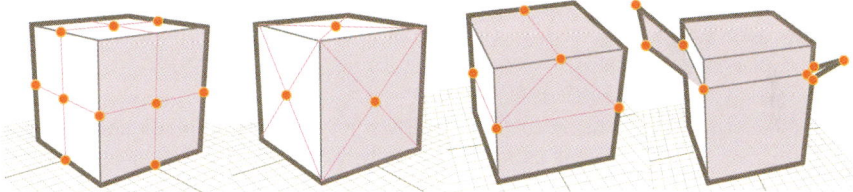

Fig 5.3
Subdivide from edge, from vertex, manual face cut, and extrude

1. *Subdivision.* This is a tool that draws new edges on every selected face, or every face if the entire object is selected. It can draw them from existing vertices toward the center of each face (diamond pattern), or from the center of each edge to the center of each face (square pattern). The first variant results in one new vertex per face, the second creates a minimum of four new vertices (one for the center, one for each edge, with a minimum of three edges).
2. *Extrusion.* Extrusion, as demonstrated in Chap. 1, detaches the selected face or faces from its neighboring faces, then connects the two groups with new faces. This results in as many new vertices as are contained in the selected faces.

(a) Extrusion variations:

- Edge extrusion. Edge extrusion creates a new edge, joins it to the original edge with new edges (creating a face in the process), and then offsets the new edge a specified distance from the original edge. A variant of this tool is a two-dimensional version. With it, the edge itself is offset, and new edges created as the sides of a new face to join the original edge and the new one. This does not create as many new vertices as the other method, and results in nonmanifold faces.

- Vertex extrusion. This tool creates a new vertex a specified distance from the selected vertex, along each connecting edge. This command creates a minimum of three new vertices. The tool suffers from the same problem as edge extrusion, if the extrusion offset is too close or overlaps the nearest preexisting edge boundary.

(b) Face extrude around edge. This command extrudes a face as in a normal extrude command, but does not cut a selected edge out of the original geometry. The result is that all of the newly created faces except two are rectangles, and the two that connect to the selected edge are triangles.

3. *Face cutting.* You may, by cutting across faces in a variety of ways, create new edges and vertices. Most applications have several tools that allow you to do this, some with greater control than others. The simplest of these tools allows you to cut any face along any edge simply by clicking. You will be expected to click on edges belonging to either the same face or connected faces.

(a) Controlled cuts:

i. Plane cuts. A plane cut allows you to define a plane and then cut through your entire model along that plane, wherever it intersects an edge on your model. This is a very handy tool for creating a relationship among vertices on an irregular surface, like a parting of hair on the skull.

ii. Distance cuts, multiple or single. This allows you to divide edges one or more times based on either number of cuts desired, center point cuts, or distance from another vertex on the same edge.

4. *Bevel.* If you invoke a bevel function with an edge selected, the selected edge will be shaved from your object, usually at a perpendicular angle to the edge. Depending on your options, you may get a straight cut or a smooth curve along the edge. Either way, the result both blunts the edge and adds vertices to your model.

5. *Smooth.* This tool will perform a global bevel operation on every vertex of your model. The result will multiply your polycount by 4, and will be much smoother in appearance. This command is often used to very quickly add curve resolution to character models, but this is not advised because at the same time as the command increases curve resolution in

your model, it also reduces detail in areas where you want sharp angles to exist, reduces the volume of the model, and it quadruples your polycount.

(a) An interesting use for this tool is to turn a cube into a sphere. Doing this will preserve the original cube's default texture coordinates. In some circumstances, this might be desirable. More on this is described in a later chapter.

Deleting vertices (all of these commands work on any component type, and all result in the deletion of vertices) (Fig. 5.4):

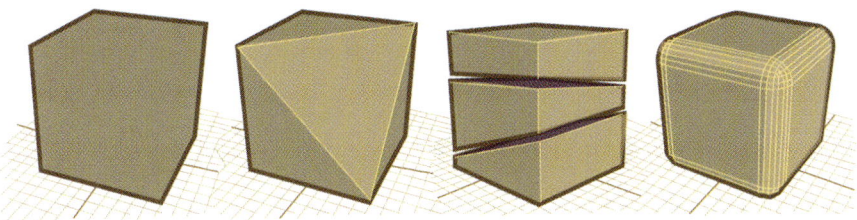

Fig 5.4
Delete, collapse, cut, and bevel. The first two are delete points only, the second two are delete, add, and move points

1. *Delete.* A true "delete" command will only delete the selected vertex or vertices without affecting surrounding vertices or edges. Some will delete the vertex and all connected edges, some will only delete the vertex if it is isolated. Some applications have a "delete" command that works like a "collapse" function (described below). These are very different tools, so be careful that you know which one you are using.

2. *Collapse.* The collapse function deletes the selected component/ components, and fills the resulting space by averaging the position of nearby vertices. The effect is of a heavy weight dropped on the apex of a tent. It pulls everything toward the weight. This tool is very helpful, especially when de-rezing an object, but if you don't want neighboring structures to be affected, use *delete* instead.

3. *Combine/weld/merge.* Unlike other commands, this one has several different names from application to application, but they all do the same thing: it checks for the selected component type within a certain radius of the selection and then averages the distance between anything found in that radius with the selected component and then collapses the elements together. This is a good way to eliminate nearly invisible vertices that are so close together you'd never find them without this command.

Booleans. A *Boolean operation* is when two or more objects are evaluated for intersection, and then a new polyset is created based on the intersection (Fig. 5.5). This can result in adding or deleting vertices from a model, and is sometimes the best way to create certain shapes that would be very time consuming to generate otherwise. Here are the types of Boolean operation available:

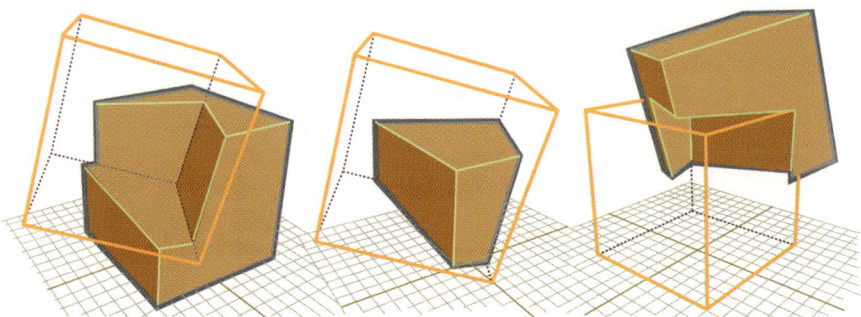

Fig 5.5
Subtract first selected, intersection, and subtract second selected. Union combines both and eliminates intersection

1. *Intersection.* Deletes everything but the portion of the two models shared within the intersection boundary.
2. *Union.* Deletes only the common area defined by the intersection boundary, and welds all vertices along this boundary, and then creates a single polyset from the original objects.
3. *Subtraction.* Subtracts the intersection of one object from another. Make sure you understand how your application defines which is subtracted from which or you will have unexpected results. Normally, it is based on the order of selection. If it doesn't work the first time, select your object in the opposite order and try again.

Booleans, while very useful in many ways, can have unexpected results that corrupt geometry. This has been getting better as the technology is improved, but these operations are still prone to error. One thing that a Boolean operation will do is cut straight through your source objects to determine the intersection boundary. Depending on the level of detail at the cut, the boundary may be represented by an undesirably large number of vertices. Another common problem is that the operation will result in floating geometry being made into a part of the polyset. Sometimes, these faces are so small that you won't notice them, but they can cause render errors. To avoid this problem, check to make sure that your intersecting objects don't intersect in such a way that you get the effect of biting all the way through the middle of a carrot, leaving both ends free.

Another thing to be aware of when using Boolean tools is that they are very picky. The geometry you use for the operation should be as clean as possible. All of their normals should be facing the right way, nonmanifold geometry will not work, and cracks or gaps in either polyset will also cause problems. Likewise, unmerged vertices, nonplanar *n*-gons, and just about any other error described in Chap. 2 could have unwelcome results in a Boolean operation.

By adding and deleting vertices, you give yourself the raw material you need to work with to modify your base primitive and change its shape into whatever you need it to be. The tools you will use to modify the model will be the basic translation tools you've already been exposed to in Chap. 1: translate, rotate, and scale. To get the effects you want, you will modify selection sets of components, and will frequently move your pivot point. This is how modeling with geometric primitives works.

Spline creation tools are based on a device used in the shipbuilding and aircraft industries by designers who needed a way to draw perfectly smooth curves with a specific shape. To do this, they would put long strips of thin wood, the spline, through slots in pegs on the floor of large design lofts. By adjusting the position and rotation of the pegs, the shape of the spline was affected. Another type of spline used weights to pull at curves by attaching them to a curve with string or wire. The weight used would determine the strength of the effect. For computer graphics, there are two primary types of spline: a normal spline and a *bezier spline*.

The types of spline are not as important at this stage of your introduction to CG as your understanding that if you invoke a curve-creation tool, that you can draw a smooth curve by clicking the points of the curve into existence. This is usually done in an orthographic viewport, and then if necessary, the points of the curve are adjusted in other viewports for truly three-dimensional curvature (Fig. 5.6).

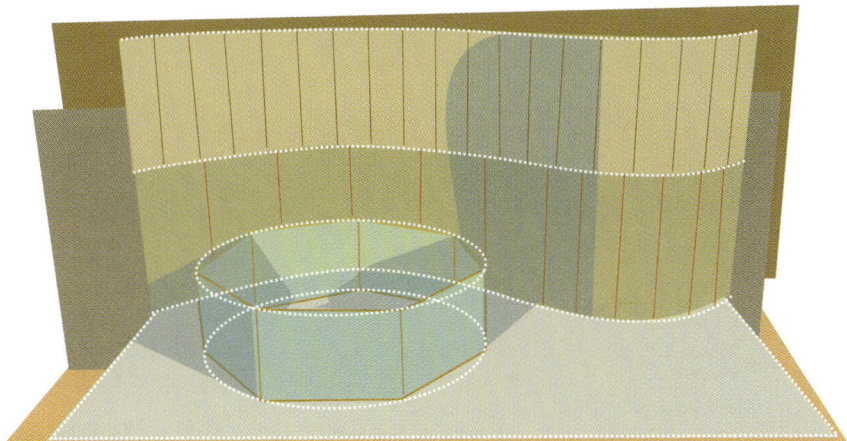

Fig 5.6

Infinite sampling points on curves are represented by *white dotted line*. Actual polygonal subdivision is *uniform*, *adaptive*, and *parametric* on each polyset

The reason you might want to build a polygonal object from a spline curve is that a true spline can be evaluated mathematically at any point along its length, whether or not it has a control point in that location. This makes curves both resolution independent (because they can be split into any number of segments without affecting the shape) and an easy way to align vertices along a carefully defined curve. This latter function is very difficult to imitate by hand, and normally would not be attempted except for models that have an extremely low level of curve resolution (five vertices per arc or less).

Working from curves allows an artist to define multiple polygons at once, with extremely smooth results. When working with curves, one of the most important factors to keep in mind is whether you want your curve subdivided evenly during the polygon creation process, or if vertices should be added based on curvature changes in the curve. The results can be quite different, so you should always bear this in mind while working.

There are a large number of curve-based tools available, too many to cover here, but there are a few tools in common that are worth the trouble to discuss, and exist in most packages. As always, the exact name of the tool will vary, but its function will be the same regardless of application. They are (Fig. 5.7):

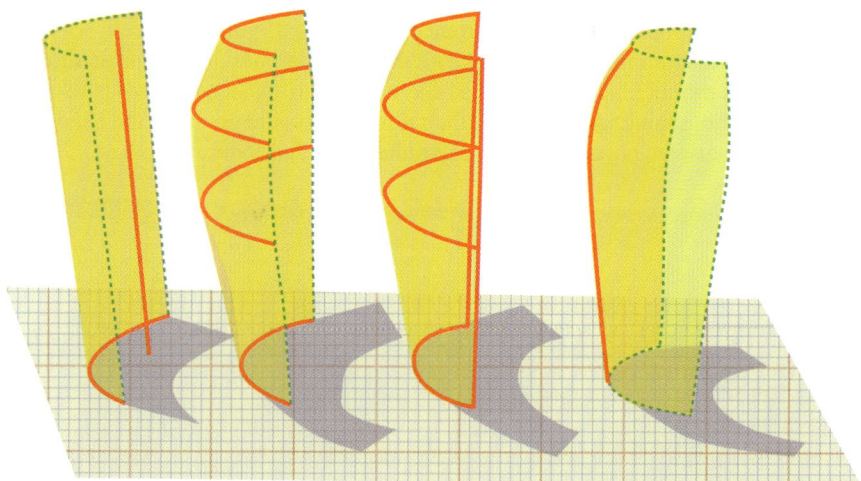

Fig 5.7

Extrusion, loft, explicit isoparm and boundary, and revolve spline-based surface creation. The *orange lines* are curves used to build the surface, *green dashed lines* are boundaries created during the operation

1. *Loft*. This tool takes two or more curves, and creates a polymesh from them. To do this, it connects the endpoints of each successive curve, usually in the order selected, and then, based on your settings for the tool,

will either connect control points within the curve or will evenly subdivide each curve into the same number of segments and connect those.

2. *Extrude*. This tool will take one curve, copy it a given offset from its current location, and then connect the two identical curves with polygons. You may have the option to modify the curve globally during the offset, and to have multiple subdivisions along the offset axis.

3. *Revolve*. The revolve command is similar to the extrude command because it copies the original curve a specified offset, and then connects the curves with polygons. The difference is that instead of a linear offset, it is radial and the end result is very much what you would expect from turning a piece of wood on a lathe. You will have the option of determining how many degrees you want represented in your final object. This can be a fraction of a full circle, a full circle, or more than a full circle. For the latter, you should also have a linear offset option, so that instead of getting overlapping polygons as an end result, you get a helix, or screw thread shape.

4. *Face*. This simple command fills the curve with a single face, usually with several to a large number of isolated vertices.

There are more ways to constrain polygon construction by using curves than described here, but these are the most basic, and most commonly used, tools of this type. They will be enough for almost all of your modeling work, and for some of you, they will be enough for *all* of your future modeling needs.

An important thing to keep in mind as you look at these tools is that the tools do not determine the results so much as your knowledge of where the points belong. Oftentimes, young modelers get caught in a trap of trying to find ever more esoteric tools to automate many of their modeling tasks, when they would finish the job more quickly by using more basic tools combined with component editing. One of the most powerful aspects of polygonal modeling is that the artist can always simply select a vertex or group of vertices and then move them to where they belong. On that level, the only tools required are poly creation, vertex addition, and translation tools.

Curves are important because they allow you to quickly describe shapes that would otherwise be complicated to build face by face or vertex by vertex. Certain types of objects lend themselves to the use of curves, like boats, airplanes, bows, and anything else where a curve is a major part of its structure.

Geometric primitive-based modeling is also a very powerful method of modeling, and one favored for compound structures like anatomical subjects, simple architecture, and organic subjects.

With both modeling types, a common workflow is to trace over a reference image using either curves or a geometric primitive. To do this, your application will have a function allowing you to load an image file into the background of any of your orthographic viewports, just as was done in the carton example. Most, but not all, applications will also allow you to load images into your perspective viewport. When you do this, be sure that any secondary images, such as a top view in addition to a front view, are the same scale as the first drawing you have loaded. If they aren't, you will have to rescale them within the application to match, and doing this accurately is not always easy.

If your reference drawing is made in a vector-based drawing program, there are various ways to import the data into your application as curves. Be aware though, that curves from a drawing program may not look as you expect them to. Depending on how they were made, there may be a large number of overlapping curves, or an excessively high level of curve resolution. The benefit to working from vector-based curves is that they are selectable, can be snapped to, can be used as-is for polygon generation, and will always match your design drawing perfectly. The downside is that the curves can be quite messy. Usually, it is worth the effort to create new curves based on the imported curves. An exception is curves used to define text.

For text, imported vector curves are fairly economical and can be very difficult to accurately trace in a reasonable amount of time. For this reason, it is usually best to use them as they are when imported.

One last thing to remember when working with curves: do not expect to be able to simply click your way to a perfect curve. Like polygonal editing, curve editing takes some getting used to before you can do it well. Even if you get the shape right, you still have to learn how to break it down properly for building either polygonal or nurbs geometry from it.

Chapter 6: Resolution

The San Francisco Museum of Modern Art once had an exhibit of electron scanning microscope photographs of very tiny things blown up into gigantic prints. Most of the images were 3–5 m on a side, and sometimes more. The pictures were of flies, the hairs on a fly's leg, a tiny bug clinging to a hair on a fly's leg, the hairs on that insect's leg, and the miniscule bug clinging to its leg hairs, then the hairs on that bug's leg, and all blown up to fill the enormous vertical height of the walls in the museum (Fig. 6.1).

Fig 6.1
Roses, 293,000 triangles. Complicated subjects such as this demand a high level of resolution, but sometimes it is not obvious *how high* is exactly right

What this exhibit should illustrate to the would-be CG artist is that there is always more detail. If you decide to build everything and thereby prove yourself to be the greatest CG artist ever, you'll never finish your first project. There is no practical way to determine an endpoint to the amount of information any given object contains, so it becomes the CG artist's job to decide at what level of resolution he will build something (Fig. 6.2).

Fig 6.2
This small chunk of mangled kneaded eraser could require tens of thousands of triangles to smoothly represent the details given here, but would it be worth it? The needs of your project will determine the resolution of objects in it, not the amount of detail in the objects themselves

More often, you will be asked to work at a certain resolution, but it doesn't hurt to develop the ability to estimate what that resolution should be. If you have no idea what a reasonable budget is, you won't know what an unreasonable budget is either. "Unreasonable" is anything beyond a narrow range of the optimal number, high or low. If you are given too many triangles to work with, the result can be just as inappropriate as if you weren't given enough (Fig. 6.3).

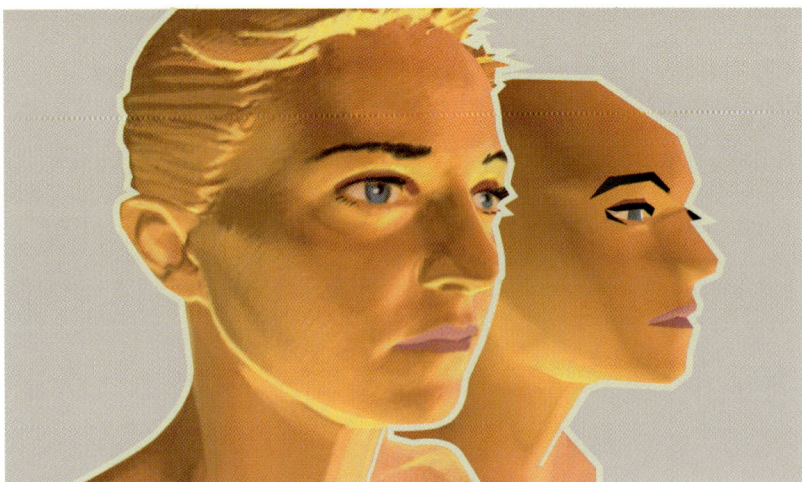

Fig 6.3
Two character heads. One is over half a million triangles, the other is 482 triangles. Either might be appropriate, depending on its use. Together though, they don't match and cannot easily inhabit the same scene

There are several ways to describe the resolution of an object. Some refer to the object itself, others to the CG "materials" used to construct its CG replica:

1. Object-based resolution:
   a. How many parts does it have?
      i. How many must be animated separately?
      ii. How many must be textured separately?
      iii. How many are distinctly separate?
2. CG resolution:
   a. Polygon count
   b. Texture maps:
      i. Texture map size
      ii. Number of maps
      iii. Number of UVs
   c. Animation controls
      i. How many bones?
      ii. How many control objects?
      iii. Etc…
3. Measurements:
   a. Nothing less than a kilometer
   b. Nothing less than a meter
   c. Nothing less than a centimeter
   d. Etc…

Most artists flagrantly waste their CG resources on their first few projects, until they learn to better understand what is and what is not necessary. In the example given in a previous chapter of dimension errors, 150% is the average error. If only CG artists limited themselves to this figure when it comes to polygon counts. It is much more common to use 400,000 polygons where 1,000 would be generous. Determining what is and what is not appropriate is a fine art that any up-and-coming CG artist will do well to master.

When building a perfectly straight line, for instance, exactly two points are re-quired to describe termination points on either end. This is all that is required. A flat, unbroken rectangular wall requires no more than four points. There are rea-sons why either of these objects, the line or the wall, might have more vertices, but these are the minimums. You should get in the habit of always trying to answer the question, "What is the minimum?" before proceeding on a project. Knowing the answer to this question will help you decide what your *resolution* scale should be. The resolution scale defines the level of curve detail, structural detail that will or will not be included, and which part classes will be included in your model (Fig. 6.4).

Fig 6.4
The *white lines* in this image represent the edge boundaries of polygonal geometry that has been subdivided to accommodate a custom texture solution

One reason to increase the vertex count of a rectangular wall is if you want to apply two different texture maps to it, in distinct locations. In this case, you would have to carve the shape of either side into the wall using new vertices. The minimum number of additional vertices is 2, to cross from one side to another, but can be higher depending on the complexity of the shape.

If the wall must fold in an animation, you would also have to add vertices along the fold line, and if it is meant to be a smooth fold, you may have to add several rows of vertices instead of a single edge. For certain smooth lighting solutions, you may want to evenly subdivide your object, to create an even distribution of vertices across its surface, each of which can be used during rendering for a more accurate, and smoother, lighting calculation.[9]

These are all examples of reasons why you might want to increase the resolution of an object, and they are all *legitimate* reasons. This is an important point. If you want to increase the resolution of an object simply to make it smoother, that might not be a legitimate reason, and frequently isn't. The terms *smooth* and

---

[9] This is usually done for the purpose of creating light maps that are added to a simpler version of the same geometry, before it was subdivided.

smoother both refer to a higher level of *curve detail*. Get used to thinking about it this way, and you'll find yourself making better choices as a modeler. You don't want your object to be "smoother"; you want a higher level of "curve detail" (Fig. 6.5).

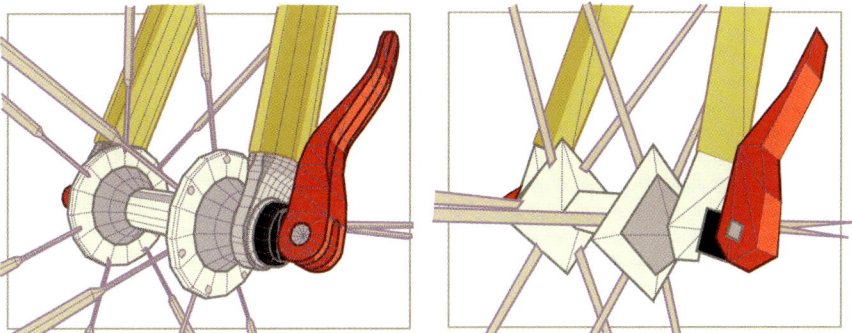

Fig 6.5
The object group on the *left* contains 6,032 triangles. The low-resolution version on the *right* has just 244. Both images reflect the same number of parts, but one has a much lower level of curve detail

Curve detail is the number of polygonal edge segments used to represent an arc of a given length. If you have a 180° arc and it is represented by two edges, you have a very low level of detail. If it has a hundred edges, it is a very high level of detail. What should be important to you, the CG artist, isn't whether it is high or low detail, but whether it is the right level of detail. Your goal, when making an object for rendering, is to determine the optimal level of curve detail for the use to which your object is put. This varies considerably on the type of project.

The first thing to consider is the output resolution. Is it going to be used in a film, a TV advertisement, a print ad, or a video game? In each of these examples, the number of available pixels defines the maximum output resolution. Here is a reference chart to give you an idea how many pixels will be used to draw your polygons to screen (Fig. 6.6):

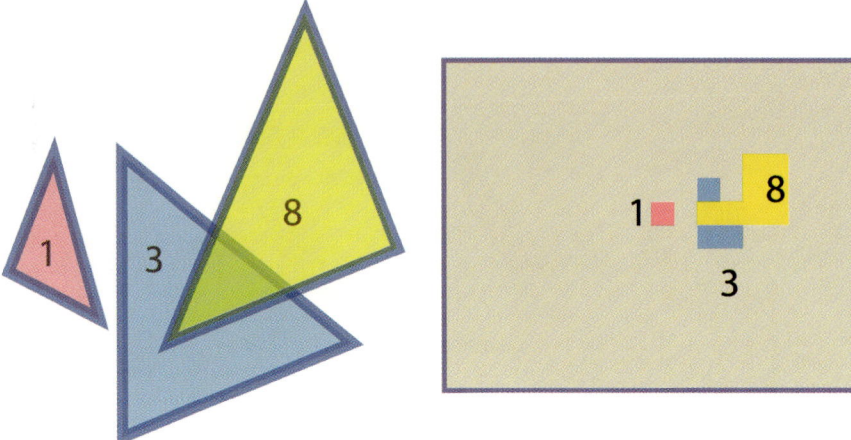

Fig 6.6
How polygons are translated into pixels. Note that only the smallest triangle is translated into a single pixel. In practice, most polygons in a scene will be represented by hundreds of pixels

1. Print (size varies): 4,800 × 2,100 = 10,080,000
2. Film (size varies): 2,048 × 3,024 = 6,193,152
3. HD: 1,920 × 1,080 = 2,073,600
4. TV (PAL): 768 × 576 = 442,368
5. TV (NTSC): 646 × 485 = 313,310

No polygon can be represented on screen or in print with less than one pixel; so theoretically, your entire scene shouldn't have more polygons than there are pixels available to draw them with. This is not entirely true however, because your shot might require camera movement through a moderately detailed scene that is, in aggregate, extremely detailed. For a print ad, where your render is a one-shot static result, the number of pixels is very closely matched to the upper resolution limit. If there is animation or movement, it is more flexible.

Even so, let's look at some of these to see how the output resolution affects the resolution of your polygonal objects, because there is an effect. First of all, most CG *compositions* (arrangements of visual objects) do not fill the entire screen with a single object. More often, there is a range of near and far objects. The near objects require a higher level of curve detail to look smooth, far objects have a low level of curve detail because there aren't enough pixels available to represent the curve detail anyway.

The highest level of detail from the incomplete list given above is for a double-page print advertisement. The most common advertisement of this type is for a car or truck. With over eight million pixels available and no animation, these models can be, and are, very high resolution, with a very high level of curve detail. CG models of vehicles for this type of image are normally provided by the manufacturer and can be several million polygons in size. For a one-shot high profile render, this is completely acceptable. These are usually combined with a live action background plate, but in those rare cases where a fanciful CG background is used instead, it would be difficult to exceed any meaningful polygon budget, except by excessively wasteful modeling techniques (Fig. 6.7).

Fig 6.7
This poster image was made at very high resolution, 7,500 × 3,750 pixels. The contents of the scene did not require high curve detail however, so the total triangle count is just 286,210

The next level of detail is for film. Here, there is a large difference from print, even though the total number of polygons, about six million, isn't a great deal different. There are several reasons for this. If you have a car that must appear on screen at a very far distance and then advance directly into the camera until the entire screen is filled with a very small detail of the car, you will have the following situation: your object will occupy a minimum of one pixel, and then advance to full screen, or about six million pixels. You may think then that you can use six million (or more) polygons for this object. This is not true. In practice, an average size vehicle in a feature film is between 10,000 and 30,000 polygons.

For the example given above, as the car advances toward the screen, it obscures other details in the scene. If they are also CG elements, then they use part of the polygon budget also. Therefore, as it advances, the overall number of polygons represented on screen goes down, not up. Depending on the shot, there may be multiple *levels of detail* (LODs) for the car as it advances, and other elements in the scene will probably be rendered separately, to make the best use of rendering bandwidth and also to provide greater flexibility when compositing various elements of the shot together for the final footage. Most importantly, a six mil lion-polygon car will render so slowly that only in the most extraordinary circum-stances, such a thing would be attempted. In addition to that, when an object is in motion (or a camera is in motion relative to a stationary object), fine curve detail is impossible to focus on, making its careful representation in your model a waste of effort.

If the point of the shot is to see in gory detail a small insect that has been squashed by a headlight, then separate geometry will be made for the headlight, insect, and nearby structures, like the fender, grill, and car hood. Even this will not be as high resolution as the sort of model used in a print ad, for the simple reason that it is not necessary.

When you build something, always keep in mind not just the maximum size it will be when rendered, but also whether increasingly fine LODs are even visible when the object is in motion. Every polygon you make is another piece of data to be tracked, and to potentially go wrong. If you don't need it, it shouldn't be there.

The last two items in the examples given are most relevant to video games. Video games are a special class of problem for the CG artist, because many of them do not use prerendered graphics. Instead, they are rendered on the fly by *real-time render engines*. This means that no posteffects are possible. Back-grounds, trees, buildings, vehicles, and characters are not rendered in separate passes, but together. In addition to this, the total number of pixels is much smaller, between 300,000 and 400,000, depending on which standard is used in the target country.

For 300,000 polygons, you will have either a few highly detailed objects or a large number of low-resolution objects. A pixel-based standard is unusual in the industry however, because it merely defines the maximum displayable resolution on screen, without regard for other factors important to a project, like animation. The point of mentioning it is that if your object has more triangles than there are pixels on the screen, you've been wasteful in your technique.

A more common standard is based on the rendering power of your computer, or the game console and it's real-time rendering software. Using this standard, an average console video game can render anywhere from 12 to 50 million triangles a second. If you take 20 million as a common number, at a frame rate of 60 frames a second, then you are rendering 333,333 triangles per frame, or about as many pixels as you have on an NTSC TV screen. A polygon budget based on this will vary depending on the game, but this is about what it will look like:

1. Characters (or vehicles, if a racing game):
   (a) Featured character: 5,000–20,000 triangles
       i. Depending on game genre. The higher number is for a one-on-one fighting game, the lower number for a role-playing or adventure game with detailed environments and multiple characters on screen simultaneously.
   (b) Secondary character: 3,000–7,000 triangles
   (c) Background character, or budget for characters in game where hundreds must be on screen at the same time: 500–1,500 triangles
2. Environment:
   (a) Buildings:
       i. Featured: 5,000–25,000 triangles
       ii. Secondary: 1,000–5,000
       iii. Background: 12–500
   (b) Terrain:
       iv. Complex/large: 1,000,000 triangles
       v. Average detail: 300,000–600,000
       vi. Low detail: 150,000–300,000

Strangely enough, the resolution level used in film special effects is starting to fall behind that used in video games, at least on an object-by-object basis. The reason is that CG artists who work in the film industry use extremely high-resolution texture maps and complicated postprocessing techniques to achieve high levels of realism, but game artists are limited to polygons for almost all visual representations due to limitations built into their real-time renderers. This is why highly realistic buildings in feature films might be only a few hundred polygons to a maximum of about ten thousand, but a video game can go well above those numbers even though its output resolution is lower.

When you build something in CG, ask yourself, "Do I really need this many edges in an arc? Do I really need to subdivide that rectangle? Will I really see this detail in the finished project?" You should get used to analyzing your target before you start work, to determine both the minimum and the maximum LODs. This will very quickly set the boundaries of what kind of resolution limit you need to work within.

There are a number of tricks used to reduce polycounts to the minimum necessary, even in high-resolution models (just because you have a 2,000,000 triangle budget is no reason to be careless with it). Here are a few of them (Fig. 6.8):

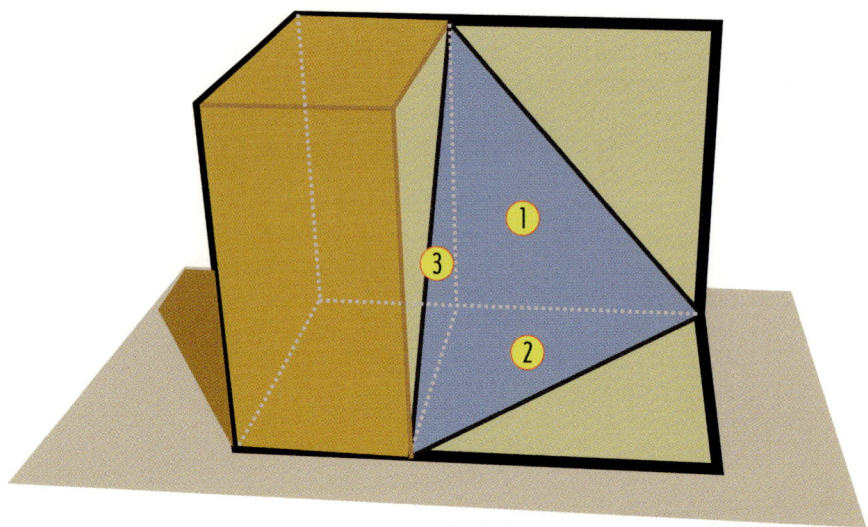

Fig 6.8

The *blue triangle* in this image hides triangles 1, 2, and 3. All three of these triangles cannot be seen unless the blue triangle is moved or is partially transparent.
Opportunities like this are common in any file

1. Do not build polygons to represent detail that will always be hidden from
    view; for example, a bookshelf leaning against a wall. If the bookshelf
    will not be animated away from the wall, or the wall broken from the
    other side, and no other event could possibly expose its missing backside,
    then don't build it.
2. Use a consistent resolution for curves. This follows the form: number of
    edges (or vertices) per linear unit. So, if you have a 180° arc that is ten
    units long and that has ten edges, then another 180° arc that is only one
    unit long would have the minimum number of edges, two. An arc of
    20 units length would have 20 edges, and so on.
3. Do not subdivide an object without a good reason.
4. Combine static elements along common edges and weld their vertices
    whenever possible. Do not do this if they must animate separately.
5. Do not add vertices that neither describe a change in surface structure nor
    are a part of a texture border.
6. Keep in mind that every additional vertex is another piece of data that
    you must personally keep track of. Do not add these unless you must, and
    be sparing when you do.
7. Use the same resolution for all similar objects in your scene. If you are
    inconsistent, it will show as *resolution contrast* whenever objects of dif-
    fering resolution are beside each other. This will cause one to look too
    sharp, the other to look too blocky.
8. Texture maps can save you from a lot of modeling work.

Texture maps represent the structural detail that is too fine or too complex to practically represent using geometry. Even spray painted graffiti on a wall is still minute particles of paint, particles that have dimension, adhered to a wall. On a more recognizable level, tiling patterns of bricks or sidewalk pavers are objects of easily defined dimensions, but because of their numbers, are often represented with maps instead of geometry. Keep this in mind when you model, because if you don't, you may not be able to make good use of texture maps later.

A CG artist, who takes care to simplify his work to the minimum possible without reducing the quality of his work below the target standard, is very hard to find, and highly prized when found. An artist who does not do this, even if his observational skills and other qualities mark him as an excellent artist, will always take second place to the more efficient artist. Keep this in mind as you work.

Chapter 7: Texture Coordinates

Texture coordinates, as described earlier, are used to attach a texture map to a CG object. Without them, textures cannot be used, and the quality of any object is sharply reduced. Without texture coordinates and a texture map, most models are not considered finished. Texture coordinates, then, are quite important (Fig. 7.1).

Fig 7.1
Cannon, model by Maarten Tops. This is a well-mapped model, with very little distortion, well-chosen seams, perfectly scaled textures, and maps of the same resolution

Assigning texture coordinates is one thing, doing it well is another thing altogether. Most CG artists find UV editing difficult, and this is just as true of texture artists as modelers. Texture coordinates, like some other aspects of CG art, contain a high number of variables. When modeling a single brick for instance, you need only pay attention to the physical dimensions of the object and then enter the data into your software. For its texture coordinates, however, there are numerous possible solutions, almost all of which are in some manner imperfect.

This is just one of the reasons why UV editing sometimes has a bad name among CG artists as a necessary evil. The truth is, those CG artists who understand how to manipulate UVs can do very well for themselves, and do not find the work as difficult as their less-educated peers.

The goals of UV editing are simple to describe:

1. Seamless textures
2. Undistorted textures
3. Efficient textures

That's it. Those three things are all an artist is supposed to accomplish when he edits an object's UV coordinates. The problem is that UVs are edited in two-dimensional space, but the object the UVs are attached to exists in three-dimensional space. For objects that are effectively two-dimensional anyway, like a one-sided flat sheet of paper, this is not a problem, but for almost anything else, it can be.

When you edit UVs, you are unfolding and cutting your object into two-dimensional space. You are like a costume designer taking a costume apart at the seams, and then flattening it out and arranging it with other sections of fabric from the same roll to reconstruct the original uncut fabric from which it was made. Unlike fabric, however, the polygons used by CG artists are not flexible.

Keep in mind as you work that a good UV solution is almost always a compromise between distortion and seams, and that most models contain some distortion and some seams. You cannot realistically expect that you can totally eliminate both. Editing UVs, then, is an art of judicious compromise. If done well, your UV sets will be a major feature of a more efficient, easier to render, better-looking model. If not, your models may not meet minimum professional standards.

Projection

To apply a texture map to an object, it must first have texture coordinates. Most polygon creation tools will provide automatically constructed texture coordinates, but by the time you are done working on your model, these coordinates may be unsatisfactory. If you need to correct the existing coordinates on a model, or create new ones from scratch, you will have to *project* the coordinates.

Projecting texture coordinates requires you to select a projection matrix type; planar, cubic, cylindrical, spherical, or any of several other more esoteric possibilities, and then align the projection matrix with your object. Most programs can do a good job automatically, but you will sometimes have to align it yourself if the object you are mapping deviates significantly from perpendicular alignment with the global axes in your scene.

Once the projection matrix is aligned and the project function is invoked, your object, or the part of it you have selected, will have new UVs. These UVs will probably, but not always, require further editing. This fact is the primary stumbling block for less-experienced artists. They want a projection type that results in perfect UVs, thus sparing themselves any painstaking UV editing. Get used to the idea that a single projection, or even multiple unedited projections, will not be enough. Expect to edit them carefully, and if you don't have to, you can be pleasantly surprised. For the rest of the time, you will get your work done faster if you assume to begin with that you will be editing your projections extensively.

A cube is a good example. As anyone familiar with the folding carton exercise will know, a cube can be unfolded into a continuous flat series of coplanar polygons. It is also true that after unfolding a cube into this flat sheet, a seam is created around its perimeter. Therefore, the cube cannot have a completely seamless texture. It will be seamless in some areas, but not all (Fig. 7.2).

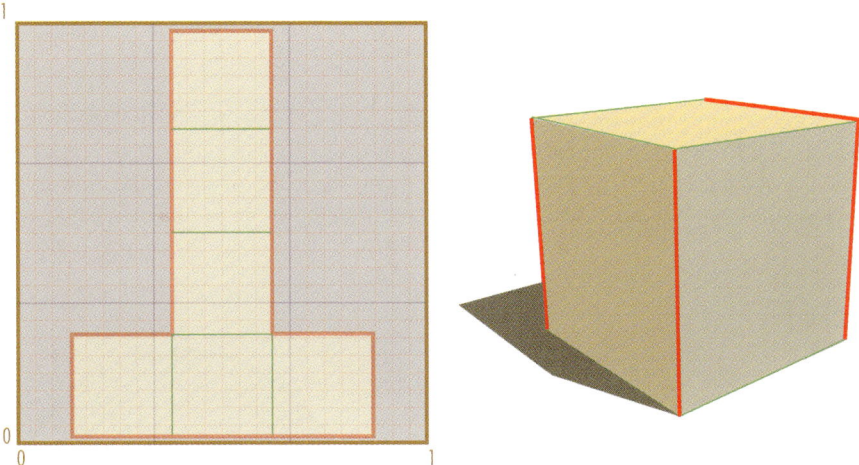

Fig 7.2
A cube and its texture coordinates. The *red lines* are seams in the UVs and *green lines* are seamless boundaries between adjacent faces

The texture coordinate layout for a cylinder is similar to that of a cube. The difference is that, while they both have a single seam tracing their entire perimeter, the cylinder has only two edges that meet in a single seam, but a cube has eight. This is because of the two flaps on either side of the cube that seal its top and bottom. If the cylinder were closed, it would have more seams because it too would have flaps at top and bottom (Fig. 7.3).

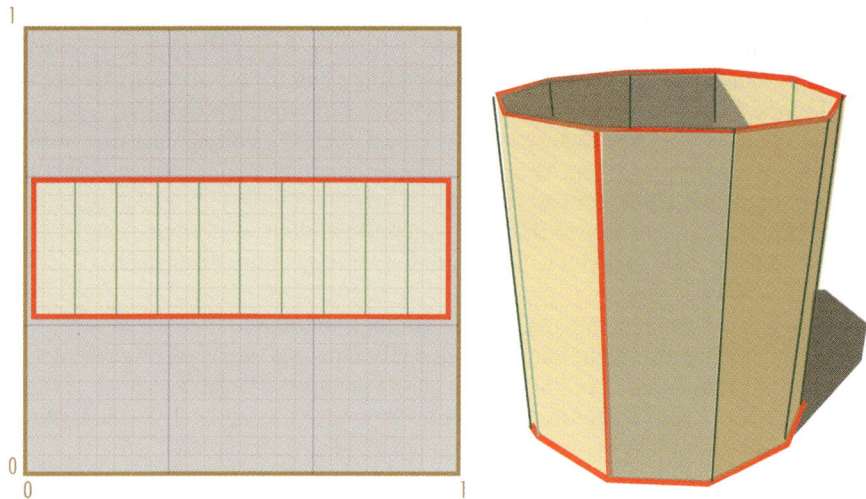

Fig 7.3
A cylinder and its texture coordinates

In the example of a sphere, any continuous row of faces may be unfolded flat, but any two rows or more cannot be, without distortion or seams. The reason is that the second row of polygons projects away from the plane of the first row, joined at a common edge that can only be represented in three-dimensional space (Fig. 7.4).

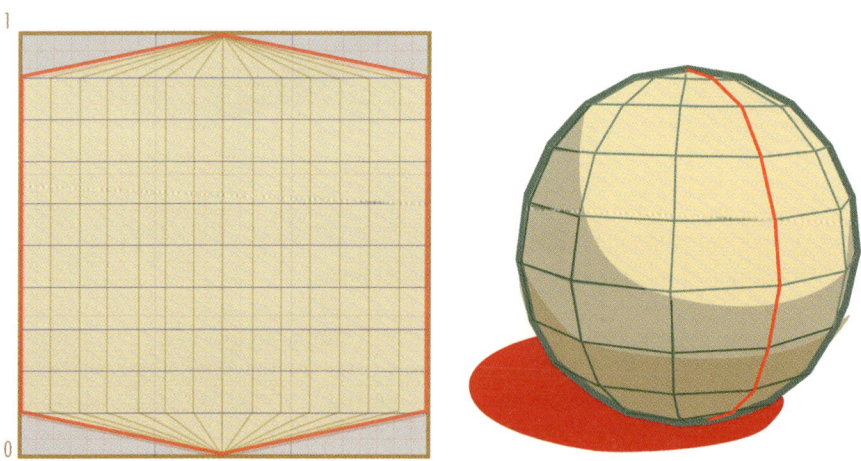

Fig 7.4
A sphere and its default coordinates

In the example of the sphere above, you can see that it has the same number of seams as the cylinder, in contrast to the description of a sphere that had to be ripped apart to unfold it in two dimensions. The reason for this discrepancy is that for the sphere in the image, there is a great deal of distortion allowed, making the object seamless in most areas. The problem is that if no distortion is desired, *then* the UVs have to be ripped apart.

Only a tiny class of objects may be mapped without distortions and seams. These are objects that have only slight topology changes and no insets. The reason is that true 3D space cannot be represented in 2D texture space. Every part of an object that is angled away from a single primary projection plane *must* be folded into that plane to avoid distortion. Folding all the planes of a three-dimensional object into the same two-dimensional plane requires the creation of *seams*. Non-manifold geometry cannot be unfolded this way, so overlapping sections must be cut away and treated separately. Polygons that share a common edge, *only because their position in three-dimensional space allows them to*, must also be cut apart or distortion will occur (Fig. 7.5).

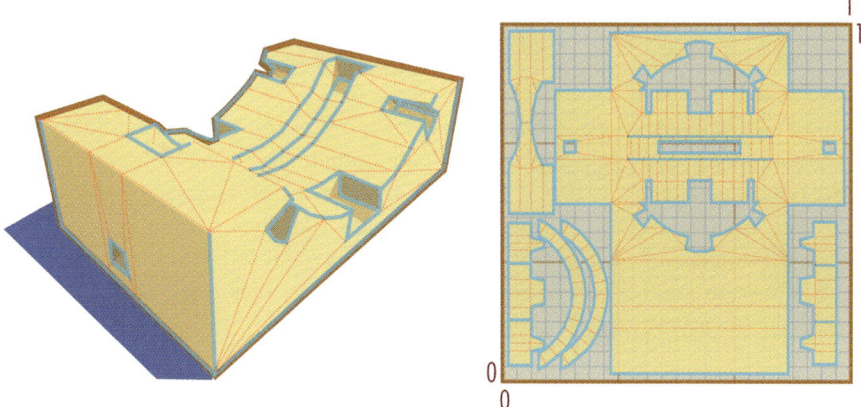

Fig 7.5
An example of an object with a significant number of insets and seams (model and UV layout courtesy of Maarten Tops)

The object represented above has a good layout for painting, despite the large number of seams. For this object, it couldn't be much better. The object itself will always dictate your limits, and every object is different. In this case, it has several insets that forced the artist to create several seams.

Painting across seams can be difficult for texture artists because it may require the precise alignment of thousands of pixels at different sections of a map or multiple maps. 3D paint programs are designed to paint across seams and they are perfectly capable of doing it. Painting in 3D is slower than painting in 2D, however, so keeping seams to a minimum is still a good idea.

Reference map. When working with UVs, it is handy to create and use a texture map to test your coordinates for distortion. These maps should be square, to fit within the square confines of legal 0–1 texture space. They should have some circles or squares in them, because it is easy to see when they are distorted.[10] Any other details, like text, that can be used to determine whether distortion is occurring are also helpful (Figs. 7.6 and 7.7).

Figs 7.6 and 7.7

Two reference maps. Maps of this type are designed to test texture coordinates for distortion, alignment, and tiling. For this type of map, the image isn't very important. What does matter is that it contains large circles or squares, to test aspect ratio and triangle distortion, asymmetrical detail (the lock of hair on one face and the arrangement of different faces or asymmetrical letter forms) to test for backward or misaligned coordinates, and a pattern that tiles easily for placement on objects of varying sizes and resolution

Distortion

The first rule of UV editing is this: If the shape of your polygon is not exactly the same as the shape of the UVs attached to it, your texture will be distorted. There is no way around this. It is always true (Figs. 7.8–7.11).

---

[10] To put it another way, it is easy to spot whether an object that should have a 1.0 aspect ratio does not.

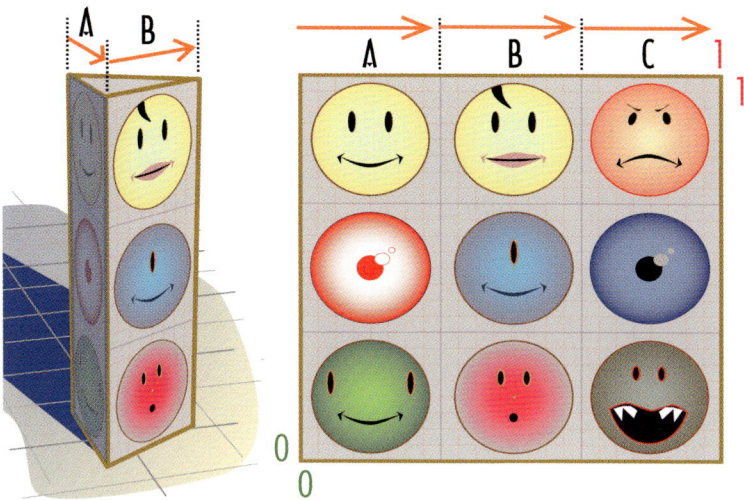

Fig 7.8
This object is mapped correctly. The shape of its UVs matches the shape of its polygons exactly

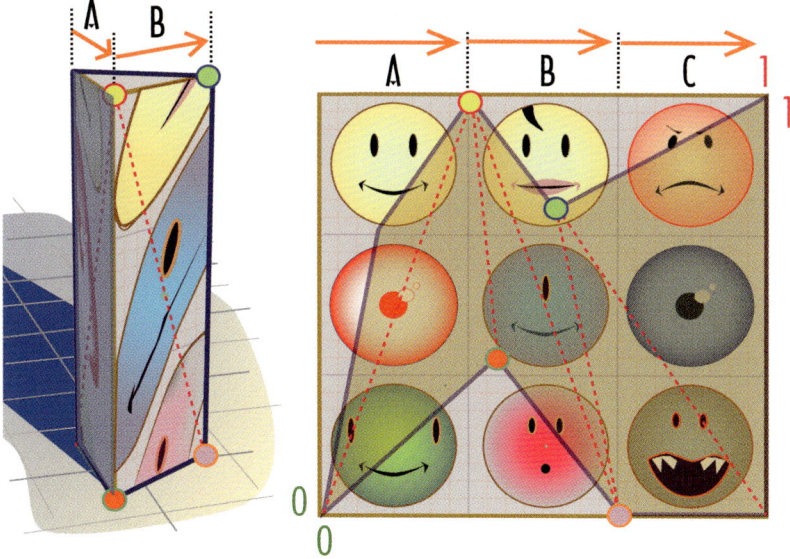

Fig 7.9
Here, the UVs have been modified, so that they no longer match the shape of the polygons they are mapped to. Most artists would never do this on purpose, but almost all of them do it accidentally all the time. Notice the distortion along the implicit triangle edge

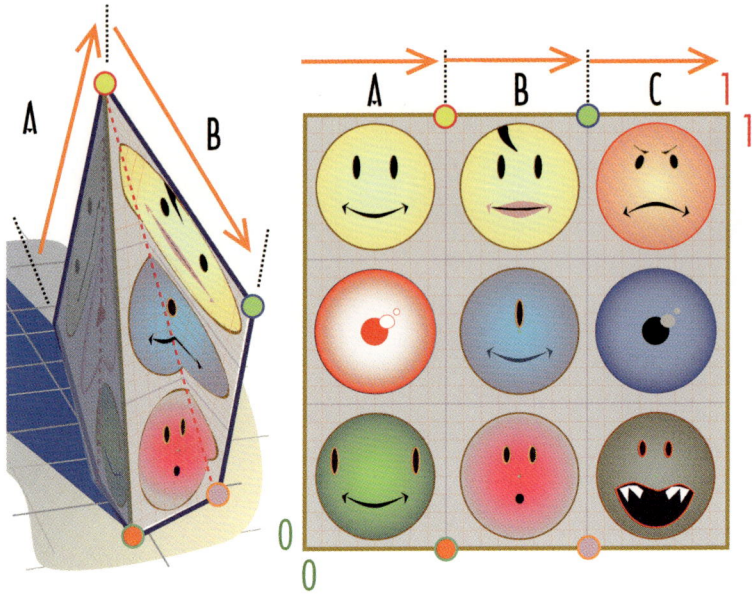

Fig 7.10
This object now has the original correct UVs mapped to modified polys. The original polys and UVs were perfectly square with an aspect ratio of 1.0. Now, the UVs still have the same shape and aspect ratio, but the polys do not. Whenever this is true, textures will be distorted

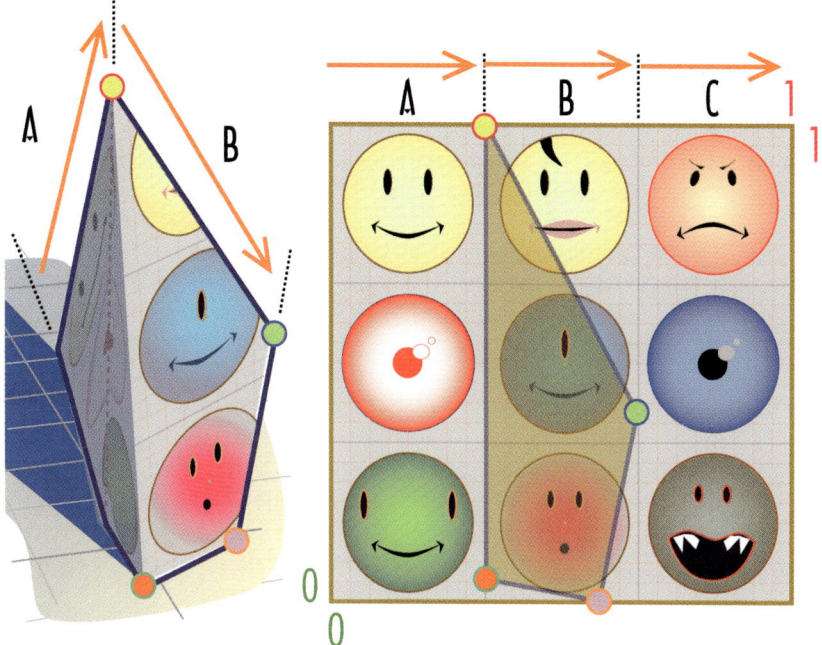

Fig 7.11

This is the same object pictured above *after* having a new planar projection applied to face B. Now the mapping is undistorted on that face. As you can see, the shape of face B matches its corresponding UV layout *exactly*. This is necessary for undistorted mapping

Whenever a model has grossly distorted texture coordinates, it *must* be painted in a 3D paint program if it is to be painted at all. In addition, the resolution of the map will need to be higher to accommodate those polygons that have fewer pixels per unit than others.

When projecting and editing UVs for a model, in only rare cases, it will be possible to accomplish *both* of the following:

- Elimination of seams
- Elimination of distortion

It is easier to eliminate distortion than seams, but it is often prudent to allow minimal distortion to significantly reduce the number of seams.

Choices

There are many UV mapping solutions that will work for any given object, and none of them is necessarily "perfect." Some methods may seem obviously wrong and yet they work for a specific purpose and vice versa. This section is here to provide a sampling of the variety of options available for mapping a sphere. All of the techniques shown are a fraction of the number of options available for any object.

The most important thing you need to keep in mind when you choose your mapping layout is to understand what you want your map to look like in the end. For this reason, it can be very helpful to make sketches on paper of various options you may think of before moving forward to projecting coordinates.

Default Sphere

Default mapping on a polygonal sphere. Notice extreme distortion across majority of object and even more extreme swirl distortion at the pole. This object is best painted in a 3D paint program, but only if the poles are to be crossed by flat or ambiguous color. For many purposes, the UVs on this object are useless because of severe polar distortion (Fig. 7.12).

Fig 7.12
Default sphere UVs and texture

Default Sphere, Cut Poles

This is the same object as seen above, but with one change: the polar UVs have been cut, separated, and moved to reduce polar distortion. This action creates a seam between each of these newly split polys and does reduce distortion, but without eliminating it. The object still suffers from severe distortion, but is now more easily painted and can have a more detailed texture treatment at the poles (Fig. 7.13).

Fig 7.13
Default sphere, sawtooth projection

Mercator Projection

Mercator projection is much more accurate than other methods, but also requires more work. To execute this properly, an artist must measure the edge lengths of any polygons to be mapped, and then match those measurements in a UV editor. To do this, coordinates will be projected, most often by planar or spherical projection, and then modified in the UV editor to match the dimensions taken from the object by manually manipulating them into position. For this example, only one half of a single polygon strip is used (Fig. 7.14).

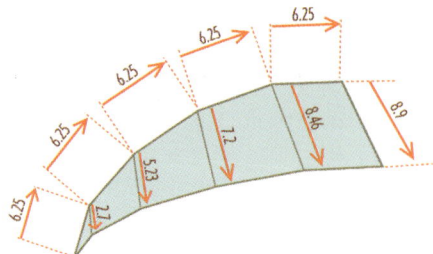

Fig 7.14
Measuring for Mercator projection

After editing the UVs in the first slice of this sphere, it is then duplicated and transformed to form a half-sphere, then duplicated and transformed again to complete the sphere. This is because modifying the texture coordinates is far more time consuming than making the model, so it is easier to get the UVs on the smallest possible section correct first, then create the model from that section.

For maximum resolution and no distortion where tiling is not a problem, each vertical slice of polygons has been superimposed on each other and the group scaled to fit the full UV space. To accommodate the distortion, the aspect ratio of the polys was checked prior to the scale operation and this was used to create a map which when applied would be undistorted. This layout could be very practical for an object with identical complicated mechanical detail in each of the slices (Fig. 7.15).

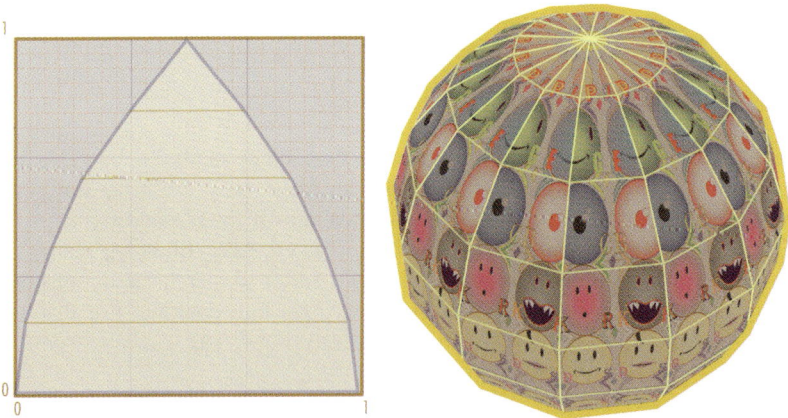

Fig 7.15
Maximum tiling, Mercator projection

Mercator, Untiled

This sphere has no distortion at all, but has more seams than most other solutions and it is a poor use of the available UV space. This is a complicated solution, but necessary for high levels of detail and accuracy in the map (Fig. 7.16).

Fig 7.16
Untiled Mercator projection

Mercator Nontiling, Scaled to Fit

This is the same model as shown in the preceding example, but its UVs have been edited to make better use of available space. The apparent resolution of this object will be higher, because a larger number of pixels will cover the distance across the sphere from top to bottom (Fig. 7.17).

Fig 7.17
Scaled untiling Mercator projection

Two Spheres Proportionate

If the above group of solutions is too complicated, here is a simple method to very quickly improve the quality of your mapping with a minimum of seams. This object was mapped using two spherical projections, one oriented at a 90° angle to the other. The objective is to eliminate the area of maximum distortion by mapping those sections of the sphere with another projection oriented so that the poles are mapped with *its* area of least distortion. The result is three seams (top, bottom, and side), and a slightly higher amount of distortion in the central horizontal band of polys because the UVs are square but the polys are not (Fig. 7.18).

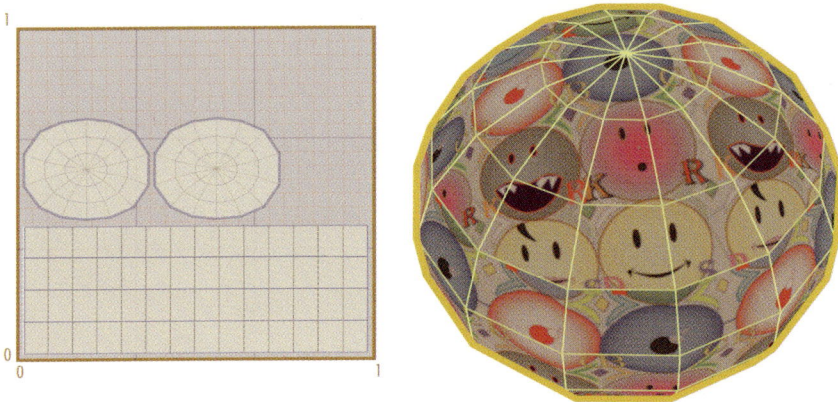

Fig 7.18
Two proportionate spherical projections

Here, the polar projections have been scaled to match the equatorial projections. About half of the available texture space is wasted. For better use of the available texture space, the UVs may be stretched to fit the legal 0–1 space, provided that the texture map is nonproportionately scaled to match. Otherwise, the map will appear to have been squashed.

Six Planar Projections Proportionate

This is a cubic projection (six planar projections) solution. This creates distortion concentrated around the edges of all seams. Overall, this solution is a good compromise between seams, distortion, and the time required to edit the UVs (Fig. 7.19).

Fig 7.19
Six proportionate planar projections

Geodesic Projection

A geodesic sphere is made entirely of equilateral triangles. These are good to work with because at low resolution, they distort the shape of a sphere less than other sphere types. The drawback is that they can only be made with 20, 80, 320, 1,280, 5,120, 20,480… triangles, each successive sphere four times larger than the last. This limits your resolution options, but it can be worth it. Another advantage is that mapping a sphere of this type is more flexible than with a polar sphere. In this case, the UVs have five seams, one for each of the star points (Figs. 7.20 and 7.21).

Fig 7.20
Geodesic layout texture map

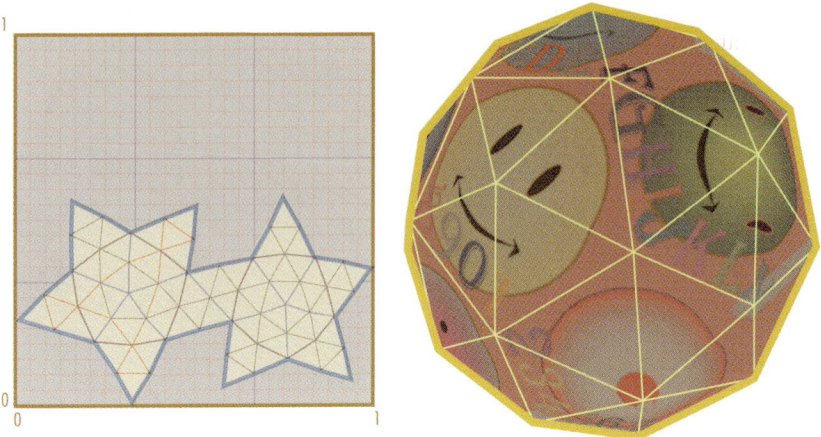

Fig 7.21
Geodesic UVs and sphere with texture

Cubic Projection

This sphere is actually a smoothed cube. Instead of smoothing the cube into a sphere and then mapping it, it was smoothed along with its original cube mapping coordinates. The result is very good, relatively undistorted UVs everywhere except where the original eight corners of the cube were located prior to the smooth operation. At each of these corners is an intersection of three faces, for a total of 24 faces. These can easily be reprojected and then the sphere smoothed again for a very clean result (Fig. 7.22).

Fig 7.22
Unedited cubic projection

Here is the same sphered cube, but with the corner UVs reprojected and the cube smoothed again. This does create more seams, but reduces distortion and it still has a very large area of low distortion seamless UVs (Figs. 7.23 and 7.24).

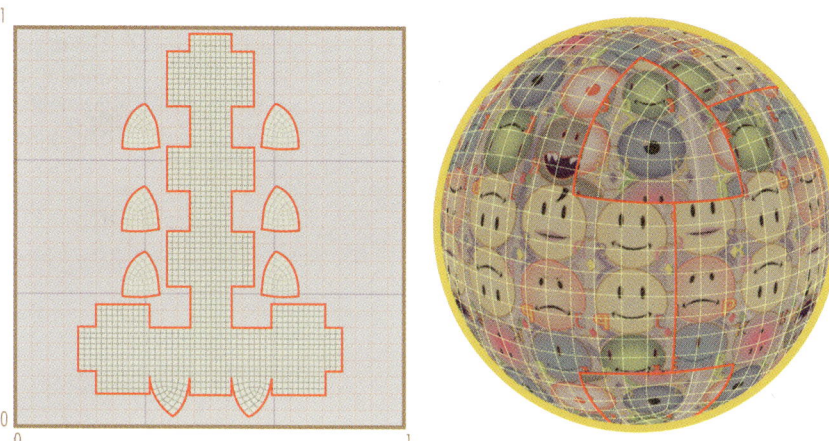

Fig 7.23
Edited cubic projection

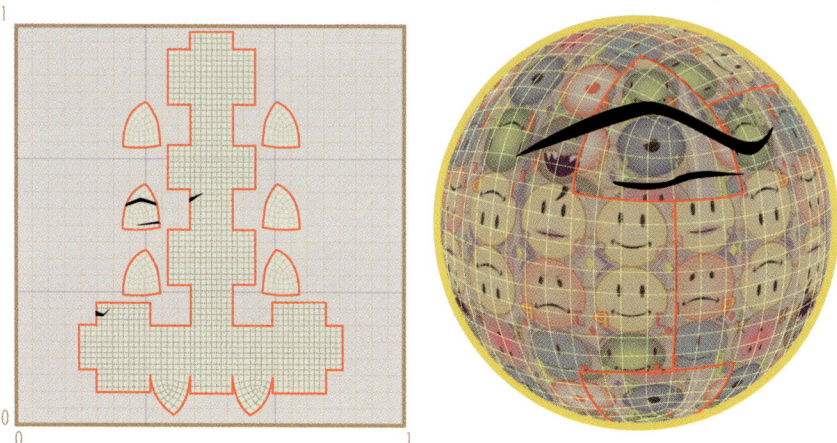

Fig 7.24
Here is the sphere again, with the addition of some seam-crossing 3D paint. On the *left*, the *black lines* correspond to the eyelashes painted on the sphere

The point of providing such a wide variety of options for something as simple as a sphere is to get you thinking of the options available for the more complicated models you are likely to make. There are many options available, even more than are represented here for a simple geometric primitive. Imagine the number of options for a character, or a skyscraper, or an automobile engine. Notice too, that the type of sphere affects the mapping results. Think of the difference between a geodesic, polar, and cubic sphere. The results are not the same. When you model, be aware of the impact your modeling decisions have on the eventual mapping of your object. Fail to do so, and you may find yourself forced to rebuild your object, or parts of it, from scratch.

Chapter 8: 3D1 Checklist and Projects

If you want to be a CG artist, you can get by without knowing some of the things taught in the previous chapters. If you want to excel in the field, you must know and understand most, if not all, of the material presented so far. It is not enough to memorize the data, you have to be able to rotate it in your mind and apply it to different situations. The concepts described so far are the underlying principles of CG, and how an artist uses CG to arrive at a given goal. It is here that mistakes are found alongside ingenious solutions. Master the material and you will not only know more about CG, you will be a better artist, in any medium.

For your convenience, below is printed a checklist you can use to determine if your model meets a "clean geometry" standard. It is not exhaustive and may differ from checklists found elsewhere, but it covers most items that any client would check for. Until you have established clean modeling habits and have memorized the error types listed below, you should check every model you make against it before handing it in.

Clean geometry checklist:

1. File naming convention must be followed: lastnameFirstnameProject-name.extension; for example: paquetteAndrewDaVinci.rar
2. File must match specified file format
3. File must contain 3D file and image file
4. All objects named
5. All objects grouped
6. All grouping hierarchies correct
7. All layers named
8. No unused layers
9. All construction geometry deleted
10. All null nodes deleted
11. Delete all transform channels
12. File saved with display set to wireframe
13. Appropriate polycount (not too low to catch important detail, not too high for game engine)
14. No coincident vertices within the same polyset

15. No gaps in geometry, all objects are solid
16. No spikes
17. No bow-tie faces
18. No smoothing errors
19. No floating faces
20. No separated faces
21. Self-penetration not allowed
22. Object to object penetration not allowed
23. Object must be centered on 0, 0, 0, with its bottommost point at $Y = 0$
24. Pivots for all parts and groups should be positioned correctly
25. Nonplanar quads must be made planar or triangulated by hand
26. No n-gons
27. No distorted geometry
28. No distorted UVs
29. No wrong-way normals
30. No misaligned textures
31. No isolated vertices
32. All extrusion-related unmotivated gaps must be sealed
33. Aspect ratio for all triangles and quads should be as close to 1.0 as possible. This does not mean that other aspect ratios are illegal, but that they are not ideal.
34. Triangulation patterns should be well ordered, neat, and follow shortest-edge rule wherever possible
35. Lamina faces are illegal
36. Coincident faces within the same polyset are illegal
37. Coincident faces between separate polysets are allowed
38. Duplicate edges are illegal
39. Holes are illegal
40. All vertices must contribute to surface or texture border definition
41. Ragged edge shapes are not ideal. Borders must follow target border shape
42. Locked normals are illegal
43. Reference map path must refer to image in same directory as object file
44. Reference map must be correctly attached
45. Zero edge-length faces are illegal

Projects

3D1
Project 1
Folding carton

Project type: Workshop only
Time limit: Two class periods
Supplies/materials required:

1. A folding carton, cleaned and unfolded
2. Scan of unfolded carton

Instructions:

1. First class:
    (a) Unfold carton
    (b) Scan carton, both sides
    (c) Stitch multiple scans if necessary
    (d) Check scan for errors
    (e) Import onto background plane
    (f) Trace carton as a single n-gon
    (g) Use transform tools as needed to straighten out model
    (h) Cut fold lines into model and eliminate n-gons
    (i) Project UVs on carton
    (j) Make shader
    (k) Attach carton scan as map
    (l) Apply shader to model
    (m) Extrude carton to give depth
    (n) Make another shader for carton interior
    (o) Apply shader to interior
    (p) Reproject UVs on interior only
    (q) Fold carton using transformation tools

2. Second class:
    (a) Check for errors against checklist, and fix all errors

Criteria:

Carton must be complete and folded. Texture maps must be present and undistorted. Geometry errors are allowed in small numbers. A large quantity of geometry errors is not acceptable.

3D1
Project 2
Skyscraper/reverse carton

Project type: Homework alternate
Time limit: Four class periods
Supplies/materials required:

1. Reference information on a skyscraper
2. Drawing supplies

Instructions:

1. Find a target subject, a skyscraper or large building
2. Analyze the subject, making drawings as necessary
3. Design a way to create a flat pattern of the building that can be folded into its final shape. Multiple parts are allowed
4. Scan the plans into your computer
5. Create texture-based reference map that contains information on actual texture elements from your subject
6. Import plans into background plane
7. Trace building as a single n-gon
8. Use transform tools as needed to straighten out model
9. Cut fold lines into model and eliminate n-gons
10. Project UVs on model
11. Make shader
12. Attach reference texture as map
13. Apply shader to model
14. Fold carton using transformation tools
15. Check for errors against checklist, and fix all errors

Criteria:

Building must be complete and folded. Texture maps must be present and undistorted. Geometry errors are not allowed.

3D1
Project 3
Da Vinci

Project type: Homework and workshop
Time limit: Five class periods
Supplies/materials required:

1. Clean geometry checklist
2. Drawing supplies

Instructions:

1. Select a drawing of a mechanical subject by Leonardo Da Vinci
2. Determine approximate dimensions of subject using *geometric reduction* technique combined with knowledge of real-world dimensions
3. Correct all visible design errors by determining how the object may be built
4. Make plans of subject
5. Construct replica of subject:
   (a) All models must be built at 100:1 scale (1 m = 1 cm)
6. Apply texture coordinates to model
7. Apply reference map to model to check for distortion
8. Check model against checklist and fix all errors
9. Deliver an archived file containing the following:
   (a) Object file
   (b) Reference map
   (c) Scans of your two best plan drawings for this project

Criteria:

Your project should be complete, delivered on time, resemble the source drawing and built to an acceptable standard of finish. All checklist errors are cause to reduce the grade. The degree to which the submitted project does not resemble the source drawing will cause a grade reduction. Texture distortion is not allowed. If there is distortion, the grade will be lowered. The reference map must be adequate to its purpose. If it is not designed in a way that allows for easy distortion checking, the grade will be reduced. Extra credit for credibly designed modifications to the original drawing, or solutions to design problems in same.

Natural resolution is not feasible for rendering, though it is required for manufacturing. Optimization allows an artist to modify an unrenderable object into one that can be used in a rendering, while surfaces allow the creation of totally accurate CG representations of objects that can be optimized for rendering quite easily.

In this part, we will explore both concepts and learn to see how they apply to any artist's effort to satisfy his artistic goals.

Chapter 9: Observation

Observation skills are one's ability to see, understand, and communicate what one has seen. It is the difference between hearing a trumpet and understanding that it is a call to battle. As it applies to the visual arts, observation skills are no less important to an artist than a soldier's ability to recognize audio military signals (Figs. 9.1 and 9.2).

Fig 9.1
The differences between the characters in this lineup are exaggerated to such a degree that it doesn't take much skill to tell them apart

Fig 9.2
Call to prayer, painting © Andrew Paquette 2006, the level of realism in this painting is made possible by strong observation skills

Some people are more observant than others. Some people see, *and remember* that a certain person has a certain color of hair, a certain type of nose, or likes to wear a certain favorite shirt. For an artist, this is the kind of information that is required to become a professional. It is only one type of information though, because within each of these observations remains a wide variety of possibilities. Exactly what kind of nose? Exactly what color of hair? What texture? The questions are generic; the answers should be as specific as possible.

Some people have a hard time noticing specific details. They see things at a schematic level only. Schematic visual information is knowledge of an object and the relationship of its parts. A car, for instance, has four wheels in two pairs, with each pair connected by an axle, and the two axles connected by a perpendicular drive train. This description is true of all cars, but is not specific enough to identify any one vehicle, tire type, or axle design. An *artist* must be sensitive to the details that distinguish one drive train from another, two brands of tire, or even two different tires from the same manufacturer (Fig. 9.3).

Fig 9.3
A schematic level of observation applied to a car

Schematic observation contains gross details that identify the type of object represented, but is missing fine details that identify the specific characteristics of the subject (Fig. 9.4).

Fig 9.4
Strong observation skills capture the overall shape of an object, and the specific shape of all its parts

A person with schematic-level observation skills will be able to make 3D objects, but will not be able to make convincing, realistic 3D objects without first improving his observation skills.

Symbolic observation is when an artist sees things in terms of simplified versions of the target subject. An example of this is a cartoon character, which is a simplified or exaggerated design, based on a human or animal subject. Artists with advanced drawing skills usually design these figures. The artists who do this take a subject they are familiar with, and then reduce it to a collection of graphic symbols that are shorthand for the character they are meant to represent. These are simplified for a number of reasons, including: making animation easier and faster, enhanced quality of expression, stylistic consistency, easy readability on a television screen, and a recognizable silhouette (Fig. 9.5).

Fig 9.5
Aheb, animation character model sheet

People are bombarded with symbolic or simplified representations of things; advertisements for exterminators, morning cartoons, signage in airports, comic books, public sculptures, etc. After seeing these artifacts of another artists' *seeing experience*, it is very difficult to forget them. Some artists have a tendency to adopt the graphic shorthand of another artist instead of paying careful attention to the subject at hand. One of the most common mistakes of this type occurs when an artist makes a model of a human head and makes the cranium too shallow. This happens because he is accustomed to stylized representations that favor the face over the entire head, a very common error in graphic design (Fig. 9.6).

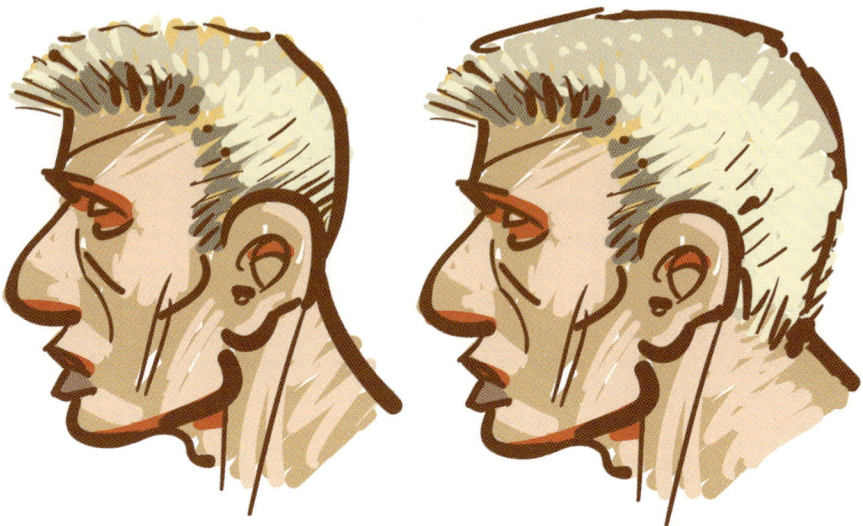

Fig 9.6
Shallow cranium on *left*, correctly proportioned cranium on *right*

Some artists don't like to be bothered with small details. They will take in an impression of the overall shape and function of an object, then invent and substitute their own designs for all of the internal details. This can create numerous errors if the goal is to replicate the appearance of a specific object, but if the artist is good enough, their stylized design will be so appealing that most viewers won't notice.

A very common observation error, usually from talented but inexperienced students, is the *myopic focus* error. With artists of this type, they focus on individual parts of a target object: the hood of a car, a tire, the interior seats, etc. Individually, the artist may see and record a great deal of detail convincingly, but the details won't match each other. Curves won't line up; edges that should be parallel are not. Size or scale errors may be present between parts, or edge patterns will not match across edge borders. In figure drawings, this error causes the artist to focus so intently on whatever part of the body he draws first, that it is far larger than it should be. All subsequent anatomical elements gradually decrease in size, for a telescoping effect. Usually, the drawing goes right off the page and the figure is incomplete.

The *gestalt* (guh-stalt) observation type is what artists should strive to achieve. With this level of observation skill, the artist will see an object as a whole, and understand how all of its parts contribute to it, and in exactly what proportion.

A trait that most people acquire as they mature through life is the ability to re-member things they have seen, and then to cease looking carefully at those things. Once we know what a tree is, we don't have to reexamine every tree we see to know what it is. Once the difference between a larch and an oak is pointed out, we don't need to look at them too carefully anymore to recognize them. Once we learn to associate the color green with the color of fresh grass, we no longer mis-take it for red, or blue, or any other color. This trait is probably helpful to the extent it saves us time, and maybe even a little bit of organic CPU bandwidth. As artists though, it can be crippling.

Think about the color green for instance. This is a color commonly associated with the color of leaves on trees, as indeed, many leaves are green. This makes perfectly good sense. The problem is that there are a wide variety of greens, and the variety alone is proof that whatever concept of "leaf green" we might have is more likely wrong than right. Let's go to a more extreme example: most people learn that tree trunks are brown. If you look at the kind of brown you get in a box of crayola crayons, or any other inexpensive paint set, you're looking at a dark, high-saturated yellow orange. How many trees actually have bark of this color? The answer is: very few.

With the exception of a small number of trees, most are closer to being light gray in color than brown, yet the idea of brown tree trunks persists. Here is an-other example that is related to color: What color are shadows? If you're like most people, you will answer either black or gray. In truth however, shadows come in a wide variety of colors, and are less often black or gray than any other possibility. It isn't even necessarily true that they are going to be low-saturated colors (black or gray being the most extreme form of this). Depending on the lighting present, shadows may be much more vibrant than whatever color the shadow is crossing. It will be darker, but not always less saturated. This *observation error* comes from the correct observation that shadows are darker than the color of the thing they rest upon. *Darker* does not mean *black*, yet this popular misconception persists regard-less. Many professional artists make mistakes related to this, as can be easily seen if you look for it in their work.

Think of it this way: An object has an *intrinsic* color, this is its *absolute color* value. The intrinsic color of an object is not visible without light. Light has its own color and intensity. It is projected as *photons*, tiny light-bearing particles. These strike the surface of your target object, and reveal its color. At the same time as it strikes your object however, it also changes its color. On collision, the color of the photons combines with the intrinsic color of the object, providing a *hybrid* color in place of the original intrinsic color of the object or the photon color. Depending on the light, the light color may have such a strong influence that it completely obliterates the intrinsic color information of the object. Where, then, would this color be preserved? They are in the shadows, where fewer pho-tons are available to affect it. This, then, is why shadow colors are frequently more saturated than lit portions of an object bearing the same intrinsic color. Light, quite simply, chips away at color saturation like a sand blaster can clean a surface of graffiti by blasting sand at the surface it is a part of. Only when the light source itself is strongly saturated, the lit portion of a target will be more highly saturated than its intrinsic color, but in those situations, the color of the object will be almost completely flooded with the color of the light.

All of these are examples of how a person's memory of an old observation can interfere with his ability to see it fresh in the present. This is not a good thing for an artist, and all artists should make an effort to avoid falling into this trap. How many times have you sat down to draw something, and then as you are drawing it, thought, "no, that can't be right," and then drawn it differently? That type of learned behavior comes from early exposure to graphic symbols for whatever your subject is. If you are drawing a person, and have the feeling that the nose you are looking at cannot possibly look the way it does, chances are good that you think so because of what you think a nose is supposed to look like based on memories of drawings in some other source, like comic books or animation.

Another type of observation error is partly a by-product of an optical effect. If you look at a modern jet airplane, you will see that almost every part of it is curved. No matter what part you look at, it curves away from you. Remarkably, the largest sections of most jet airplanes are totally straight. The error in seeing curves where curves don't exist comes from a couple of factors combined: first, airplanes are so large that they cannot be viewed in one glance unless from a great distance. Up close, every edge is beveled to the point where each perfectly straight wing edge, for instance, has a graceful curve running its entire length. This contributes to the overall impression of a great many curves, and can result in incorrect models if you don't pay careful attention.

Models of characters are usually crammed with observation errors, at least, if they are made by artists with little absolute knowledge of anatomy. The reason is that throughout life, we are bombarded with information about the human body and what it looks like. So much that we forget to really look when given the chance. Probably, the easiest to describe error of this type comes from the focus of popular images of the human body. We look at photos of eyes, beautiful full lips, gorgeous hair, large breasts (or a muscular chest in a man), ample hips, and long legs. Is it any wonder that so many artists make all of the other parts smaller than they should? What about the nose? Ears? What about hands, knees, and feet? These parts are all frequently misrepresented at a fraction of their natural size. Worst of all, particularly in female characters, the abdomen is almost entirely absent, unless she is supposed to be pregnant. This happens with men as well, but less often, thanks to the popularity of "six-pack" style abdominal muscle groups in magazine layouts.

Think of a Photoshop gradient tool and then think of the gradient you would find on the side of a bag of bright orange and yellow Cheetos (or any other snack food). If you had to make a texture map of the bag, you would have to be very careful to match the colors and the gradient, right? Except it isn't a gradient at all. It is two colors, orange and yellow, totally unmixed, unblended, sitting side by side. Yet it looks like a gradient. Why? The reason it looks like a gradient is because these two colors are broken up into circles that gradually diminish in size as they move through each other. This never actually produces any intermediate mixed colors, but it does give the impression of a smooth gradient. If you used Photoshop's gradient tool to mimic this, it would be a mistake because the gradient tool does create intermediate colors, a large number of them, to bridge the gap between the two source colors (Fig. 9.7).

Fig 9.7
Gradient(s)

Measurements are where CG artists have the most problems, and this is why it is important to take as many empirical measurements as your project's schedule and your ability to find measurable reference allows. For those occasions when you do not have access to something you can measure, you will be most prone to making measurement errors. Be aware of this tendency, and stay focused on making your estimates as carefully as possible.

Sometimes, what happens when an artist does not have access to his target, but does have either a photo or a drawing, is that the size of the reference causes errors. What if, in a scale drawing of a helicopter, a single pixel covers an area equal to about one foot? The drawing will still look like a helicopter, but the detail lost when the photo was reduced could result in very poor results for you if you are working from it. Do you draw your helicopter from the center of each pixel, the outside, or the inside? This is a *pencil-width* error, and it used to happen to architects and engineers if their pencil width was so thick in a scale drawing that the pencil line itself had a measurable dimension. This is a much bigger problem in CG, when so much reference is acquired from low-resolution images on the Internet. Your best defense against this kind of error is to be observant enough that you can detect whether this flaw exists in your reference.

In the first stage of your work then, the most crucial stage of any project, you have to learn to trust what you see, even if it conflicts with what you think it should be. It will more often conflict than match your expectations. Get used to this and rediscover what things actually look like in your work as an artist.

To help you as you work, it is useful to constantly pose questions about your target, and then answer as objectively as possible. If you have access to a helicopter, for instance, ask yourself, "How many blades are on the primary rotor?" Instead of walking around and counting them (which risks forgetting which one you started with), see if you can get a photo of the helicopter from above, so that you can see where they all come together, and all at once. If you are building a plane, and can't see enough detail from a distance, and can't see the entire plane close-up, find a middle distance so that you can see which borders are perfectly straight and which aren't. Ask yourself if an edge is convex or concave, or whether a border is longer or shorter than another one in view. Ask anything you can think of to help you understand your target better.

The number of questions you can ask to elicit more accurate observations is too long to attempt a representation here, but the important thing is the idea of doing it. If you are drawing a pine cone, ask yourself, "Where is this double helix I keep hearing is a part of a pine cone's shape?" and you'll find it. Even better, when you start asking questions like this, you may even make original observations and discover things that no one else ever noticed before.

Do be careful that you keep in mind the level of detail you are aiming for however, or you may find yourself bogged down. If your subject is a tennis ball for *wii tennis*, then you do not need to go to the trouble of checking the fuzz on the ball all that carefully. Spotting the shape of the glue strip on the ball should be enough to identify it as a tennis ball, and you can be done with that part of your job much more quickly than if you ran rampant with highly detailed observations. If you had to build a container of floss for an advertisement, you might be surprised to find, on opening it, that the container is far more complicated than expected. If it is not going to be completely taken apart in the ad however, you can, and should, ignore this detail. The point of being observant isn't that you catch every tiny detail, it's that every detail you catch is correct, and at whatever resolution you are working.

The quality of your observations determines your maximum level of success. After executing the exercises in this book, your observational skills should improve considerably. Every exercise is meant to enhance these skills while simultaneously illustrating important concepts about 3D graphics. Do not forget that your success as a CG artist is more dependent on your observation skills than your technical skills. Technical skills are easier to acquire than observation skills, so take advantage of every opportunity to improve the quality of your observations.

3D artists can practice their observation skills by making 3D models, though the facility can be developed more quickly by learning how to draw. If you learn how to recognize and accurately record details related to your target object, you will be able to utilize this enhanced sensitivity in your 3D projects.

Chapter 10: Optimization

In Chap. 9, we discussed object resolution and how to arrive at the right level of resolution, or resolution target. Optimization will help you achieve this resolution goal, in addition to streamlining your scene for final use, whatever that might be (Figs. 10.1 and 10.2).

Fig 10.1
High-resolution bicycle render

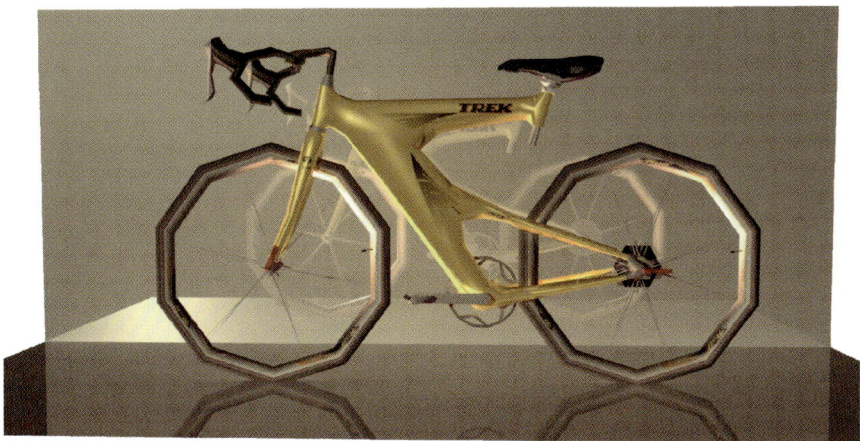

Fig 10.2
Low-resolution bicycle render

The primary goal of optimizing your model and scene is to have an efficient file. *Efficient* doesn't necessarily mean "as small as possible," though that is also a goal. Sometimes, efficiency demands more information in a file, such as in longer, more descriptive object names within a scene. An efficient file will not contain unnecessary information, but it will not be missing crucial information either. You do not want to cut out every single triangle around a joint in a character, simply because it does not contribute to the overall shape of the object. If those triangles are used for animation to ensure smooth limb motion, they should remain. Reducing for the sake of reduction doesn't always work. Like editing UVs, optimizing a model is also a series of compromises.

The principal compromise is between amount of information (as little as possible) and inclusion of all necessary information. Your ability to determine what is, and what is not, essential will determine your success at optimizing a file. If you have insufficient experience or comprehension, you will probably make many errors when optimizing a file. Generally, it is only through trial and error that an artist learns what is and what is not needed.

Check Curve Detail

Architectural models are built of polygons that are positioned at sharp angles to each other, usually right angles. Some modern buildings employ the use of segmented arcs for the appearance of arcs, but these are not common. The angles of an architectural subject are often sharp, or *acute*, making them a poor subject for optimization based on curve detail. In addition to plentiful acute angles, even when an architectural subject has curvature, it is usually single-axis segmented curvature. This means that it has already been optimized to at least a limited extent by the designer of the building, and remains a poor prospect for curve detail optimization (Fig. 10.3).

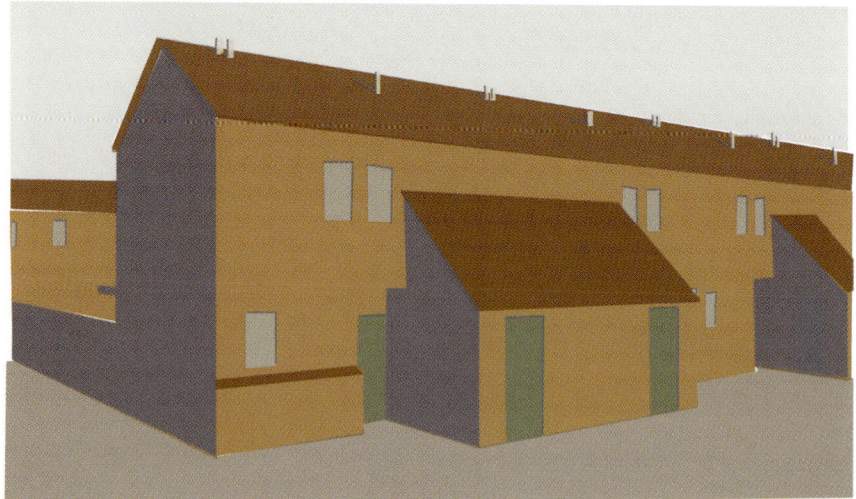

Fig 10.3
Hard angles like those pictured in this illustration cannot be reduced in detail without radically changing the shape of the object

   More promising are organic subjects, or CAD-designed objects like cars, planes, vacuum cleaners, and anything else built predominantly of curves. This class of objects will not only have more curves, but also they will be *two-axis* or even *three-axis* curves. What this means is that the edge of any given curve is not extruded at a 90° angle, but blended with a curve in one or more axes. Objects of this type are extremely easy to de-rez based on curve detail (Fig. 10.4).

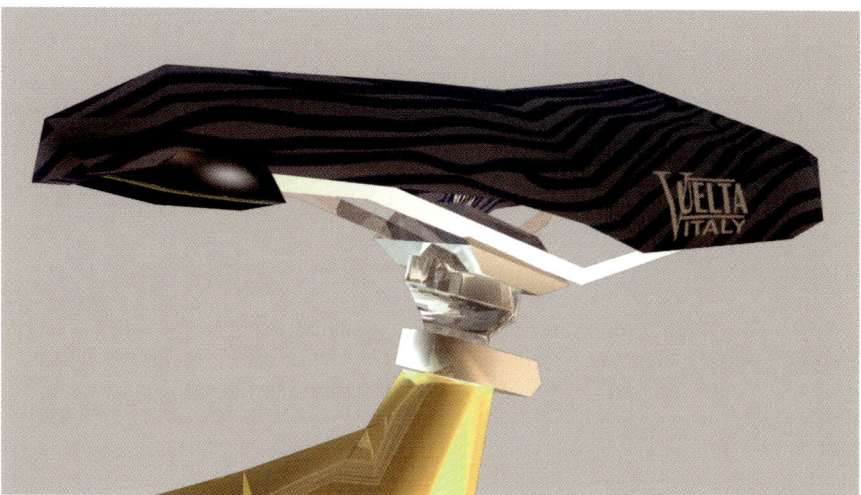

Fig 10.4

Curve detail in this object is very low, yet it remains a recognizable object. One factor that favors this object is that it has parts where one would expect to find them. In some cases, like the seat rails, individual parts are made of only 6–10 triangles. Low triangle counts can be very effective when care is taken to retain all parts required for easy recognition. When done properly, each part is represented by such a small number of triangles, that it is almost a 3D pixel instead of a representation of the object itself. With such a small triangle count, it is enough to be the right size and in the right position relative to other parts

   Curve detail is the number of segments per linear unit of distance. It is easy to make a rule that you will have so many segments per meter, but it gets more complicated when dealing with face angles. In addition to the number of segments per meter, you must ask yourself at what angle a pair of edges is considered to be part of an arc. Ninety degree is out of the question, and represents, for our purposes, the maximum deviation from a zero angle possible because it is only the difference between parallel and perpendicular that we care about for optimization.

If 90° is the maximum, and is not optimized, and zero is parallel and so not part of a curve, where is the line drawn? It could literally be 89°, if you have enough segments to create a smooth arc at that angle. More often, you will optimize curves that are 45° or less. Some programs allow you to set an angle tolerance for ridding yourself of *shallow angles*, but these often create difficult to undo errors, so their use is cautioned. What these tools can do, however, is highlight which edges are most likely to be lost at any give angular threshold. If you test it at 80°, then 70°, 60°, 50°, 40°, etc., you will be steadily selecting more and more polygons to be fused together and can decide for yourself which is most optimal.

When considering curve detail, the first question you should ask is whether you can see the detail at the resolution your object will be seen in the final render. If it isn't detectable, then it is too high and you can afford to lose some curve segments. When you delete curve segments, or collapse them, you can also delete every connected edge all the way around your object. This can save a large number of polygons.

Next, you should determine if the structural integrity of your object is compromised when a segment is removed. If not, it can safely be taken out. Often, a model is built with high curve detail within a large surface. Because it exists entirely within the larger boundary of another object, the larger object conceals much of its silhouette detail. For this reason, deleting or collapsing edges and replacing them with smoothed edges can save you many polygons with no apparent degradation of quality.

You should also make sure that your level of curve detail is consistent throughout your model. This does not necessarily mean that you must have the same number of segments for a given distance, it could also mean that you always have a minimum number of segments no matter how much distance it covers. Whatever you do decide, you should be consistent about using the rule throughout the model.

An easy way to spot unneeded curve information is to look for *edge-star* formations in your model. This is when five or more edges connect to a single vertex. Any time you see this, there is a good chance that the angles represented are shallow enough that the central vertex of the star may be safely collapsed. Be ready to undo your actions however, because it isn't always the case.

Check Part Detail

Parts can be defined in three ways: as a *selection set*, a *material grouping*, and a separate grouped object. A selection set is any collection of elements that have been named as a set. This is like a group except it does not take the set elements out of their parent polyset. If they were broken out, then they would no longer be elements, or components, but a separate object. A material grouping is like a set, but it is based on any given face's material assignments. Most software allows artists to select based on material assignments, making this a quick way to designate a separate layer of model information. Separate grouped objects are exactly what they sound like, an object that is grouped into another object or group.

The number of parts in your object is important to control with your object's end-use in mind. You can easily have an overwhelmingly high number of parts, or an irritatingly low number of parts, making sections of your object impossible to animate. When you consider parts, also consider the difference between parts that are literally separate objects but grouped together and selection sets of faces that share vertices. Selection sets of faces are a good way to reduce your vertex count, but bad for certain types of animation, while having too many grouped parts can be unwieldy (Fig. 10.5).

Fig 10.5
In this model, each part of the model is designed to animate independently. This requires all parts to be whole, solid objects. Optimization for hidden faces is not possible here (model by Marein Könings)

It is typical for a low-resolution car to be made of a single polyset for the body and interior, and then grouped parts for tires and steering wheel. In some cases, the doors, trunk, and hood are also separated for animation. This *moving parts only* rule is very common, and you can expect it to be the primary decision maker when you examine your parts' list to see which may be safely combined and which must remain separate. For a high polycount vehicle to be rendered in a film, you would likely have to build a very long list of parts and then group them together (Fig. 10.6).

Fig 10.6

In this illustration, the *pink dashed line* describes sections of the model where texture borders are incised into the geometry. This technique ensures a hard edge along borders and can save a lot of trouble when texturing

After checking to see which parts are animated independently from others, you can ask yourself if any of your parts have been carved into, and then extruded from another polygon as *incised detail*. If so, you can safely detach the extruded element as its own object, eliminate the resulting hole (and a number of useless vertices), and then group or add the extruded part back into the original polyset. Many artists use incised detail often as part of their construction technique. One reason is that it is easy to ensure that any parts extruded from another are aligned perfectly, but it also causes a higher polycount because the vertices that define any common edge between the original object and the extruded part will have to be connected to the surrounding face(s) to prevent holes. These connections are unnecessary if the polygons of the original face are recreated without the shape of the incised detail carved into it. Some modelers devote as much as 20% of their models to this kind of detail. Eliminate it, and their models are now 20% more efficient.

Welding parts together after combining objects is another good method to save vertices. Unlike eliminating holes, which also recovers polygons, welding edges of adjacent polysets will only recover vertices, but they are important also, and if you can save them, you may as well do it. Not only does your model render faster and with fewer opportunities for render errors, but also your peers will get accustomed to seeing clean models from you and your reputation will be enhanced.

Check Texture/Structural Detail

Texture can represent structural detail that is too fine to be included in your model. Even if you already took this into consideration when you originally built your model, look at it again and ask yourself if there is any other detail that can be represented by a texture map instead of geometry. Ideally, you will be able to add UVs to an existing map, and you won't have to make any new maps, but will instead modify an existing one.

Some types of detail should not be attempted with a texture map; others work very well with one, and can be done very efficiently. For instance, what if you want a simple incised groove in your object, to represent the space between a door and its frame? That type of detail would require a minimum of two rows of very small polygons. Instead, consider using a two-pixel high black and white bump map. The width of the map will vary, depending on the width of the polygon(s) it is attached to, but a black and white two-pixel high map is going to be very efficient compared to polygons.

Check for structural detail vs. color detail. Sometimes it is better to cut the shape of a change of color into an object, sometimes it is better not to, and define the curve entirely with paint. Look at your object and ask yourself which is best. The result can be a more efficient model, depending on your answer. Take a look at the following low-resolution vehicle model as an example (Fig. 10.7).

Fig 10.7
Arno Schmitz. In this model, the headlight is built substantially out of texture maps instead of polygons. Is this a good way to optimize the object? This ia a very low-resolution object, where optimization was a primary concern. In this case, the number of additional polys was small, so the tradeoff for a ragged edge in the texture map probably wasn't worth it. Remember, you can optimize too much also and you do not want that

Optimization Goals

It is important to never lose track of your optimization goals. Your first goal should always be to eliminate everything that does not contribute to your scene. After that, you should search for anything that could impair your scene. After these two things are done, you should look for opportunities to improve your scene through optimization, and last, you must compare the results with your limits. If you are over your limit, you must continue to reduce, regardless of other concerns.

The method outlined above presumes starting with a highly detailed, high-resolution treatment of an object, and then bringing it down to an optimized level. Optimization can also work in the other direction. Instead of working from high detail to low, you can work from low detail to high, adding detail until you reach your resolution ceiling. With this method, your work will probably progress more quickly, but you are also less likely to include certain types of detail that might otherwise have become a part of your model.

Organic models usually look better if they start as high-resolution objects and are then de-rezed. This is because it is very difficult to predict from a low-resolution model how to average the many complex curved structures in an organic model. Mechanical and architectural subjects, on the other hand, do not lose a great deal when started as a low-resolution object and are then increased in detail until a resolution limit is met.

Compare to Checklist and Cleanup

After you have your object reduced to its optimal polycount, it should be checked for errors. This error check should always be done before handing off a model to another artist for animation or rendering. If you are the artist who will be doing these other tasks, it is still important to check the model for errors. All too frequently, errors left over from the model construction process create problems later. Therefore, you want to make an effort to catch these before those errors cost you time when you cannot afford to spend hours looking for them.

Your error check should always be considered part of the modeling process, with no model considered complete until it is done. The type of errors you will be looking for are technical errors, such as those described in Chap. 2, functionality errors, presentation errors, and efficiency-related errors.

A well-built model will:

- Be a good likeness of the target
- Contain no illegal geometry

- Have well-balanced texture coordinates
- Be well organized
- Have all detail represented at the right resolution

Optimization Cheats

Optimization is almost by definition a way to cheat your model into a convincing state despite being incomplete in some way. The techniques described so far are standard methods of optimization however, and not regarded as true "cheats." To really cheat your model, you have to be more daring, more outrageous with your optimization technique. This section is for the more unusual optimization methods you may have occasion to encounter, though these are only recommended if your poly budget absolutely forces you to use them:

1. *Opacity maps.* If you cannot spare the polygons to create a complex shape, consider using an opacity map (also known as a *transparency map*) to describe the information (Fig. 10.8).

Fig 10.8
Arno Schmitz. Many of the details in this model are made of simple polygons with opacity maps. The spokes, tail rack, brake cables, and gears are all examples of this

2. *Silhouette.* Depending on how your object will be used, you may be able to reduce the number of triangles to the minimum required to retain its silhouette in most angles. This can drastically reduce your triangle count, depending on exact circumstances (Fig. 10.9).

Fig 10.9
Power of silhouettes

3. *Fake perspective.* For models that are meant to represent large areas of terrain, if the camera will never stray outside certain clearly defined areas, terrain well beyond its path may be artificially shortened to reduce overall polycount. To be effective, a consistent scale must be used, where concentric contour rings (whether they are ring shaped or not) describe a certain distance from the camera, and objects between each successively distant pair of rings are scaled down and brought closer. This means, for instance, that if all objects are built at 1:1 scale within the nearest camera range, the next group out would be 75% their original size, the next group beyond that would be 50%, then 25%, and so on. This method is most effective if used in combination with environmental fog, nonflat terrain, and an irregular (not square) terrain border.

4. *Card geometry.* This is often the most extreme form of optimization. Card geometry describes objects that are usually rectangular in shape and are as flat as a card, with a texture map to define all its details instead of geometry. For this to work, there is usually a color map, sometimes based on a render of a more complex object, in addition to an opacity map to define the object's silhouette, and sometimes a bump or normal map to enhance the model's depth. Card geometry is often used to represent complex objects such as plants. An enhancement to the technique is to use multiple intersecting cards to cause realistic overlap of elements.

5. *Use two-sided geometry sparingly.* This should be obvious from previous chapters, but is easy to forget. Using two-sided geometry immediately doubles the number of triangles your renderer has to deal with.

There are many other ways to cheat your way out of a low poly budget, or to simply make a more efficient scene, but these should suffice as a general idea of the limits one can go to and get away with when optimizing a scene.

Optimized Geometry and Rendering

Optimized geometry will render much more quickly than geometry that has not been optimized. The difference can be startling. On the feature film *Space Jam*, for instance, optimization was a major priority because the effects crew had to make over 1,400 shots in a very short period of time. This meant that the render stations could not be kept busy with hour per frame renders with hundreds of thousands of frames of animation waiting in the queue.

Because of the throughput problem presented by the combination of number of shots and the deadline, tests were done and an optimal render time was arrived at: 1 min per frame. Anything more had to be for a very special shot only. Some frames rendered at only a few seconds each, so great was the optimization of some scenes. This time-based standard was effective at identifying problems in scenes, and usually led to improvements in overall quality at the same time as the renders were made to execute more quickly.

In video games, there is also a time-based standard; frames per second. For a game to be interactive, player responses must be communicated to the screen with a result given very quickly or the illusion of interactivity is lost. For most games, this means that they must run at between 30 and 60 frames a second, preferably 60.

To test frame rate, game objects are brought into the game engine and tested. If the engine cannot maintain its desired frame rate due to the complexity of the geometry or other problems related to inadequate optimization, the objects will be rejected. Rendering, then, becomes the ultimate test of successful optimization, whether it is for prerendered graphics in a film or real-time rendered graphics in a game.

The first way to test an object's renderability is to put a light in your scene and render your object. This should always be done at least once before proceeding to the next step. Some modeling errors are difficult to detect, but if they are severe enough, they will cause an error message or an error in the render itself that will help you find the problem. It is not necessary to make a beautiful lighting setup for this test, but it isn't a bad idea to put together a set of *test lights* to help you evaluate your model.

These lights should illuminate your model from all sides, and at least one should cast shadows. If you save the lights to a separate generic file, you can import them as needed to test your geometry.

Testing your object for real-time rendering is best done in the game engine used for your project, but the hardware shader used in most applications is a reasonable approximation. One thing that will almost certainly be different is that your computer will probably be more powerful than the target platform of most games, so it will not give an accurate fps output. Instead, it will tell you only if you have errors that interfere with the renderers' normal performance.

Chapter 11: UV Editing

UV editing, unlike UV projection, is where the hard work of texturing a model is done. It is here that a texture map layout is decided on, and here that an artist succeeds or fails to make the best use of the pixels available for texture maps. In the first section of this book, different projection methods were described as an introduction to concepts related to UV editing. To illustrate the different projection methods, some discussion of editing took place, but not a great deal. This chapter explores finer details of the UV-editing process not covered earlier (Fig. 11.1).

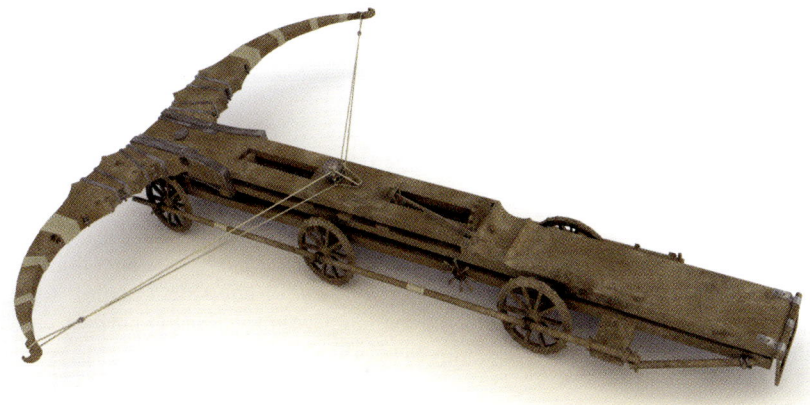

Fig 11.1
Textured giant crossbow and render by Arno Schmitz

Box Projection to Avoid Scale Errors

Frequently, parts of an object or components of an assembly are not projected together. The result is the scale mismatch seen in the plane on the left (Fig. 11.2). It is important to note that although the objects in the image for each quadrant appear at a different size, this by itself isn't necessarily a scale mismatch. What makes it a mismatch is that it is the same image, mapped to a different number of linear units. Therefore, the number of pixels used to cover each same length edge is not the same. The images were generated in a vector-based drawing program and could be easily recalculated at different resolutions. If this were done to match the scale of the polygon each section of the image is mapped to, there would be no scale mismatch.

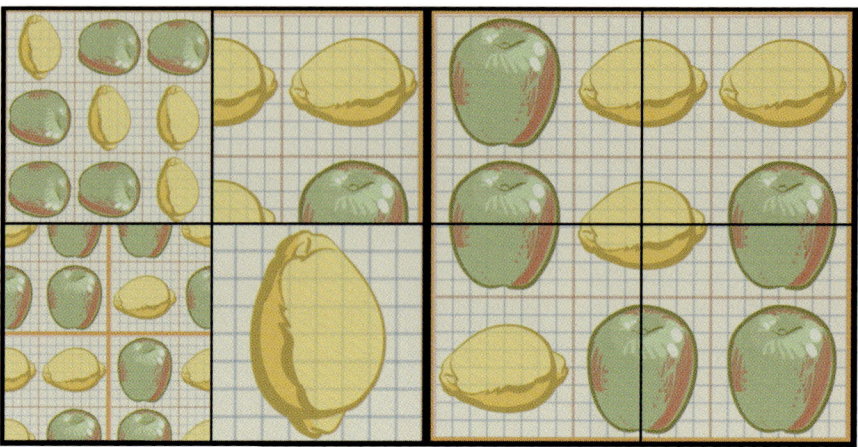

Fig 11.2
Both of the two planes pictured above have been subdivided once to create four
quads each. The plane on the *left* has had its UVs projected separately; the one on
the *right* was projected together

For mapping large assemblies that must be proportionately consistent, a *reference cube* may be employed. Some software allows for equivalent control simply
by typing in absolute dimensions for the mapping volume. For the purpose of ex-
planation, the cube is used here. In both cases, the principle is the same (Figs. 11.3
and 11.4).

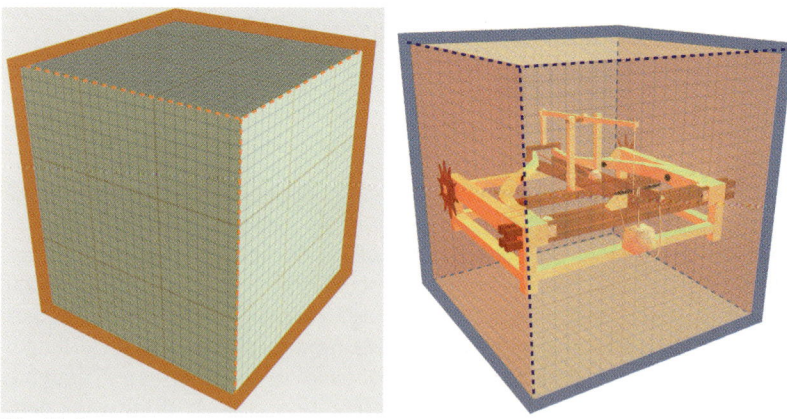

Fig 11.3
A reference cube
Fig 11.4
Model by Elsje Bakker. A reference cube and the object it is meant to contain for
mapping purposes

A reference cube should always be large enough to contain all objects that must have proportionate texture coordinates, so that its parts may be included in any projections. It is very important to scale the cube proportionately. If you do not, the aspect ratio of some faces will be changed and corresponding texture coordinates will be distorted. Because each of the six projections contains a 1.0 aspect ratio face of the same dimension, all of your other faces will be proportionately consistent.

Different applications vary in the method required to make effective use of the reference cube. In some, you will have to project each axis separately, in others; you can project them all simultaneously. The difference is whether your application always projects into legal 0–1 texture space and whether it allows overlapping projections. Your goal is to project in such a way that each projection does not overlap the other. All applications have a way to do this, but whether it is automatic or manual will depend on the application.

In the following illustration, (Fig. 11.5), the cube has been scaled to be a little larger than the height of the target object. After getting it close to the desired size, it was scaled up to an even number, 5, so that cylindrical projections could be scaled to an easily remembered value. Notice that the cube does *not* hug the borders of this object as a bounding box would. That is so that the 1.0 aspect ratio of the mapping across all projections is maintained. The UVs for none of the projections will come close to filling the UV space, but that is permitted because they will later be combined and at that time they *will* fill the space.

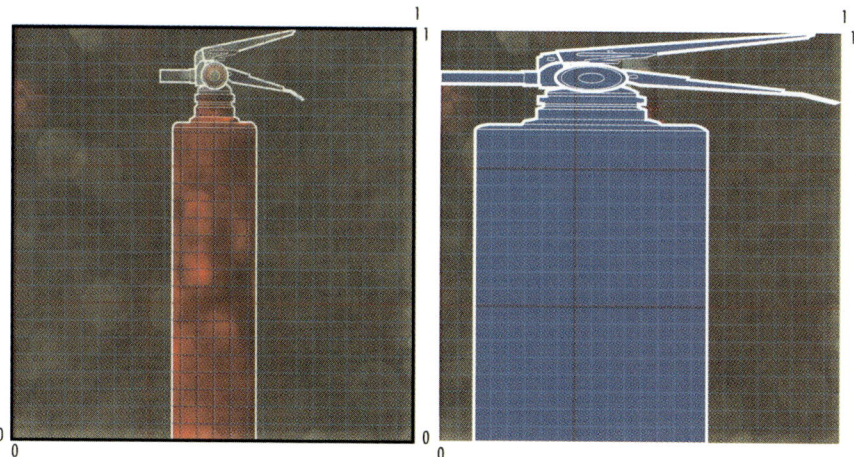

Fig 11.5
The fire extinguisher on the *left* is mapped proportionately. The extinguisher on the *right* was mapped based on its own bounding volume, the default mapping method used by most UV projection tools

An object to be mapped is completely enclosed by a reference cube object. If it were not completely enclosed, the reference object would be of no use because it would no longer constrain the outer bounds of a projection to the size of any of its identical faces.

Fig 11.6
Model by Andrius Drevinskas. Rotate mapping plane to fit object

Note in this image (Fig. 11.6) that some parts of this object are not aligned with the global axes. To project this without distortion, the projection should be oriented to each plane's normal, or as close as possible. The white dashed line shows the proper orientation for a projection, though it is the wrong size. If possible, it would have been better to model this object in a more neutral position to eliminate the extra effort of aligning the UV projection plane with faces at odd angles.

The size of the reference cube should remain constant. It may be rotated and moved as necessary, but never scaled. During the course of making projections for a complicated object, a reference cube will have its faces mapped many times over. Don't worry about overwriting its UVs or whether the cube's UVs look acceptable, the only thing that counts is that the object you are mapping gets the UVs it needs. That will occasionally result in poor UVs for the reference cube. When you are finished, you may want to hide the cube, but keep it around in case you need to make changes later on.

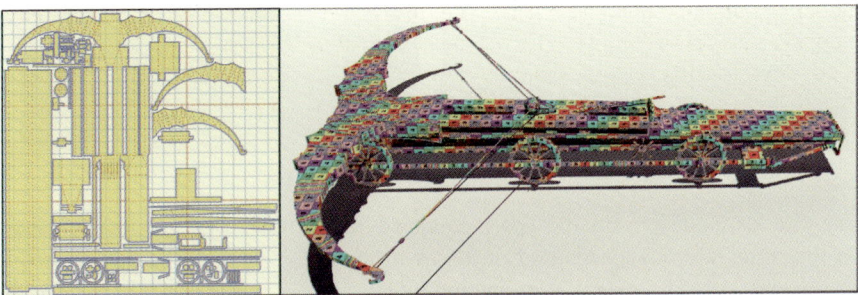

Fig 11.7
Model and map solution by Arno Schmitz

The UVs for this object, (Fig. 11.7), were projected using a reference cube. The resulting UVs were then edited with a high-resolution texture treatment in mind. For this reason, the object is almost entirely distortion free. Seams are kept to a minimum, straight edges are aligned to X and Y, and there is no scale mismatch.

How Modeling Technique Affects UVs

Here is a complex object built along a path that would be difficult to paint because of its UVs. It is not a very good use of the texture space, the UVs are distorted, and the projection is not oriented to match the orientation of the object. This type of object is fairly common, like multiple arched columns in a cathedral entry, or mouldings on the exterior of a building. If an object like this is made without thought to its UVs at the time of modeling, the above result is about as good as you are likely to get. It can be much worse (Fig. 11.8).

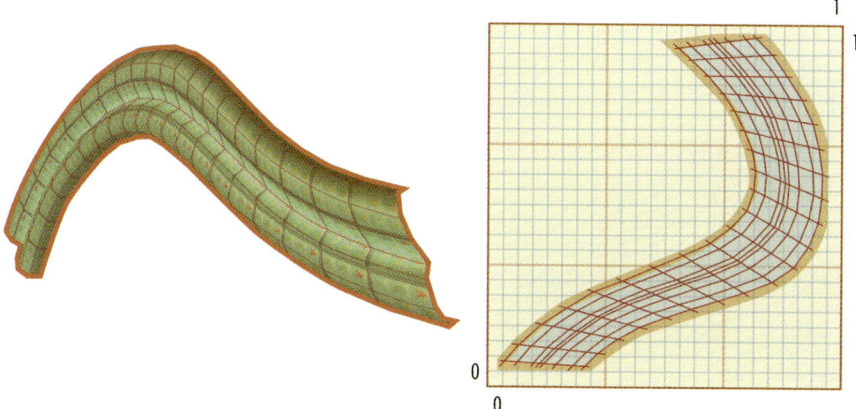

Fig 11.8
A complex path-built object and its UVs

The best-case scenario is to always have an idea how your object should be mapped before you build it. Mapping and texturing can take much more time than modeling, and take much less if they are planned for. In this situation, the default mapping you get with most tools will be sufficient as long as you are careful to set it up properly and don't accidentally destroy the UVs in a mistaken effort to make them better.

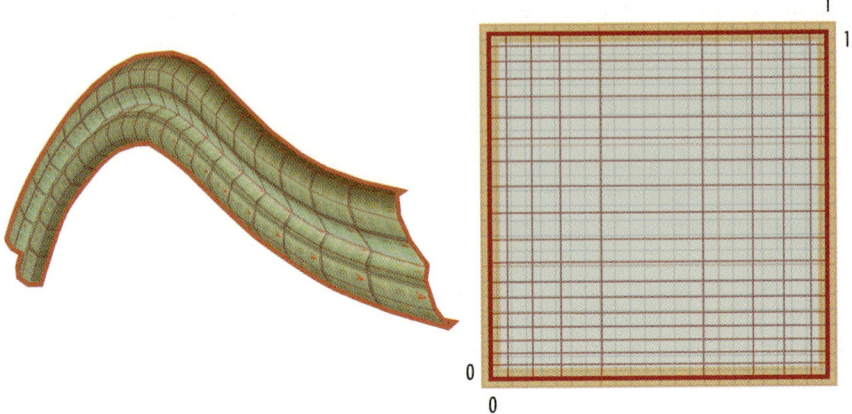

Fig 11.9
This is the same object shown above, but with better UVs. In some studios, the texture artist has to work with whatever the modeler provides. These coordinates, clean, undistorted, and well packed, are what a texture artist should be able to expect from any modeler

This object (Fig. 11.9) will be much easier to paint than the previous example, will yield a higher quality map, and will require a lower resolution map to achieve the same apparent level of resolution. It is also about five times the resolution of the previous mapping, not an insignificant advantage when considering how costly texture maps are to render speeds.

Notice that the UVs have been disproportionately scaled to completely fill the UV space. To avoid distortion in the texture map, the map will be scaled to fit the original unscaled proportions of the UVs.

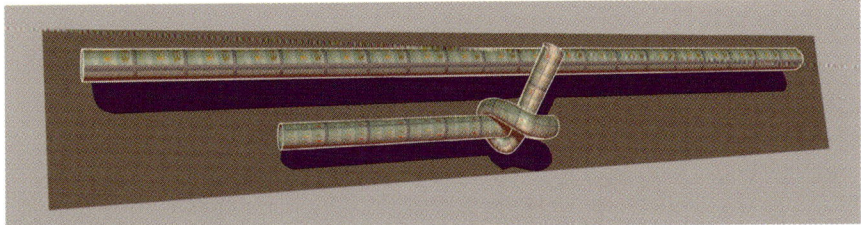

Fig 11.10
The texture coordinates of a knot can be very difficult to edit if you don't know what they are supposed to look like (a long grid), or how to do it

The problem presented in the above image (Fig. 11.10) is similar to the lofted profile problem described earlier. The difference here is that (1) this object overlaps itself and (2) many modelers like to build these objects in their final position, that is to say, knotted rather than straight. The easiest method to edit this object's UVs is to avoid it entirely. This can be done if the modeler simply uses the default coordinates that come with the cylinder it is built from, and then takes care not distort them as he adds points and moves them into position to create the knot. Some artists will use a skeleton to move an object like this into shape.

Texture Alignment

An improperly aligned set of texture coordinates can cause problems of various levels of severity. At the first level, it is simply easier to paint certain textures that have been aligned in a certain way. For instance, you would not want two adjacent faces mapped so that one had to be painted upside down or sideways. To do so would require extra modifications to the texture map that, if avoided, would save you time and trouble. Another issue is that straight lines can be made to be perfectly straight, without antialiasing, if the underlying UVs are aligned to allow these straight lines to be perfectly aligned to the *XY* coordinate system of UV space (Fig. 11.11).

Fig 11.11
Orientation

In both of these models, their texture coordinates do not match the orientation of the map, thus causing the text on the map to tilt across some faces. The object on the left has an additional problem. All of its UVs are backward. This is evident by looking at the type on its map. This is why, when making a reference map, you should avoid symmetrical characters like A, M, and O. In this example, it is from the letters B, C, E, J, K, G, R, and L that *UV* direction can be determined. The "A" is useless.

Fig 11.12
Rotated texture map to match misaligned UVs

The problem with this object, (Fig. 11.12), as with many others, is that its UVs cannot be rotated into a position where all of its contiguous faces are oriented at 90° angles to the *U*- or *V*-axis of texture space. This is why many artists will modify their texture map, as shown here, to match the orientation of their object instead. If this UV solution is desirable, the map must be rotated off axis for each edge to be aligned to the object, for instance, as a label.

How to Determine an Acceptable Level of Distortion

The type of error discussed in this section would not normally be considered a serious problem for anything but a close-up shot. However, it is always good to keep in mind that these are errors and if the opportunity presents itself, they should be corrected. Every one of them can in certain circumstances delay the texture artist or make it impossible to paint certain parts of model in the manner desired. In this case, there were a few polygons with slightly stretched coordinates that cost an extra 40 minutes or so before the texture artist realized that the polys could not be painted properly without first fixing the UVs.

From a distance, there is no distortion evident, but in the close-up shot of this character's back (Fig. 11.13), distortion is clear in the shoulders. This was not true when the arm was in its neutral position, but in this pose, the distortion is fairly strong. The amount of distortion visible on the right could be a problem, depending on the complexity of its maps and the type of animation planned for it. If it is not meant to hold this pose for any length of time, it may not be a problem at all.

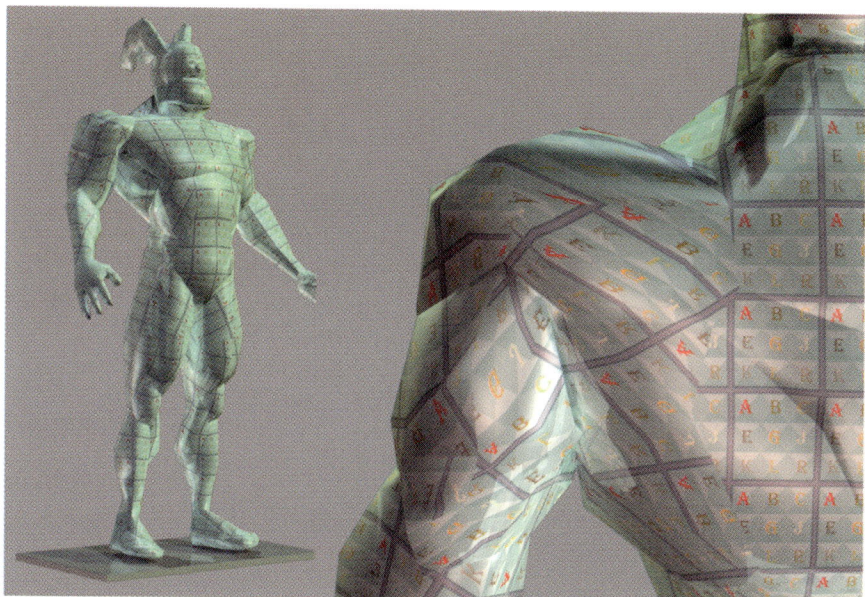

Fig 11.13
Distorted UVs on character at shoulder joint

In this case, it was not anticipated that the camera would linger on this part of the character's anatomy during animation, so the distortion was allowed. For characters, this is a very common problem for shoulder and hip joints because they both enjoy a full three degrees of freedom in the X-, Y-, and Z-axes.

This (Fig. 11.14) is one of those objects that make you wonder if you want to take that one last extra step to make it just a bit better. As it was originally mapped, there is a sawtooth seam running around the edge of the topmost and bottommost faces of this object, as can be seen in the version on the left. Even though it can be easily painted without distortion, the number of seams is daunting. On the left, the top faces have been reprojected with a planar projection, so that they may be painted together. This does not change the number of seams; it just modifies their position to a more logical border. Now, the seam runs entirely around the group of triangles in a circle, instead of the ragged sawtooth edge it started with.

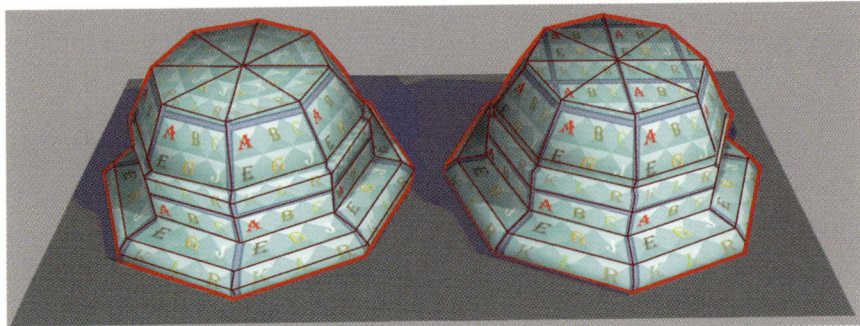

Fig 11.14
Seam decision

Overlapping UVs, How to Eliminate with Seam Ripping and Stitching

These are showstoppers. If you see anything like the examples below (or if you made them), you will eventually be asked to fix it (Fig. 11.15).

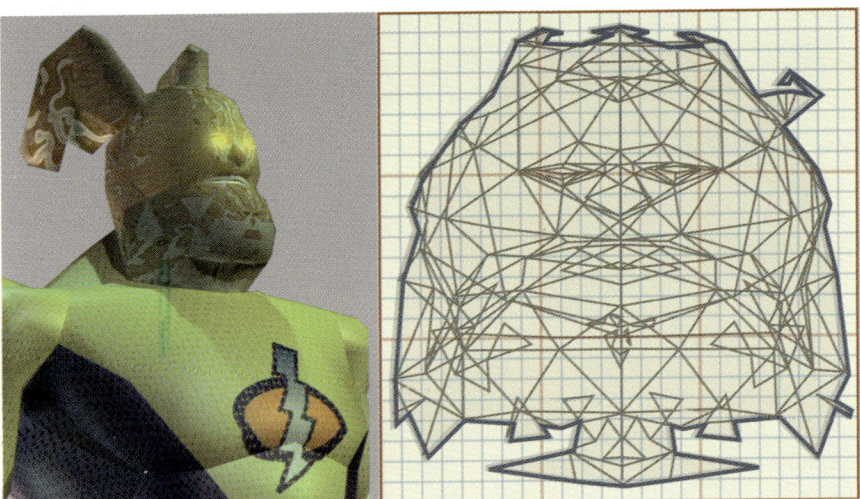

Fig 11.15
Overlapping UVs

Although this character's body is mapped properly, his head would in almost all cases be so difficult to paint that it would be sent back for a considerable amount of UV projection/editing.

The problem is that the planar projection used is:

- Not aligned to most of the faces
- Creates a considerable amount of overlap

Even in 3D paint, the overlap problem makes this object an impossibility to paint with any degree of accuracy (Fig. 11.16).

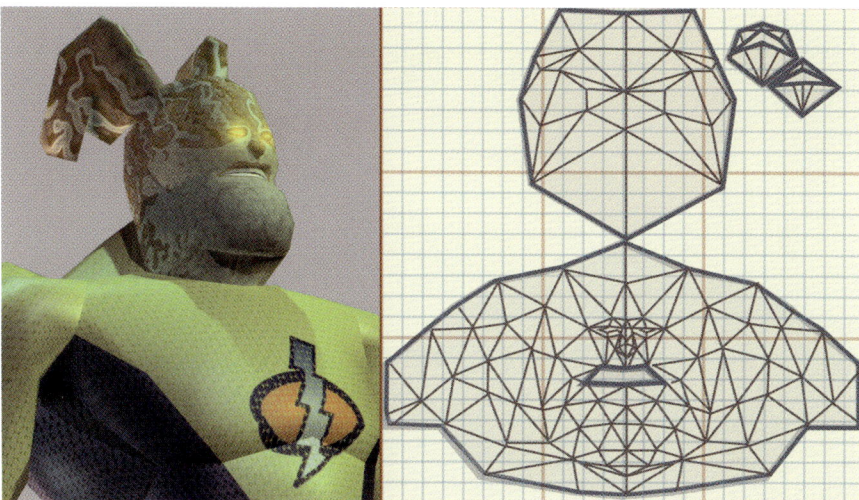

Fig 11.16
Here, the head has been fixed with multiple projections and some editing of UVs

Grouping and Its Effect on UV-Editing Workflow

One way to organize a large number of parts is by material type, like wood, rubber, cloth, steel, etc. Most often, you will have fewer parts than you have materials, so some parts will share the same material. This is already an improvement over having everything assigned to the same material, and is usually workable. On some occasions, your parts will be so complex that you will want to keep your objects separate while texturing them. When that is true, you may want to create temporary shaders, to keep the UVs separate while you work with them, and then combine them when you are done (Fig. 11.17).

Fig 11.17
These are the texture coordinates for an object that has all of its hundreds of parts
attached to the same material. Artists who do this create unnecessary work for
themselves, and fail to take advantage of one of the advantages of having separate
parts: the ability to also separate their texture coordinates

Here, the various pieces for a character have been scaled to match each other
and separated to prevent overlap. This UV solution can work for a low-resolution
treatment, but is insufficient if the character is meant to use multiple material
specifications, like for his skin and clothing. What this shows is what the UVs are
supposed to look like to you while you are editing them, clean, separate, and organized. It is also what any artist working with your file should be able to expect
to find (Fig. 11.18).

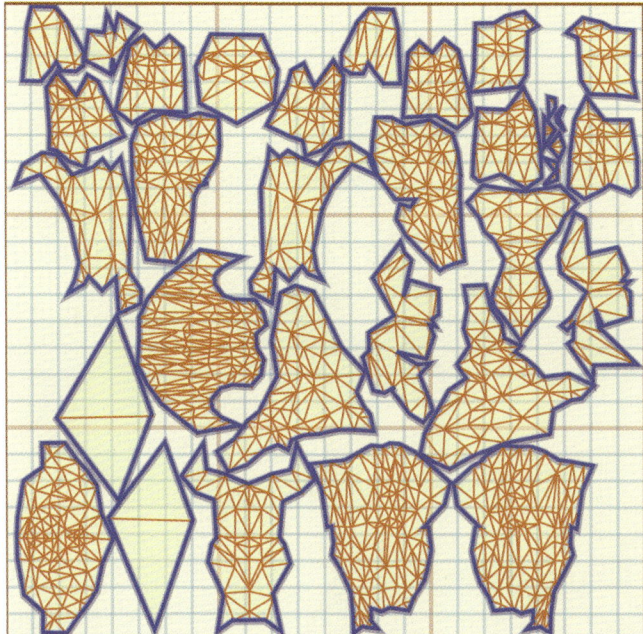

Fig 11.18
Character UV layout

Neutral Poses and Projection

Nobody is perfect, but some choices seem designed to prove it better than others. Here are a couple examples of situations that might make you seriously wonder if you made the right decision right up until your CG supervisor tells you to do it over. In these examples, the common denominator is a choice of saving time over improving quality.

How will this hand be mapped? A fast planar projection with minor editing will not be satisfactory, and if it is to be seen close-up, a complicated multiple projection solution is required. Ideally, this hand would have been modeled in a neutral pose prior to UV projection and then moved into position afterward (Fig. 11.19).

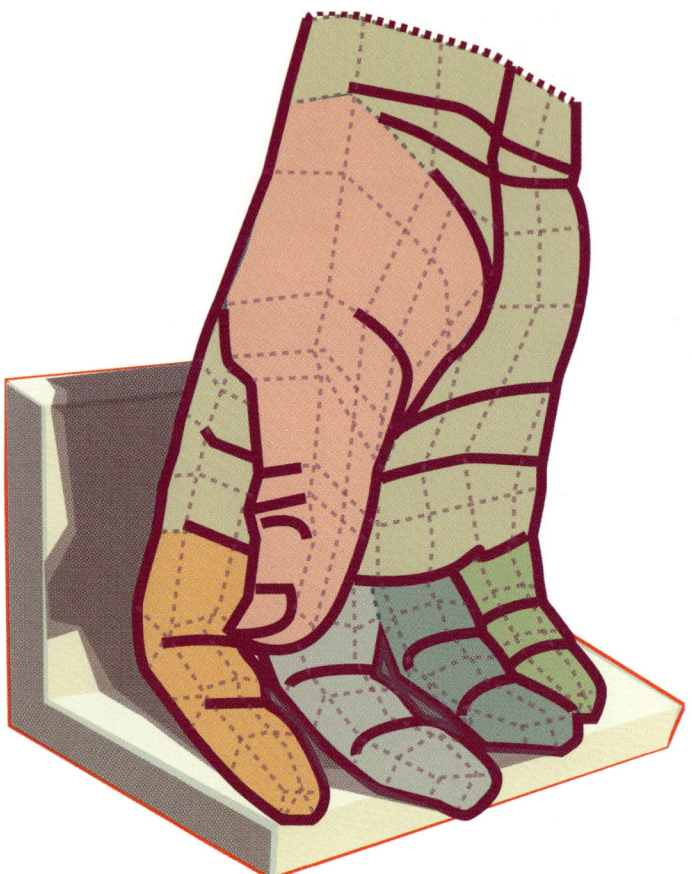

Fig 11.19
A difficult mapping problem

If this had been modeled with some attention paid to how it would be used, each finger would have been modeled in a neutral position, then mapped, then attached to the palm. For an animated hand, a skeleton would be added to the model to move the fingers into position. When modeling, always consider the purpose of your object. Many modelers find their work returned because they failed to do this simple thing.

UV Packing

"Packing" describes the process of arranging UVs, so that they fill the available texture space as densely as possible. A well-packed UV set will reduce the amount of unused pixels in a map. Some objects will naturally use almost all of the space because they are made entirely of right angles, but many objects are the wrong aspect ratio, or have to be combined with other parts on the same map, or are not built of right angles. Most objects can be packed into about 80% of the texture space without distortion (Fig. 11.20).

Fig 11.20
A texture map for a PS2 real-time character. In area, about 8–10% of this map is not used. This is an acceptable ratio

A number of factors affect packing decisions. The most important factors are these:

1. *Alignment*. If your object has any straight lines, you may want to align its UVs to make this possible without any antialiasing artifacts.
2. *Grouping*. You should put objects that are related to each other close to each other on the map. This way, it will be easier to find the parts you are looking for. Because of their nature, it is sometimes difficult to know what part you are looking at on a map, so grouping related objects reduces the amount of time it takes to locate a certain object.
3. *Margins*. A 1–3 pixel border should surround each discrete group of UVs. Otherwise, it is possible that a pixel meant for one polygon will bleed into another, but only if it is too close. The reason there is a range given instead of an absolute value is because it depends on the resolution of

your texture map. The lower the resolution, the farther apart the pieces must be to avoid *overspray*.

4. *Orientation.* Generally, you want all parts to be oriented with their topmost points at the top, bottom points at the bottom, and so on. The reason is that it is usually easier for a texture artist to paint things that are oriented properly than to paint them at an angle. Sometimes, you may want to rotate the UVs at an odd angle, to make the best use of texture space. If you do this, the texture artist may have to paint the object with a 3D paint tool, or he will have to exercise greater care when painting. Either way, it will slow him down.

For this low-resolution character, a high-resolution texture treatment was used. Because the texture had a tiling pattern as well as identifiable details, seven different projections were made for the four maps used for the character. In each case, care was taken to make sure that the texmap did not distort on the character. Although this map appears to have significant wasted space, this is not true. Overlapping polys used the same map, but are not displayed to make the image less confusing (Fig. 11.21).

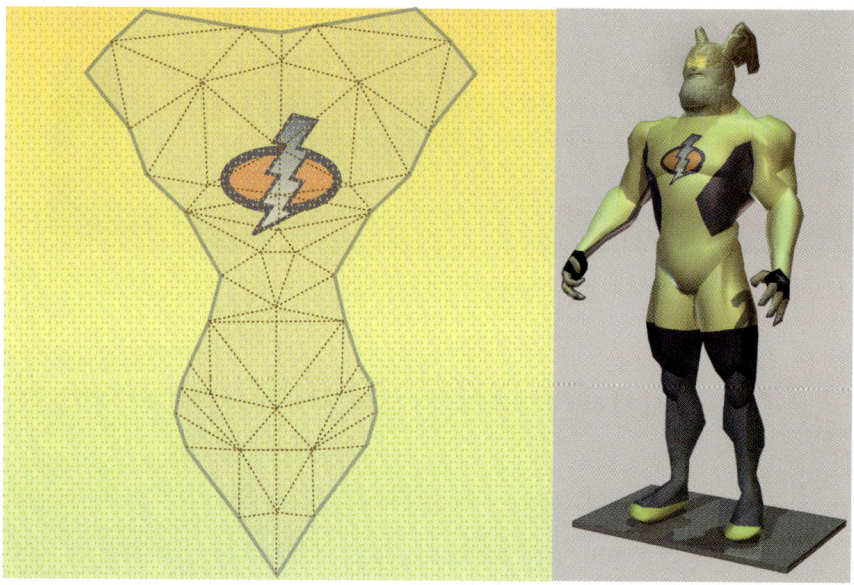

Fig 11.21
High-resolution mapping

Keep in mind the difference between the resolutions of your map and the resolution of your UVs. They are not the same thing. The most obvious factor that is relevant to UV resolution is the percentage of undistorted UV space. The higher this percentage is, the higher your UV resolution is also. The other factor is the number of maps required by your UV solution. Generally, the more maps there are, the higher the resolution.

Packing is where some artists lose most of what they have gained by clever projection and editing. Take care to understand the available space and how your objects can best be made to fit into it and your texture map will be higher resolution without having to increase the pixel count. The more space you fill, the more pixels will fill each polygon. The more pixels you have in your polygons, the higher resolution the texture treatment is.

How to Calculate Ideal Texmap Size

Resolution contrast happens when adjacent objects are textured with maps that have different pixels per linear unit ratios. Regardless of what the difference is, if there is a difference, one object will look crude compared to the other. Projecting your coordinates while using a global size reference will avoid this problem for objects that share the same material, but what if they don't? What if you have several materials, and you have to use as much of each map as you can by filling the texture space completely? If that is the case, simply projecting the UVs to scale is not enough. You must also modify the size of your texture maps[11] (Fig. 11.22).

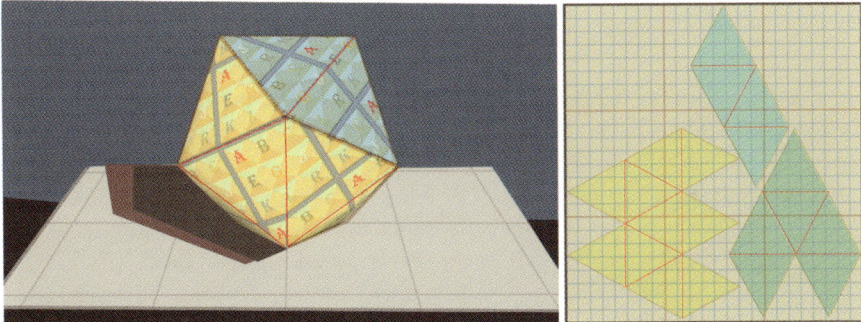

Fig 11.22
Calculating ideal texmap size, three materials

This object has three shaders for each of three face groups: yellow, blue, and green. It will have one map for each of these sections. The three sections must match because they are built out of faces that are adjacent in the model. In this image, the UVs have already been edited after projecting them together to eliminate scale distortion. They have then been separated within UV space to keep them distinct for editing purposes.

---

[11] Modifying map sizes outside of power of two or square sizes is not recommended in all situations. Map size limitations are primarily meant to speed up rendering in real-time games, but the same limitations exist in many renderers. It is almost never a hardware-related limitation, but a software flag that can be set by the user. This is not commonly known, and artists who deviate from power of two or square maps on group projects may encounter resistance.

As you can see in the illustration, the text in each reference map for the three materials is about the same dimensions, indicating that the scale is correct across all parts of the geometry.

Because the largest of the UV groups extended more than 1.0 unit in *U*, it had to be scaled to fit within legal UV space. Because all of the pieces have to match, they must all be scaled together. Left at this scale, each of the three maps would require a map of the same resolution, though two of those maps would use much less of the available pixels than the third (Fig. 11.23).

Fig 11.23
Here, the UVs for all the maps have been scaled, so that the largest of them fills the legal 0–1 texture space

By using the grid squares in your UV editor as a reference, you may determine exactly how much of the UV space is being used relative to the largest of the three. Based on this analysis, if map "3" is 1,024 × 1,024, then "2" will be 717 × 973 and "1" will be 307 × 840. If you had a square power of two size limitation, you could add the maps for 2 and 3 into one 1,024 × 1,024 map. Instead of three maps, then, you'd have two (Fig. 11.24).

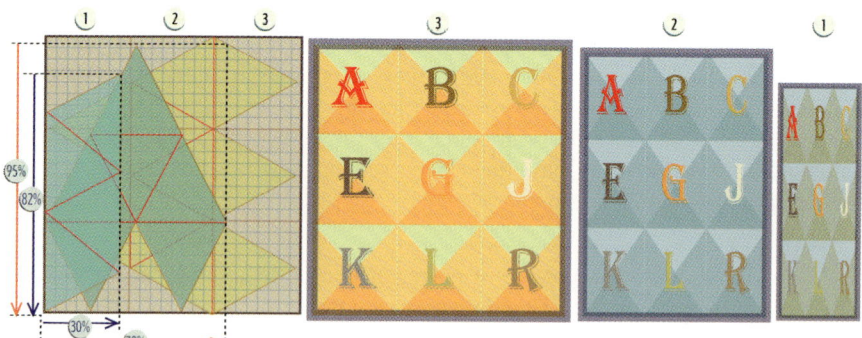

Fig 11.24
Calculating map size

These UVs have now been scaled nonproportionately to fill UV space in both directions. If you look at the polyhedra on the left, you will see the original object, and to its right, the new one. The reference map repeats more times on the new version than the old, indicating that the texture treatment is higher resolution than it was originally (Fig. 11.25).

Fig 11.25
Calculating ideal texmap size, overlapping UVs

The information contained in this chapter is not comprehensive, nor could it be. It should be enough to get you thinking about the kind of objectives you should have in mind when editing texture coordinates, and how to go about making the best decisions you can as an artist to achieve those goals.

Texture-editing tools are improving every year, but these can only improve how the coordinates are manipulated. Because each project is different, they can never be a substitute for an artist who knows what his project needs and can supply it by making appropriate choices during the editing process.

Chapter 12: Nurbs Curves

Using curves to build a model is about as different from polygonal modeling as drawing is from sculpting. Conceptually, the differences between the two modeling techniques are difficult to reconcile until you understand them both. When you do understand them, you will find that both techniques work well together and enhance your abilities as a CG artist (Fig. 12.1).

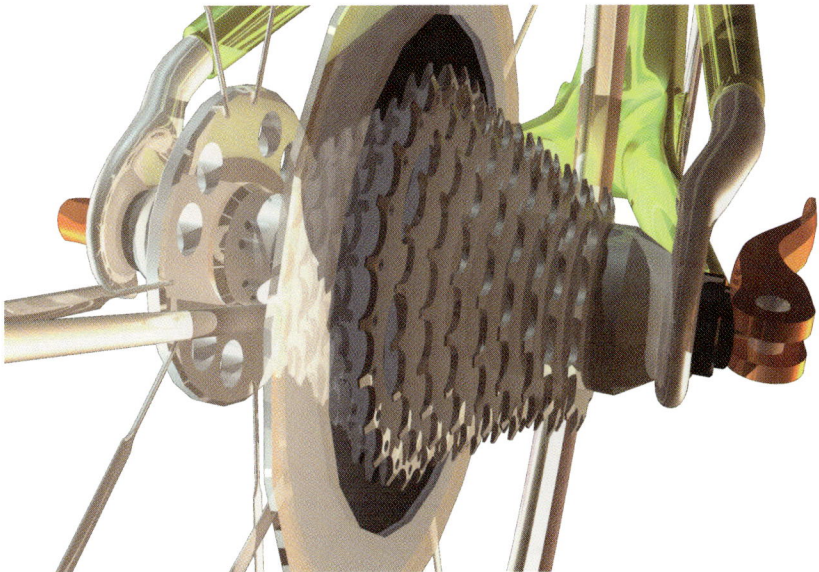

Fig 12.1
Y-foil rear hub and chain rings. All of these parts were built from curves

A polygonal arc that is broken down into ten edges can be fairly smooth in appearance compared to an arc that has only three edges, but a true nurbs curve can be broken into an infinite number of edges, and these edges can be arranged based on either even subdivisions of the curve length, or CV weighting. This simple difference results in a radically different approach to modeling with these geometry types. On an extremely simplified level, polygonal modeling is *additive*, in the sense that a base object has points added to it, then moved, and more points added to it, and so on. With curve-based modeling, it is more *reductive*. This is because, to derive a good likeness of any given object, the artist usually must learn to visualize a shape from which the final object is cut, and then carve it out by successive reduction of the initial object. Another reason for looking at it this way is that curves have an infinite amount of detail that must be reduced into a finite number of polygons.

Nurbs is an acronym for *nonuniform rational Bezier spline*. To understand this best, you may read the acronym backward and start with *spline*. A spline is a tool once used in shipbuilding to design smooth curves for boat hulls. Not all splines are the same, but the idea behind the various types is similar. The two most popular varieties are these:

For boats. A rod with slots cut into it along its length. These rods are the spline. They are inserted into holes in the floor at different distances. Strips of wood are then passed through the slots of successive splines and then fastened to them. Once this is done, the splines may be rotated and their rotation fixed with a ratchet or by other means. This has the effect of modifying the curvature of the wood running through each spline.

For autos. A thin strip of wood with heavy weights connected to it by flexible cords or by other means. The weights could be changed to increase or decrease their effect on the wood. These splines were used in much the same way as the rod and plank splines in ship design, but were meant for tabletop use instead of the massive warehouses used for boat building.

In the illustration below, the *black line* is the curve itself, the *green line* shows the *U* curve direction, *yellow triangles* highlight control points, and knots are located in the same locations as edit points. Knots at the beginning and end of the curve are full-multiplicity knots (Fig. 12.2).

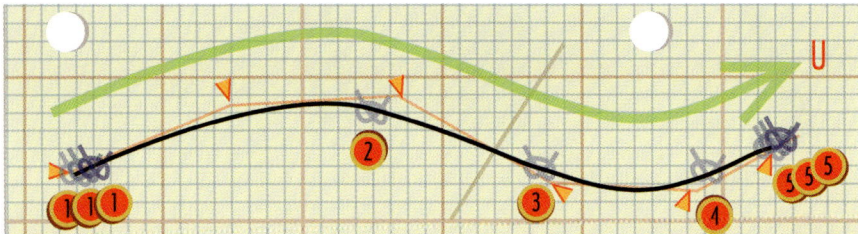

Fig 12.2
Curve components

The word *Bezier* refers to Pierre Bezier, a French automobile designer who published the first paper on nurbs curves, as used in the auto design industry. Bezier did not invent the method, but his name has become linked to this type of curve because of his paper on the subject. The word *rational* refers to the fact that the curve can be rational, depending on *weighted values* at each control point. Most curves are nonrational. They are rational only if the weight of each point is the same. The term *uniform* refers to a curve that is evenly divided based on *knot* position. Knots control curvature at control points. The more knots there are, the tighter the curve becomes at that point until it can form a sharp edge, instead of a smooth *tangent*. In a uniform curve, it starts and ends with *full-multiplicity knots*, with evenly spaced *simple knots* between them. For example, the following group of knot values in a three-degree seven-control point curve is uniform: 0, 0, 0, 2, 4, 6, 8, 8, 8. In the previous example, the knots at values 0 and 8 are full-multiplicity knots. Full-multiplicity knots are hard knots that can have a tangency break. Simple knots have no tangency breaks. A *nonuniform* curve does not have evenly distributed knots, as in a uniform curve. A *nonuniform rational Bezier spline*, then, is a spline of the Bezier variety, with weighted control points, and knots that usually follow a nonuniform curve definition.

Nurbs curves come in a variety of *degrees*. A *one-degree curve* is a perfectly straight line because it has only two control points. To make it into a *two-degree* curve, an additional control point is inserted. This makes the curve more complicated, but also allows it to become a true curve. For greater control, a third control point may be added, for a total of four control points. This would be a *three-degree* curve. Three-degree curves are most commonly used for rough modeling and animation, but lack sufficient accuracy for industrial and vehicle design. For manufacturable objects, five- to seven-degree curves are most commonly used.

A higher-degree curve, or *higher-level* curve, gives its user greater control over its shape, but is primarily used to achieve either *tangency* or *curvature continuity*. Achieving either of these two goals is probably the greatest source of frustration for any modeler with insufficient experience working with curves.

The simple definition of a *tangent* is a line that touches but does not intersect a curve or surface. In CG, it is a little different. In CG, a tangent can intersect the curve it touches, but not at its origin, and only if the curve is not a *conic section*, or circle. Also, in CG, a tangent line begins at the point it first touches a curve, and then extends in the same direction as the curve a certain length. This is unlike a tangent in Geometry that is a line extending indefinitely in both directions at the point of contact. The length of the tangent helps define the strength of the control point that marks its origin.

Curves *A* and *B* are tangent in this illustration. A quick way to see this is that their tangents intersect at a 180° angle (Fig. 12.3).

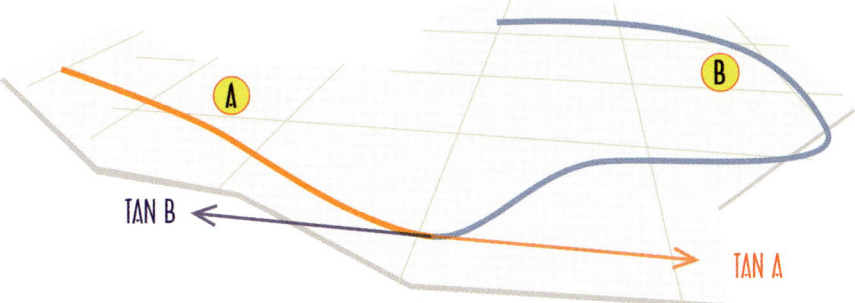

Fig 12.3
Tangent curves

In this illustration, the tangents for curve *A* are almost at a 90° angle to curve *B*'s tangent at the intersection point. For this reason, the two curves cannot be tangent (Fig. 12.4).

Fig 12.4
Nontangent curves

Tangency is when a curve's *out tangent* is equal to another curve's *in tangent* at a common point. If you have a three-degree curve connected to another three-degree curve at a common point, then aligning the last two points on the first curve with the first two points of the second curve will cause the two curves to be tangent, because any pair of control points that starts or ends at an open end of a curve will define the tangent at that location. By aligning them, you ensure that they are the same for both curves.

These three surfaces are *tangent* but not *curvature continuous* because they only have three tangents aligned at each intersection. This is acceptable for rendering, but not for manufacturing (Fig. 12.5).

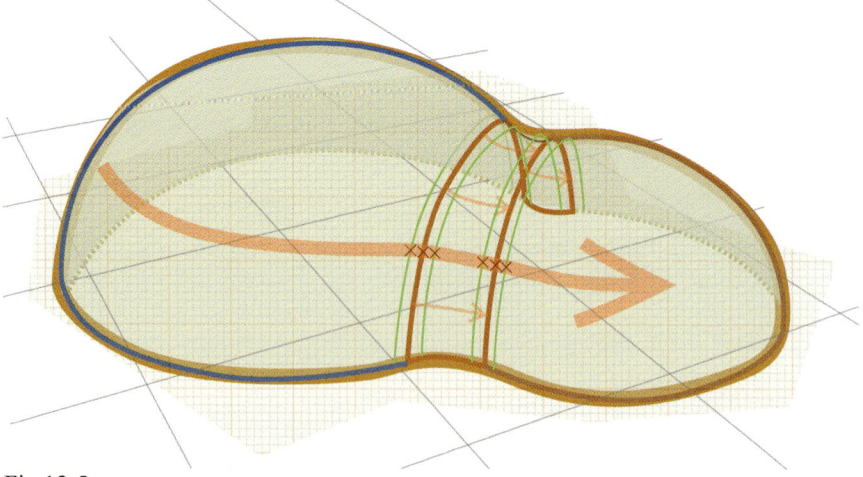

Fig 12.5
Tangent surfaces

These two surfaces have been made curvature continuous by the addition and manipulation of four new isoparms to either side of the intended connection border of each surface (Fig. 12.6).

Fig 12.6
Curvature continuous

Curvature continuity is similar to tangency, but to a greater degree. Instead of tangency being held by one control vertex on either side of the respective endpoints of two curves, there will be a minimum of two control points with matching tangents on either side of the join. This increases the strength of tangency at this location by providing a set of control points that serve to absorb the weight of control vertices that come before or after them and smoothing the tangent flow into the next curve. This results in a five-degree curve. If it had three control points on either side, it would be a seven-degree curve.

Curvature continuity is desirable for manufacturable surfaces or objects that will be rendered at high resolution in close-up. Curvature continuity requires significant additional modeling effort and is not recommended for most projects, particularly in CG animation for games, film, or television advertisements. For most projects, unless a high-resolution final render will be made directly from your nurbs objects, even tangency is not required, if adjacent surfaces are close enough that any mismatched vertices may be merged after converting to polygons.

When modeling with polygons, simply merging vertices and then smoothing the edge between formerly discontinuous faces achieve the equivalent of tangency. To do the same thing with curves can be more difficult, but the reward is a much more attractive surface.

A polygonal model can be made out of one piece, with many insets and extrusions. This is not true of a nurbs object. If you are accustomed to modeling in polygons, you will naturally want to take a nurbs base object and modify it by adding and moving control vertices until you have what you want. This can work with certain simple shapes, but for more complex objects you will find that you very quickly have a model with so many control points that it is unwieldy to work with. This is the central reason polygonal modelers find nurbs objects difficult to use. By treating a nurbs patch as if it was a polyset, it is made too complex. Instead, a modeler who is using nurbs, especially if he is working with curves, must instead think of an object as a collection of surfaces, each of which is individually defined by:

1. Curve boundaries
   a. These are the four boundaries of a patch, either an actual patch boundary or the curves that will be used to make it.
2. Internal control points
   a. These are points along internal surface isoparms and between curves at surface boundaries. They may be moved or reweighted to alter the shape of a curve or surface.
3. Curve direction
   a. The control point designated as the first point in the curve and the next control point define a curve's direction.
   b. A surface's direction is determined in a similar manner, though for both *U* and *V* directions. The start point for *U* and *V* will always be at the same control point.
   c. If the directions of curve or patch pairs do not match, any surfaces, blends, or attempts to join across mismatched curves will result either in failure or a seriously distorted curve or surface.
4. Trims
   a. A *trim* is a section of a surface defined by either a closed *projected curve* or a group of open projected curves that together completely enclose an area. The area within the defined region may be defined as either *cut away* or *remaining*. The renderer will then render either the area outside of the trim curve(s) or within them.
   b. Trim surfaces effectively double the amount of geometry for an object, because the original untrimmed surface is always retained as a reference for the renderer.

How a trimmed surface is made. First, a curve is projected onto the surface, usually using orthographic or two-dimensional projection. Then, the object is defined as two separate parts, based on the new curve within the surface. Next, the two may be separated (Fig. 12.7).

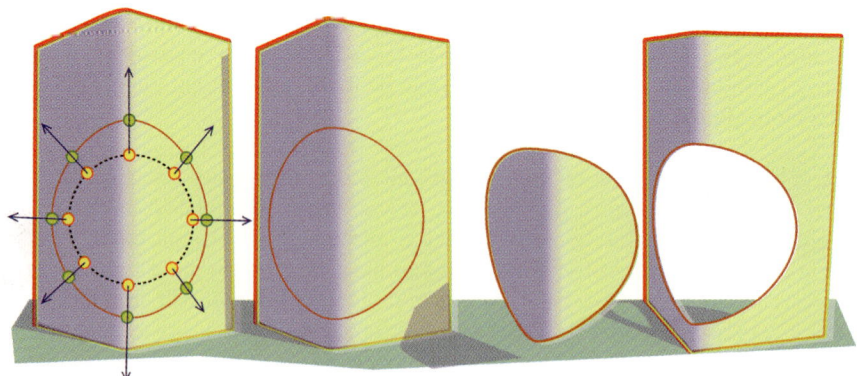

Fig 12.7
Trimmed surface

These four elements are crucial to the proper definition of an object and must be understood by any artist who wishes to work with nurbs.

To make curves tangent, one must align the tangents of two or more curves where their endpoints are coincident. If you do this, any surfaces generated from those curves will be tangent or continuous, depending on the degree of the curves you use. Where this gets difficult is when you have to align more than two curves at a common point. If, instead of a linear connection where one curve flows smoothly into another, your intention is to create four tangent patches arranged in a grid, you have a more difficult problem. The reason is that now, you have eight curves to deal with instead of two.

Depending on the shape of the curves you are using, this can be easy or difficult. If they are all planar, your task is simple. If instead they have been heavily manipulated, the likelihood of matching all eight tangents at the same location is reduced. Not only that, but now you also have to match tangents at the other side of each curve, and every tangent/isoparm in between. If you haven't got the same number of isoparms on either side of a curve, you probably will not be able to achieve curvature continuity, though you may be able to achieve near tangency in most places. Sometimes, tangency is extremely difficult to achieve accurately because of the position of tangents. When this is true, most applications have tools to force tangency.

Here are some simple rules to follow that keep tangency problems to a minimum:

1. If possible, first make all your curves as coplanar objects and adjust tangency before adjusting their shape. When you do modify their shape, take care to move tangency-holding control points together.
2. Align your tangents with the global axes, or use a construction plane for control point alignment.
3. Design your curves so that endpoints that are meant to be tangent do not have sharply divergent tangents.
4. Count the number of control points in your curves, and make sure that all curves used for the same patch have the same number of control points.

Other types of curves:

To make a pair of curves intersect is not difficult. To keep them that way while editing either one of them can be difficult. In this example, if an artist caused the bend in the green curve to intersect with the red curve, but wants to eliminate the bend after the fact, the intersection will almost certainly be lost (Fig. 12.8).

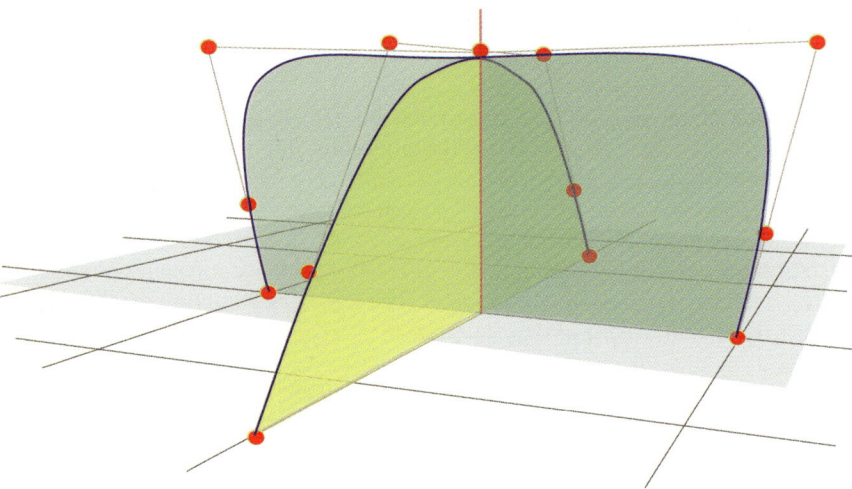

Fig 12.8
Intersecting curves

Here, it is easy to see why it can be difficult to cause some curves to remain intersecting while editing. The control points do not live on the curve they affect, but they affect the area of the intersection. Only if three control points in a row, on both curves, were snapped to the same *Y* value (in this example) *and* they intersected at some point, it would be possible to easily keep them intersecting. This would be possible if, either all six of the control points responsible for the intersection were moved together, or no edits are made to them (Fig. 12.9).

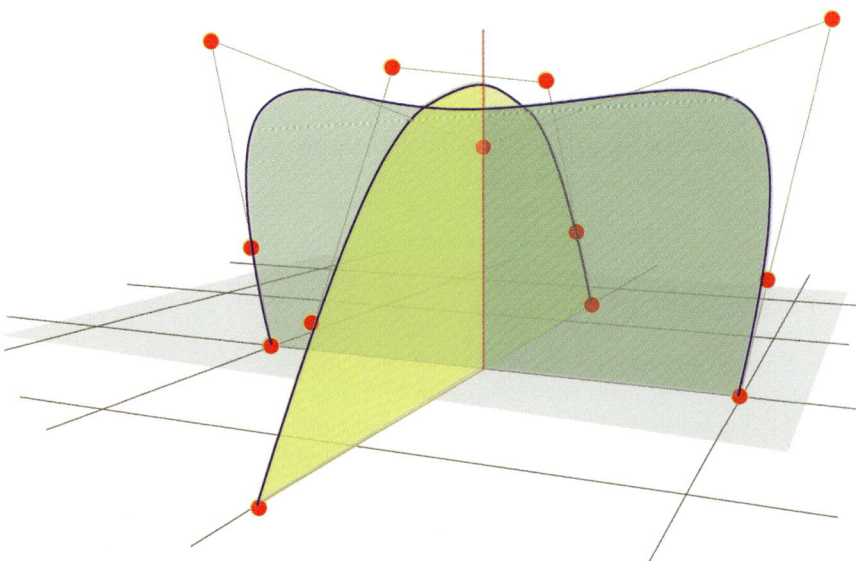

Fig 12.9
Nonintersecting curves

Although all curves in any CAD program are splines of some kind, they are not all defined at the user-interface level by laying down control points with your mouse. Arcs and circles can be defined parametrically and are very useful because it is more difficult to generate curves of this type by hand. A two-dimensional arc can be plotted in a number of ways. These are the most common:

- Radius and center point
- Radius, center point, and arc length
- Two points and center
- Three points on curve
- Tangent to two curves or surfaces
- From point to tangent to a curve or surface.

The red curve in this illustration is built from three separate tangents on three circles. Notice that a curve can be tangent to another curve without touching it (Fig. 12.10).

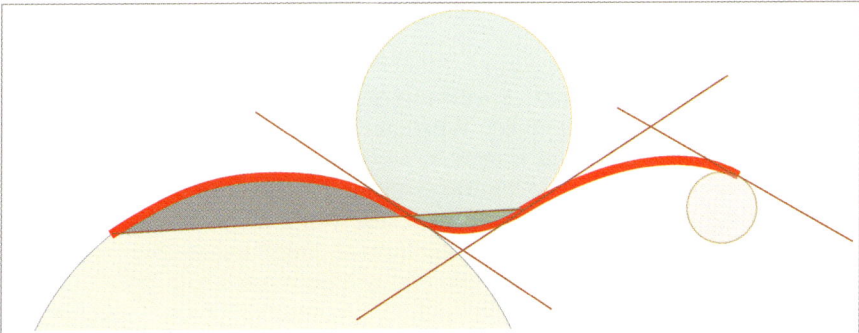

Fig 12.10
Tangents and curves

Tangent curves are curves created based on tangency with other curves. The difference between this type of curve and a tangent arc is that a tangent arc will always have curvature characteristic of a circle, but a simple tangent curve does not have this limitation. A tangent curve can be calculated based on the tangent vector of two curves at any given selection location. The new curve will blend between these tangents in the middle, and flow smoothly into both source curves on either end.

To build a surface from curves, you need only select the appropriate curves and then invoke a surface generation tool. Unlike polygons, which normally require considerable editing before they resemble your target object, if you have built your curves properly, the resulting surface will be either an exact match or very close to one. If it isn't, the most likely reason is that it needs to be cut into shape. Ideally, you will always plan your curves in advance, so that any surface built from them matches exactly the shape you intend to build. Any further editing should require either the addition of new surfaces or the cutting away of existing ones with trim borders.

The idea of planning your modeling process is important to success with nurbs objects. Because they are reductive, it isn't always obvious what the original shape of an object is before it is cut into a different shape. You will have to become sensitive to the steps necessary to build certain objects, so that when you build them in nurbs, you are able to layout the steps properly. This is not much of a problem when designing an object from scratch, but if you are copying an existing product, it can take some time to reverse engineer how it was built.

Curve Topology

One way to ensure that all of your curves have the same properties, or *topology*, is to first build one curve, and then copy it as the base curve for all your other curves. If you do this, all of your curves will have the right number of control points and the same direction. This strategy is very effective for creating clean surfaces from curves.

You will notice as you practice with curves that it is not so difficult to create the boundaries of your target object. What takes more work is to define the interior portion of the surface. This is because nurbs surfaces are very sensitive to the curves used to produce them. If the curves themselves do not contain the tangent information necessary to represent a certain shape, then it will be absent from the final object. For example, if you build an object of three curves, where each curve is offset the same distance from the last, you will get a patch with three isoparms to match your three curves. That will define one direction of the object; in this case, we'll call it U. What defines the V direction? How many isoparms will it have? The answer is that it will have as many isoparms as your curves have control points. These *implied isoparms* become actual isoparms during the surface creation process, and their direction from the first point in U will define their direction in V as well. The tangents created by these V control points determine the shape of your object's interior portions. If you only have three control points in V, then the center row of control points has an equal effect on the first and last tangent of each isoparm. This cannot result in a full-bodied curve, if that is your intention. In this example, you would have to add at least one new isoparm, and then adjust its position to create the curve you desire.

Surfaces Are Very Sensitive to Tangent Direction and Length

One of the first things you will notice after you build a surface from curves is that small changes to the curves it is built from have a powerful effect on the surface. If your software allows you to display tangents, turn them on and you will see why. If a tangent is quite long, and then is paired with a short tangent or one moving in the opposite direction, the surface must be reconciled between the two.

To accomplish this, it is often forced to create an absurdly long or twisted curve connection. The result is a surface with obvious distortion. The types of distortion you are likely to see are:

1. *Twisting.* This is the equivalent of a bow-tie face in polygons, where a pair of misaligned tangents causes the bow-tie effect.
2. *Rippling.* This is caused by a full or partial row of control points that have been moved together from a position between two rows of control vertices. This happens when an artist doesn't realize that the selected vertices are close enough to others that moving them will require severe distortion in a small area to maintain the shape of the surface after the move.
3. *Shredded.* Excessively long tangents near the last row of control points before reaching a surface boundary cause this. In an effort to reconcile the surface out tangents and these long tangents, the surface's maximum display subdivision limit is exceeded beyond your application's ability to represent the geometry. When this happens, your patch will appear to be shredded, or torn, around these long tangents. It is not actually torn, as you will discover if you change the subdivision level to a higher number.
4. *Empty.* It is possible to create a surface with such serious tangent problems that it will not display at all. It is more common to make a legal surface and then modify it into this state. Either way, the effect is caused for reasons similar to a shredded patch. In this case however, the tangents are so bad that none of it can be displayed. If you ever invoke a create patch command and don't seem to get a result, check your scene node diagram to see if an object was created. Sometimes, you will find that this is the case. If so, you should delete the error geometry.
5. *Cracked.* This only happens between two adjacent surfaces. There are more than one reason for this error:
   (a) The surfaces have a different number of control points along the common edge.
   (b) The subdivision level for either patch is different.
   (c) Although the surfaces may be partly tangent, they are not tangent at the crack, causing the surfaces to move away from each other at this point.

Periodic Curves

A periodic curve is a curve without beginning or end. This isn't literally true, but conceptually, that is what it is. To define a periodic curve, the endpoints must cross with at least two overlapping CVs on either side of the join, for a total of five CVs. These must all have the same tangent. If these conditions are satisfied, *and* the curve is identified to your software as "periodic," then it will be periodic. The reason it has to be identified as periodic is that otherwise the endpoints will be free to move away from each other. As a periodic curve, they cannot be pulled apart. Most programs have only two ways to make a curve periodic; either make it that way to begin with, as a circle, for instance, or invoke a close command that will make it periodic. Some close commands will only make it tangent, making it worth your while to check your tool options to give you an idea what to expect.

Surface Modification with Curves

Adjusting a curve will modify the surface built from it, and the results may be wild. This usually happens because of the effect of undisplayed tangents. Compared to the effect of moving a vertex, moving a control vertex can have a severe effect on the surface it is connected to. A face that is adjusted by moving a vertex will only change exactly as far as the vertex is moved. A control vertex has a more powerful effect because it is not just the CV position that is adjusted, but also a tangent that in most applications isn't even displayed.

It takes some practice to get accustomed to adjusting CVs, but the practice is worth it. Not only will you be able to control more complex surfaces that render more smoothly than any polygonal surface, but you will become sensitive to *surface tension* as well.

Surface Tension

Surface tension is just another way of saying that a surface tightly adheres to the shape of the surface it is meant to represent. When a surface has the right surface tension, it sags where it is supposed to, and doesn't sag where it shouldn't. Surface tension is something that is difficult to describe accurately with polygons because polygons are by nature rigid and do not have any surface tension from face to face. It can be imitated, but can be more time consuming than with nurbs. In nurbs, not only is it easier to represent, but also using nurbs will sensitize any artist to surface tension. This will improve the artist's observation skills and his ability to make a good likeness of a target object, even when working in polygons.

Surface tension is important if your objects are meant to be convincing. If the surface tension is duplicated correctly, the object will have more life to it than one where this is not true. Poor surface tension will make a sail on a sailboat look like it is made of rock instead of fabric, or the skin of a character look like metal instead of a pliable organic substance. It might make metal look dented where it should be smooth, or the elegant arc of a television screen look like the bulge of a partly inflated soap bubble. Surface tension can be described simply as an accurate representation of a surface, but it is more than that, because it is not accomplished by positioning an infinite series of points exactly where they belong, but by positioning just enough points that their tangents accurately describe the rest of the surface.

A Note on Curves on Surface and Trims

A curve on surface is a curve that has been projected onto a surface. The easiest way to visualize this is to imagine the curve extruded straight through the surface it is projected onto. The points of intersection are used as the basis for a new curve, and their tangents adjusted to ensure that they lie perfectly within the target surface. By itself, a curve on surface doesn't accomplish a great deal, but when combined with curve duplication, a curve on surface can be used to create a shape that would have been very difficult to make without the aid of a reference surface. Combined with a trimming tool, unwanted sections of a nurbs surface may be cut away into almost any shape you like.

The real disadvantage to using these tools is that if you want to render them as nurbs objects, they do increase the complexity of your geometry significantly. If you are using the nurbs objects as the basis for a polygonal finished model, trim rendering concerns will be irrelevant to you.

For industrial design and manufacturing, you may not have any choice. In those specialties, the output is almost always pure nurbs objects. For these objects, there is no practical way to completely avoid using trims, regardless of the impact on rendering speed. It is not possible to create certain types of shapes with a nurbs surface unless it is cut to match the shape of a projected curve. This is a limitation, but not so great that it makes a good argument not to use this geometry class.

Power of Curves

Curves allow you to "draw" in 3D, to create a simplified yet totally accurate 3D image of your object, and then build it into a renderable or manufacturable object based on those same curves. Curves allow the construction of extremely complex shapes with resolution-independent accuracy. The degree of precision and flexibility afforded by nurbs curves is not equaled in polygonal modeling tools (Fig. 12.11).

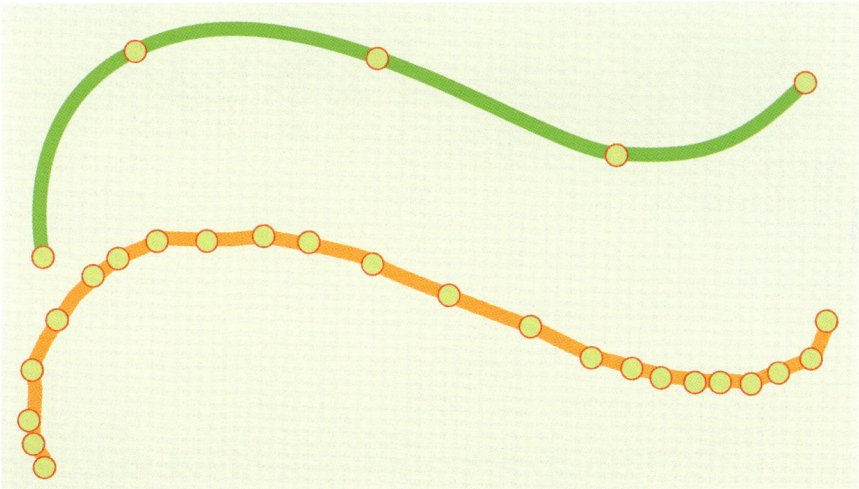

Fig 12.11
Unlike polygons, with curves, less is almost always smoother

Curve Limitations

Working with curves is always a two-step process. First, you have to make the curve. Next, you build the surface. In polygons, you just move the polygons or their vertices. This is one of the reasons why simple objects made from linear segments are most often built in polygons. The more complex an object's curve definition is, the more justified nurbs become.

Nurbs must satisfy certain conditions that are irrelevant to polygonal modeling. Their direction must be correct or surfaces built from them may be twisted, their knot definitions must be correct, or they may have unwanted kinks (or not enough). It is not enough for the endpoints of two curves to be coincident, they must be tangent as well or there will be a visible tangent break in the render.

In this illustration, the ends of the middle cylinder are no more tangent than the one on the left despite being coincident. Furthermore, because they are not tangent, a cusp is made, causing an unwanted shadow on the surface of the object. The smooth transition across endpoints in the rightmost cylinder is only possible with true tangency along the entire length of the seam (Fig. 12.12)

Fig 12.12
Nontangent and tangent surface

Chapter 13: Nurbs Surfaces

Nurbs surfaces are geometric primitives that are the equivalent of an infinitely flexible thin square sheet of rubber. One of the trickiest issues to deal with for these objects is that they must have four sides, as in a square, but that they can be manipulated into the shape of a sphere, perfect circle, or almost anything else. An easy way to visualize this is to literally draw four-sided boundary edges (in two colors for horizontal or vertical sides) directly onto various objects, with a simple grid in between. Any area you can describe in this manner can be built as a nurbs surface (Fig. 13.1).

Fig 13.1
Nurbs jeep (courtesy Andrius Drevinskas)

When you model with polygons, you are working with the thing itself, the final product. There is no *representation* of your geometry on the screen that differs from what your final product will be. It is the final product. Although curves are mathematically accurate, and no polyset can compete with them for accuracy, when a nurbs object is converted to polygons for rendering, it may not look as you expect it to. The reason is that when a nurbs object is drawn to screen, the number of renderable polygons it converts to at rendering time is not displayed. This makes it difficult to judge what it will look like at render time. Instead, the totally accurate nurbs surface is drawn. This usually makes your object appear to be completely seamless, even if seams may appear after triangulation. This difference is limited to renderings.

For manufacturing purposes, computer-aided machining (CAM) software will understand a nurbs description of a surface and build it flawlessly. It will not convert the surface to triangles because it understands curves and doesn't need to create any intermediate geometry. For manufacturing, this makes a nurbs object much more accurate than a polygonal object, because it has an infinite number of sampling points embedded in the mathematical description of each surface. It is this accuracy that makes nurbs essential for industrial design, and highly desirable in certain animation applications.

A nurbs surface is a *parameter-based object*, meaning that it may be edited by modifying parameters. A *parameter* is a variable that can be modified to change the shape, position, orientation, or surface type of your object. A nurbs object contains the following primary editable variables:

1. Edit point position
2. Control vertex position
3. Control vertex weight
4. Tangent length
5. Tangent direction
6. Number of isoparms
7. Position of isoparms
8. Curve direction
9. Surface direction/orientation
10. Subdivision level in U
11. Subdivision level in V

Nurbs objects also contain noneditable values that artists familiar with polygon editing might be surprised by. The principal noneditable values are:

1. Texture coordinates
2. Normals (they can be reversed, but that is all)

Texture coordinates and normals (apart from reversal) are not editable because these properties are embedded in the surface itself. Because a nurbs surface, or *patch*, is always made between four connected edges, the edges may be mapped to the four sides of UV space where U is the horizontal direction and V is the vertical. This allows a patch to have texture coordinates always mapped to it without regard for the actual shape of the object (Fig. 13.2).

Fig 13.2
The difference between polys and nurbs; rubber and glass

Embedded texture coordinates in a nurbs surface are just one example of their flexibility. *Flexibility*, in the context of nurbs primitives, is one of the primary justifications for using nurbs objects. A nurbs surface is not a simple collection of individual vertex coordinates that can exist independently of each other, as in a polyset. Because every component of a nurbs surface contains surface information that is shared by or related to the surface information of neighboring components, changing the position or other values of any part of a surface will automatically affect others. This does not happen with a polyset without attaching special controls. As a result, a polyset is like brittle glass, causing it to crack into very sharp edges when its components are adjusted, but a nurbs surface is like flexible nylon, and may be stretched a great deal without ever tearing.

Examples of Plane to Torus Transformation

To give you an idea how this works, the following illustrations describe, step by step, how a simple nurbs plane can be made into a torus-like shape. In this example, the plane will not literally become a real torus, because its ends will be *open*, or *coincident*. To make it into a true torus, the surface would have to be *periodic*. A periodic curve is a closed curve. A periodic surface is a closed surface. A curve can have only one direction, from the start point to the endpoint of the curve. A surface has two directions, labeled U and V. These two axes are perpendicular to each other in a square patch, and remain nearly perpendicular in most patches with moderate distortion. To make the patch periodic, it must be closed in both U and V, so that there is no endpoint separate from a start point (Fig. 13.3).

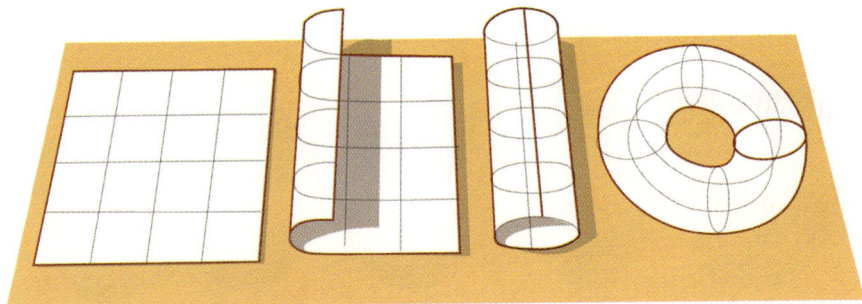

Fig 13.3
A plane is rolled first in *U* and becomes a cylinder. Then it is rolled in *V* and becomes a torus

Nurbs Modeling with Primitives

Modeling with nurbs primitives can be done for simple or complex objects, but work best for shapes that have no significant insets or extrusions. A model of a car exterior, for instance, can be made easily with a single nurbs patch, as long as you leave out things like door handles, antenna, windshield wipers, and headlights. If you want to show the other objects, you are better off using custom-drawn curves to define them. If, on the other hand, you are looking for a simple representation of a car, or are merely roughing out the shape of a more finished model to be made later, then working with primitives can be a sensible method to achieve your goals.

When modeling with nurbs primitives, it is always best to keep the number of control vertices and edit points to an absolute minimum at all times. This means that you should not add isoparms (which also cause CVs and EPs to be created) until you have done all you can with existing elements of your model. Usually, this means that an artist will start by moving CVs to match a border of the target object. The next step is usually to add a centerline, adjust its shape, then another, adjust it, and so on (Fig. 13.4).

Fig 13.4
When you have as many isoparms as are present in this model of a dog, each additional isoparm becomes very costly because it adds control points to every other isoparm it crosses. It's like compound interest, but worse. With each new isoparm, you have that many more isoparms for the next one to intersect

The technique becomes limited with extremely complex objects because, as detail is added, the number of isoparms increases. Each new isoparm creates a new row of CVs all the way around an object, drastically increasing its complexity. There are a few ways to know if you have gone too far:

1. *Isoparm count*. If you have more than ten isoparms in U and V, your model is starting to get heavy. Some models have, and need, hundreds of isoparms in both directions, but this is rare. More often, if you have ten divisions along both edges of your patch, you are at your limit. At this point, you would normally use another patch to model additional detail.
2. *Branching topology*. If you have started making branching shapes with your patch, you have probably gone too far. Four-sided patches do not branch, or extrude, very well. If your target branches, then you are normally better off using multiple patches to represent the branch than trying to build it out of a single patch (Fig. 13.5).

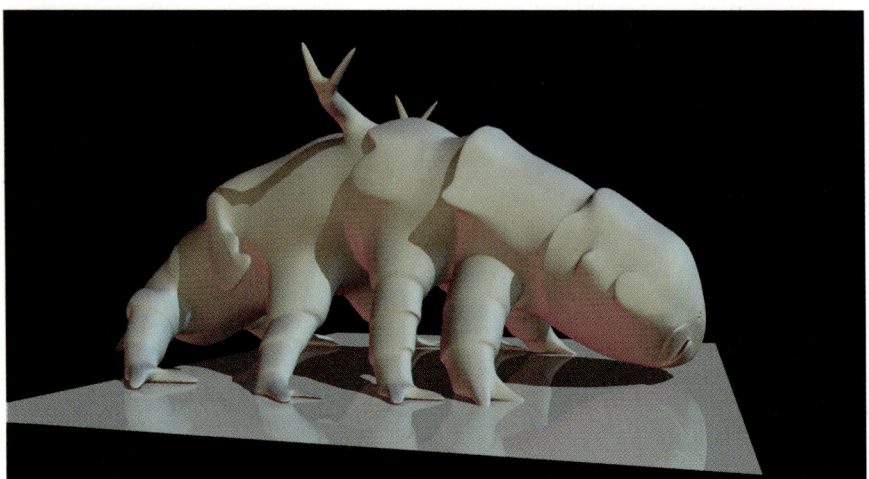

Fig 13.5
This creature begs for multiple patches because of the large number of branching shapes

3. *Overlapping geometry*. If your geometry significantly overlaps itself, especially if it is in several separate locations, as opposed to a single overlap of the entire object, you probably have too much detail in this part of your model. There are times when this is acceptable, but like a high isoparm count, it is rare.

Apart from watching your isoparm count, modeling a nurbs patch is quite simple. It involves selecting nurbs components and transforming them. It is literally as simple as that. This technique becomes less practical when tangent or curvature continuity is desired across surface pairs. If this is required for your model, you are usually better off starting with curves, rather than primitives.

To give you a better idea what this looks like, here is what it looks like to take a simple plane and turn it into a more complex object (Fig. 13.6).

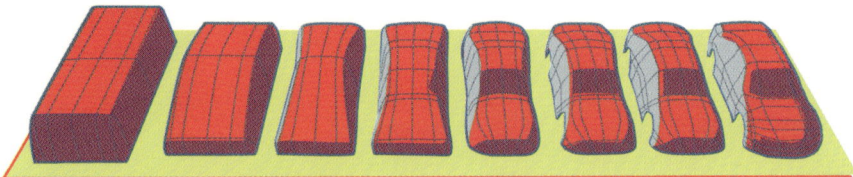

Fig 13.6
Draping a plane to make a car

Taking a plane and transforming it into a simple auto can be done very quickly. This technique is not suitable for a detailed treatment of an object, but can be extremely effective for roughing out a design in 3D. Most objects can be represented simply this way in under an hour. Some modelers will then convert their nurbs object into a polyset and add detail. The value nurbs adds, as a layout tool, is superior curve information.

As you can see from the above examples, a very smooth nurbs object can be represented with only a few curves. This is one of the advantages of working with nurbs. To build a polygonal model with the same level of curve detail would require thousands more edge loops, the poly equivalent of curves, than are evident here. This simplification of your model is not an insignificant advantage. It allows you to work more quickly, and you will be less prone to mistakes. You will not, for instance, have to sort through a confusing mess of thousands of edges to find the one you need to work on. Instead, because of the extremely small number of isoparms, you will more easily find the elements you need to work with, and all of your transform edits will be accomplished more quickly.

Because a nurbs object can be displayed at a high smoothing value, while manipulating the equivalent of low-resolution geometry (the curves), you will be able to see a perfectly smooth version of your model. This is also not to be underestimated. In polygons, if you want to see your object as a smooth mesh, it must be smoothed. The smoothing process reduces the volume of your object uniformly, unlike a nurbs object, where its volume is maintained better by the nonuniform triangulation pattern used for rendering.

In this image, a polygonal object sits beside the nurbs object it was built from. Which would you rather look at while editing the model? Their shapes are identical, apart from the loss of detail in the polygonal version that comes with its lower level of surface definition (Fig. 13.7).

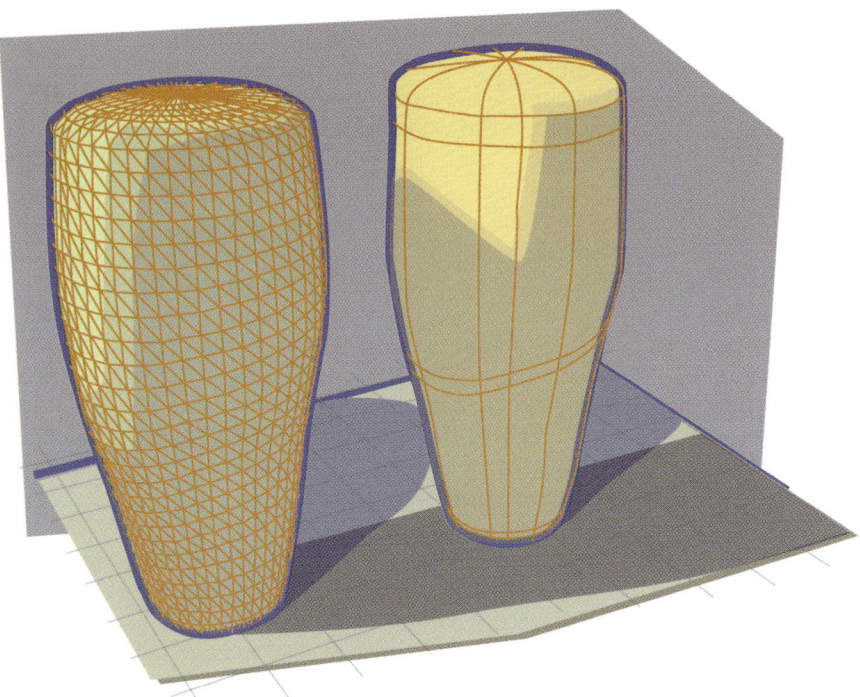

Fig 13.7
Nurbs display vs. poly display

Nurbs objects allow you to preview your object at high and low resolution at the same time. They also reduce your memory needs, thus improving system performance, because drawing nurbs surfaces to your screen is less memory intensive than drawing an equivalent level of smoothness with polygons.

The following object types make good subjects for nurbs modeling, either as a finished object or an intermediate starting point for a polygonal finish object:

1. *Characters*. Characters are built out of the same homotopic parts. This allows one generic nurbs model to be a starting point for any character, and then through manipulation become that character. Characters are most often defined by skin stretched over hundreds of muscles in discrete limb segments.

This type of topology is easily represented and manipulated with nurbs, and can quickly be made into a desired shape for this type of object. Because of branching problems, nurbs are recommended as an intermediate stage of the character building process, rather than the final product.

2. *Vehicles.* Many vehicle types, particularly automobiles, are designed with nurbs to begin with. This means that a nurbs modeling solution will more likely match the overall shape of a target of this type more quickly than polygonal techniques. Simple models of these subjects may be generated very quickly with nurbs primitives.

3. *Industrial design.* Most modern examples of industrial design are built from curve-based models, like vehicles.

4. *Objects that will be seen close-up in prerendered graphics.* Because nurbs have a very large number of normals compared to polysets, renders made from them have much smoother lighting than polygons.

5. *Simple organic objects.* For reasons similar to those for building characters with nurbs start primitives, other organic objects are likewise quite easy to build with nurbs primitives.

Problem Object Types

Objects with an odd number of branches, as in this five-sided starfish, require special treatment to comply with the four-sided rule of nurbs modeling. It can be done so smoothly that you'd never know how difficult it was to do, but it may not be easy. Solutions range from making one point of each of a group of square patches coincident, and then stretching them into parallelograms instead of rectangles, to allow as many branches as are required. The primary difficulty with this solution is maintaining tangency or continuity across surfaces (Fig. 13.8).

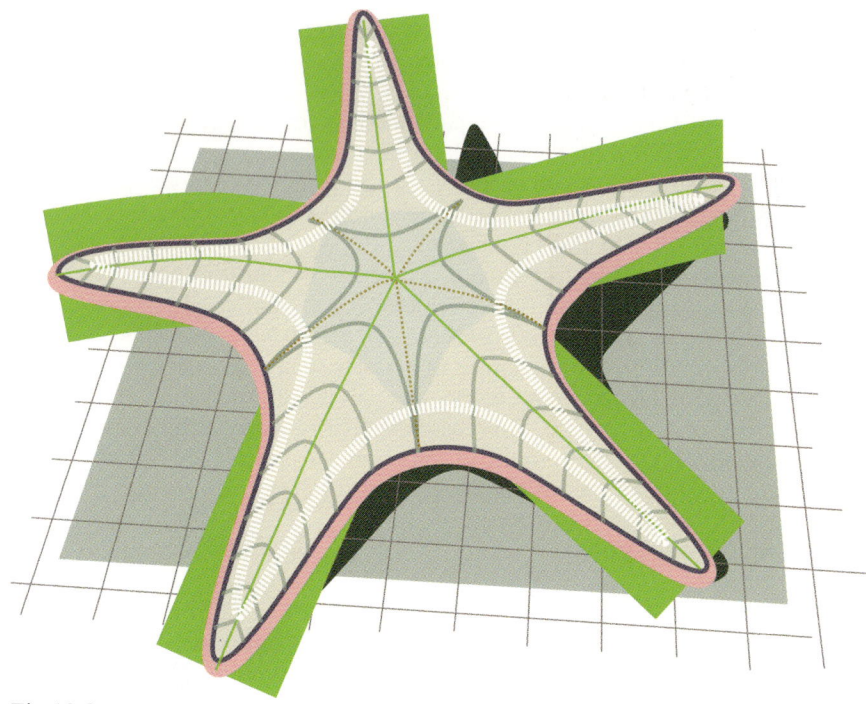

Fig 13.8
Five-sided object

Here is the worst-case scenario of what you may have to work with from time
to time when using nurbs: "triangles" and odd-numbered parallelogram edge intersections. The patch on the left is not a true triangle, as you might have figured out
by looking at its isoparm layout. Instead, one edge of the patch has been collapsed
to zero in length. As a consequence, all of the isoparms along that edge have also
been compressed to the same coordinate. This object will be very difficult to paint
(Fig. 13.9).

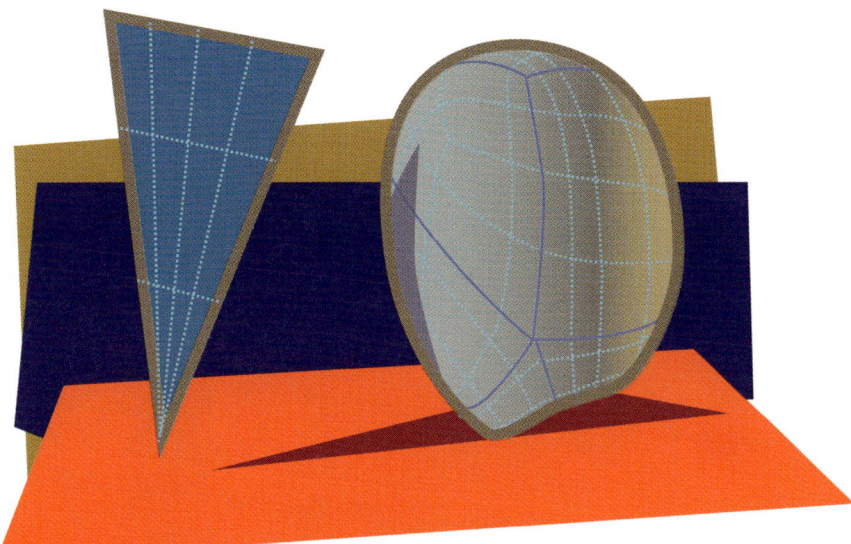

Fig 13.9
Triangle and odd-numbered edge-star intersections

The other object, on the right, suffers from some very difficult surface tangency. In this example, each patch is tangent with its neighbors, but at the cost of a very high number of control points. Because of the high number of control points, the object itself will be very difficult to edit any further.

These objects are better to work with than the last pair but do have their difficulties. The patch on the left has non right-angle corners, thus making it harder to paint, though in other respects it is fine. The second object has that problem and it is a trim surface. As a trim surface, it has double the visible geometry, and depending on your application, may require special treatment to render (Fig. 13.10).

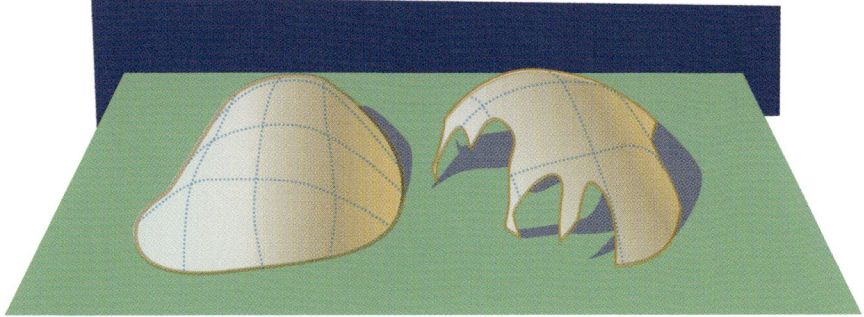

Fig 13.10
A trim and the object it derives from

These two surfaces, apart from both being trims, are very easy to work with. Their edges are right angles, the one on the left is planar, and neither is distorted (Fig. 13.11).

Fig 13.11
Right angle planes

These objects are the best nurbs type to work with. There are no trims, a perfectly square texture layout, and 90° corners are formed at the end of every edge. Believe it or not, many objects are just a large number of parts just like these. To properly take advantage of the power of nurbs however, you will make much more complicated shapes (Fig. 13.12).

Fig 13.12
Revolve and planes

Making Nurbs Surfaces from Curves

Greater care is required to build a surface from a curve than to work from a predefined primitive. The reward is that you will have much greater control of the shape of your surface. This is the preferred method for building in nurbs for industrial design subjects where fidelity is a major concern. In this case, *industrial design subjects* can be taken to mean these subjects, whether or not they are made by an industrial designer and whether or not they are made in CG for the purpose of CAD design or manufacturing. Industrial subjects, like automobiles, airplanes, boats, vacuum cleaners, and bicycles, are generally more easily built with nurbs than polys. The primary reason is that every part of these objects, even examples that date to before the invention of CAD technology, can be accurately described in drawing form with lines that are the equivalent of curves. Therefore, even if the output geometry is meant to be polygonal, most artists will still use curves to define the shape of the object (Fig. 13.13).

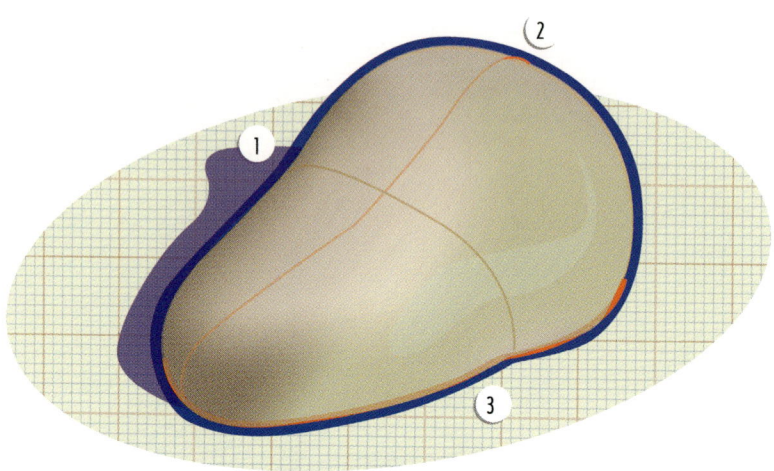

Fig 13.13
An example of a simple three curve nurbs surface and two interior isoparms

The trick to working with curves is to remember that the curves you built must describe your target object completely. Every change of curve direction, every tangent created by a stacked group of curves, and every bit of data you create in your curves must belong to your object and be accurate. The good news is that working with curves does not require you to use a high level of detail. Instead, you usually only need to ensure that a few parameters are correct and you may generate your surface.

The two orange curves that are the basis for this surface are both pointing in the same direction. The result is a clean surface (Fig. 13.14).

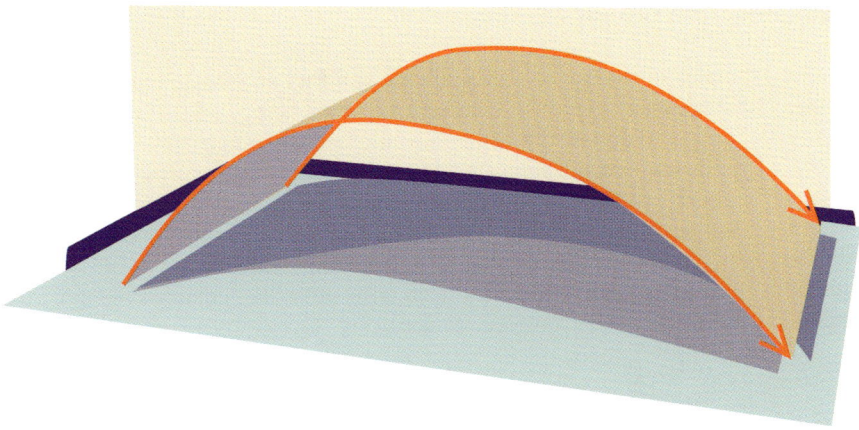

Fig 13.14
Matched curve direction

The two orange curves here are not pointing in the same direction, causing the start and endpoint connections to be reversed and a faulty surface created. This is conceptually exactly the same as a polygonal bow-tie face, but with much greater complexity (Fig. 13.15).

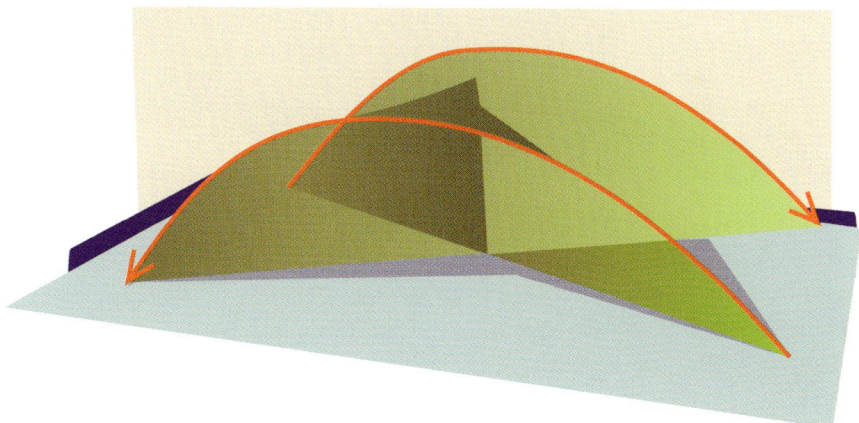

Fig 13.15
Crossed curve direction

The two most common industrial subjects an artist will encounter are simple extruded or revolved shapes like a tube or a torus, and vacuum-formed or injection-molded objects like the hood of a coffee maker or the base of an engine block. The first type of object is quite easily made, with very little investment of time required.

Building from Curves

Good examples of the use of curves are the majority of parts found in a typical bicycle. The shapes are simple for a variety of reasons, one of which is that the easier they are for you to define, the easier they are to manufacture. This is one of the reasons why industrial design subjects with extremely complex surface definitions can often be more expensive to buy at the retail level than their simpler counterparts. A typical seat tube for a bicycle seat is usually just a tube of common dimensions for just this reason. Most CG applications will allow you to build it without even making a curve. All you need do is enter the length of the tube, its inner radius, its outer radius, and you are done (Fig. 13.16).

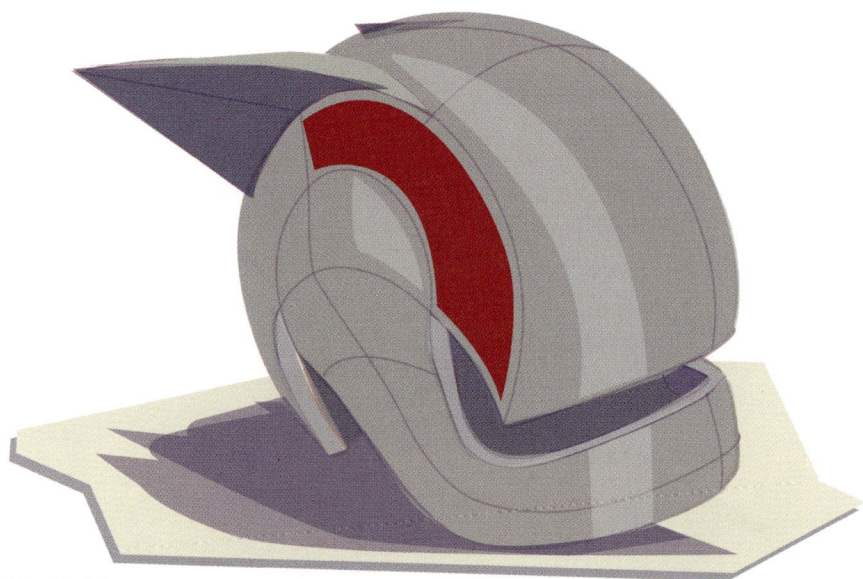

Fig 13.16
This battle robot head was built from curves. Designing them to be curvature continuous was no easy task, despite the small number of parts

For these types of objects, your ability to make a convincing CG model will not require anything more than accurate measurements of your target. Fancy modeling techniques are not required. If it is measured properly, and you put the parts where they belong, it will be a credible model.

If the part in question cannot be described entirely with parameters entered into a basic primitive formula, you will have to make some kind of a curve, even if the finished object remains quite simple.

A skewer lever can take some ingenuity to build, even if it is made of only a few curves. In Fig. 13.17a, all curves for this object have been built. In Fig. 13.17b, the sides are lofted. Figure 13.17c shows how the end of the lever is cut into the right shape by using a projected curve and trim, and then a top surface, also a trim, is created. In Fig. 13.17d, a hole is passed through the lever by first trimming the top surface, then by creating a cylindrical loft through to the other side.

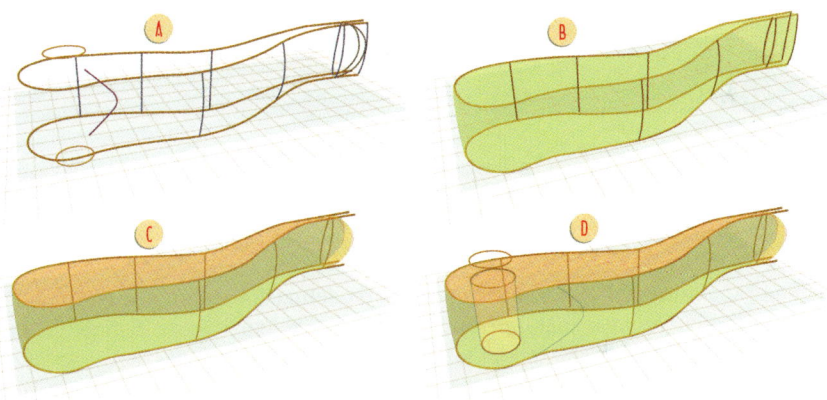

Fig 13.17
Surface construction order

Custom parts can be more challenging. These are parts that are made of things like compressed powdered metal or fluid casting techniques. The parts in the illustration below are an excellent example of this type of object. Building something like them correctly not only requires the use of curves, but also requires some skill (Fig. 13.18).

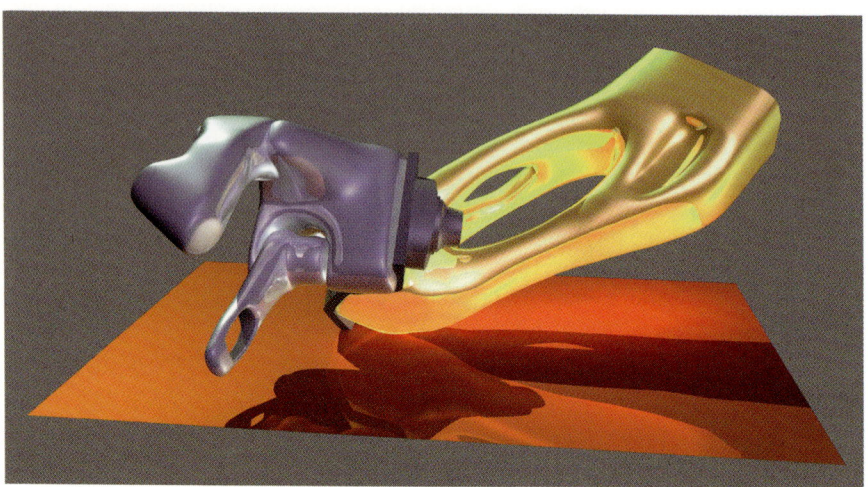

Fig 13.18
Custom bicycle parts; a real challenge to the modeler's skill

Nurbs and Grouping

One of the most difficult aspects of nurbs modeling for an artist accustomed to working with polygons is that nurbs modeling often requires more distinct geometry parts than a polygonal model of the same subject. This is because nurbs patches are the equivalent of a polyset, but they rarely represent as much information as a typical polygonal polyset. This differs depending on the type of target in question. A character, for instance, can be very efficiently modeled in nurbs. It would probably have a separate patch for each limb, the head, ears, and the torso, plus fingers, for a total of 18 parts. A polygonal model of the same thing would probably be one polyset. If the subject is architectural, a nurbs model could easily have six patches for every cube-shaped object, but a polygonal model might be broken down into different polysets only where certain parts need to be animated separately from the main polyset, like for windows and doors. In such a case, the nurbs scene will have a much more complicated grouping of parts compared to a polygonal model. This is another reason why nurbs objects are sometimes converted into polysets after they have been molded into the right shape. Despite the large number of parts however, nurbs make up for this drawback with increased fidelity to target, ease of use while modeling, more efficient curve detail, improved quality at render time, and simplified on-screen display (Fig. 13.19).

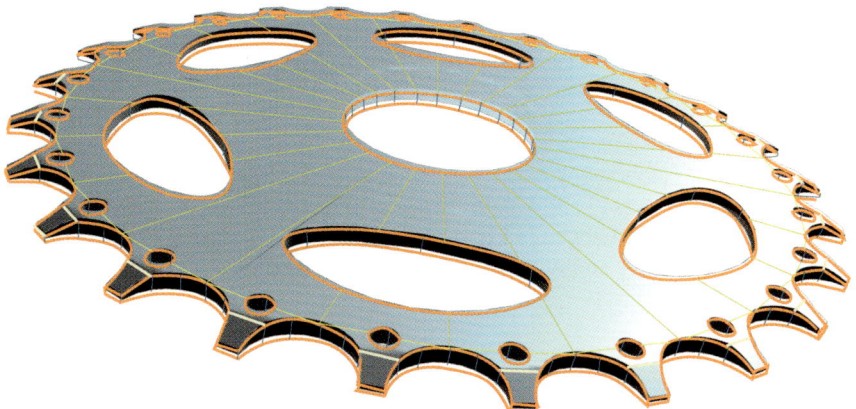

Fig 13.19
This nurbs model of a chain ring is made of 35 separate patches. They cannot be combined into a single object, like a polyset, so they must be grouped instead

Here is an example of efficient curve detail, courtesy of a nurbs to polys conversion. Here, the gear teeth have only six edges per 180° arc, but they are completely convincing (Fig. 13.20).

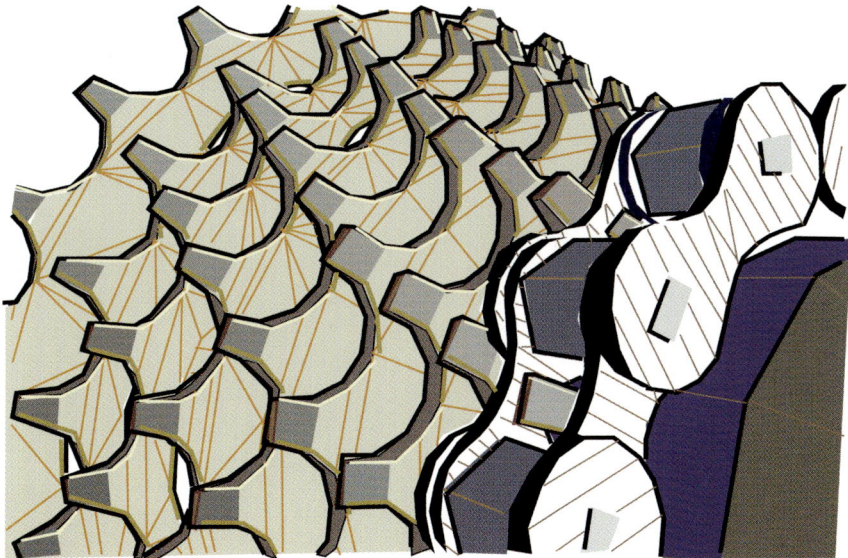

Fig 13.20
Curve detail

Nurbs Normals

It may not look like much, but this illustration demonstrates one of the reasons why nurbs objects render so well compared to polygons. It is because they have more normals, an infinite number in fact. The only limit to the number of normals used for lighting calculations is the surface subdivision level, a parameter set by the artist. This can be set so low that the nurbs object has a very small number of used normals, but this happens only rarely. Practically speaking, a nurbs object will always render more smoothly than a polygonal one (Fig. 13.21).

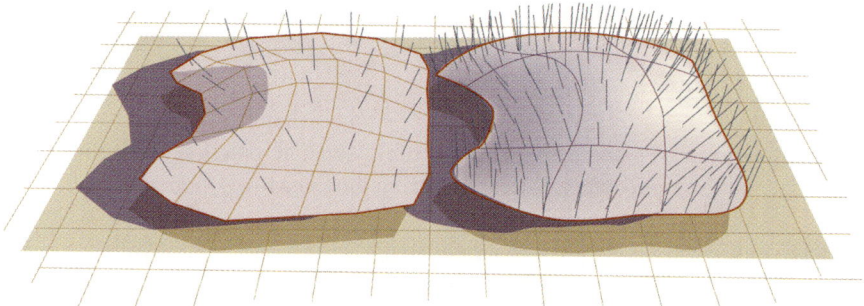

Fig 13.21
A polyset on the *left*, a nurbs object on the *right*, both with displayed normals

Poly Conversion

Converting a nurbs object into polygons can be accomplished with the push of a button. It is helpful, however, to know a little about how it is done, to get the most out of the conversion operation (Fig. 13.22).

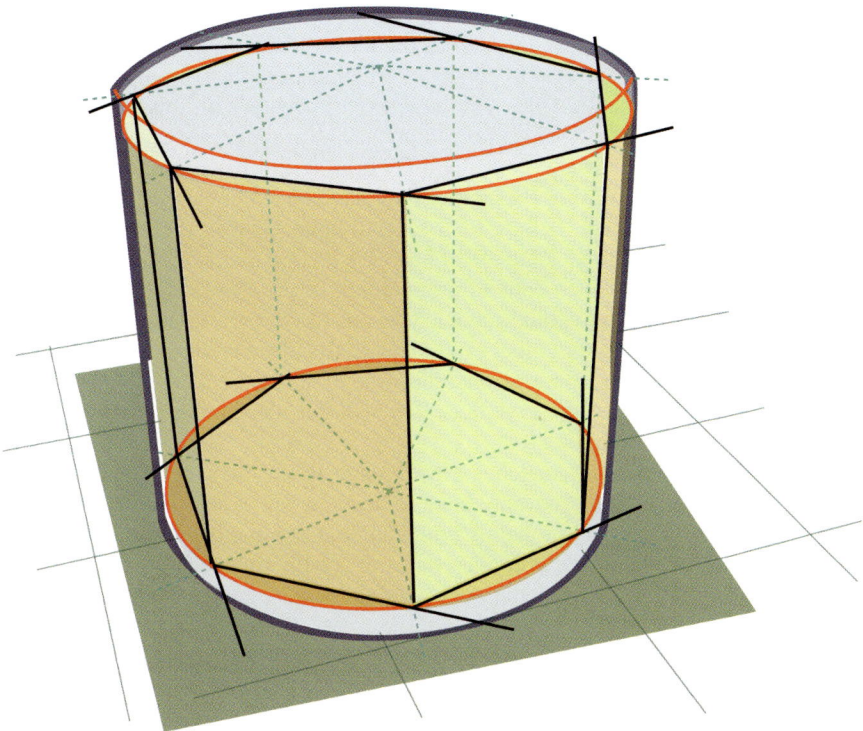

Fig 13.22
When a nurbs object is converted to polygons, it will always lose volume, for the simple reason that nurbs surfaces contain an infinite degree of surface information and polygons do not

If you intend to make a polygonal object out of your nurbs model, you should keep the following in mind:

1. Subdivision type; nonuniform nurbs objects will usually place vertices based on your objects' curve weighting. The result may not be what you expect. It is possible that the product will have a high number of small polygons in a dense cluster near CVs with a high weight value relative to their neighbors. To eliminate this, you can ask your program to divide your surface based on its isoparms. If you do, you will see that a great deal of your curve detail is cut away. This is because the curves occur between isoparms. To retain this curvature, you will have to subdivide the surface between isoparms one or more times, or add isoparms between them, to catch this curvature.
2. A nurbs object can be subdivided uniformly, but if you do, know that the polycount of your polyset will be very high and you may cut out curve detail that you would rather retain.

3. Keep an eye on areas of greatest curvature. These are the parts of your model that benefit the most from the nurbs primitive geometry type, but also the areas that tend to generate the largest number of polygons in the conversion process. Once you have experimented with this a few times, you will have a better idea how to prepare your model for conversion.

4. If your model has any coincident CVs, as it will have on a sphere, then you will want to weld these after they have been converted to vertices in a polygonal model. Failure to do so will unnecessarily increase the complexity of your model and affect how it is texture mapped.

5. If you want the open ends of any number of primitives to be seamlessly joined in your polygonal model, you must take care to ensure that they convert to the right number of vertices at all adjacent edges.

    (a) By counting isoparms on either side of an adjacent edge, you can determine how many vertices you will get, depending on the conversion method.

    (b) If you need to match a closed edge to an open one of shorter or longer length, you may have to account for vertex count discrepancies in the poly model. A limited amount of manual control can solve the problem, but you must be careful with your technique, to ensure that either side of the edge gets the right number of vertices.

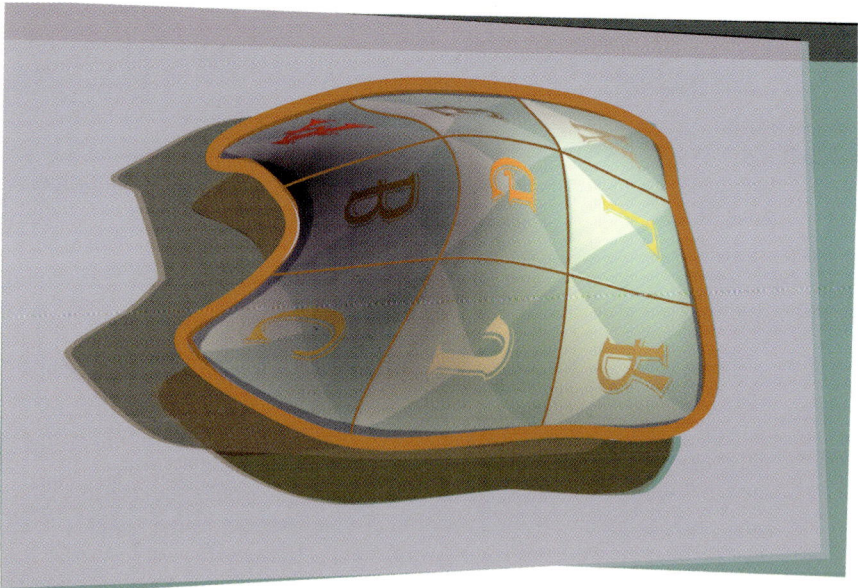

Fig 13.23
These backward, distorted texture coordinates are typical for a nurbs object. This can be overcome with either 3D paint or very careful planning, but isn't always worth the trouble

6.   Polygonal objects are usually easier to map than nurbs objects (Fig. 13.23) because of the more flexible rules that apply to polygonal UV editing. After you have converted your nurbs object, you may want to edit its UVs, to improve its texture layout. This will almost always be something you wish to do. The only time you won't is if you are modeling in nurbs specifically to take advantage of its embedded coordinates.

(a) Some objects are difficult to project as polygons, but can derive ex-celent coordinates from a nurbs base object. For these, you should retain the coordinates automatically generated for you during the conversion process.

Chapter 14: Shapes and Topology

Topology, or the part of it that is most closely related to CG, is the study of surface properties that remain the same regardless of deformations made to an object. When working with nurbs, it is especially useful to understand these properties because nurbs surfaces are made from a very small number of topological types. If you understand these surface types, you will be able to more quickly construct your target object out of nurbs surfaces (Fig. 14.1).

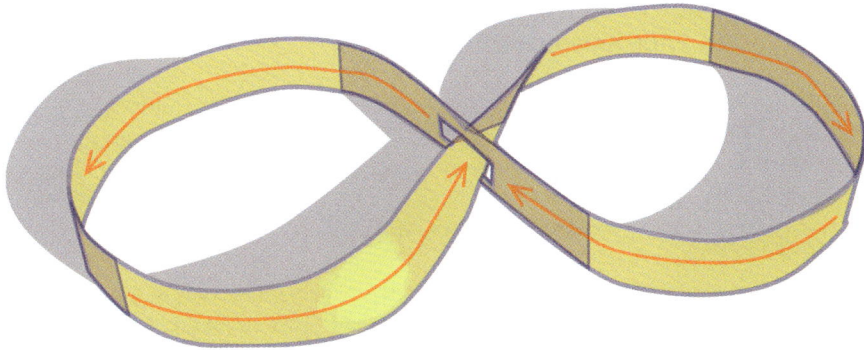

Fig 14.1
A Möbius strip. Because the ends of this object have been twisted before connecting them, one may trace a line across the surface of both sides of the strip without ever breaking the line or changing sides. This property is sometimes called *one-sided*, although at any given point on the object's surface, it does have another side

The mathematician Leonhard Euler wrote the first major proof on topology in 1736. The problem he described in the paper is known as the *Seven Bridges of Königsberg*. In it, he was asked to find a way to cross each of seven bridges bridges exactly once. By abstracting the problem into nodes that represented each endpoint and lines that connected them, he was able to prove that it could not be done. He went on to show that it could only be done if either none of the end-points or two of them (and only two) had an odd number of connections.

What is important about this problem is that it showed that the exact shape and dimensions, as well as the location of the bridges, were totally unimportant to the solution to the problem. In the same way, topology, at least the branch of topology relating to surfaces, studies surfaces that are, or are not, *homotopic*, or topologically identical. A nurbs sphere, cylinder, and plane are all homotopic surfaces because they are topologically identical. They could each be made into the other simply by moving their included control vertices to the right position.

All nurbs primitives are four-sided. This is a topological limitation. To use them effectively, you will have to be able to *see* this four-sided topology in everything you intend to build. The easiest way to accomplish it is to remember the unfolded carton from the first exercise. When you look at objects, analyze your target to discern how it will unfold in two-dimensional space. By doing this, you will be able to understand its topology, and know how to build the object using four-sided nurbs surfaces.

Certain shapes can be made with certain topologies, others cannot. Learn how to recognize opportunities to use one shape to create another.

How to See Four-Sidedness in Targets

Because nurbs objects are always four-sided, if you intend to build with them, you need to be able to break objects down into four-sided pieces. To do this, you must learn how to see four-sidedness in objects. For some things, like a sheet of paper or a cube, it is easy. For other things, like a triangle or the Y-shaped intersection of branches in a tree, it can be more difficult.

A cube is made of six grouped four-sided surfaces, the cone is made of one four-sided surface that has had one edge collapsed to zero in length, and a cylinder is a simple rolled four-sided plane (Fig. 14.2).

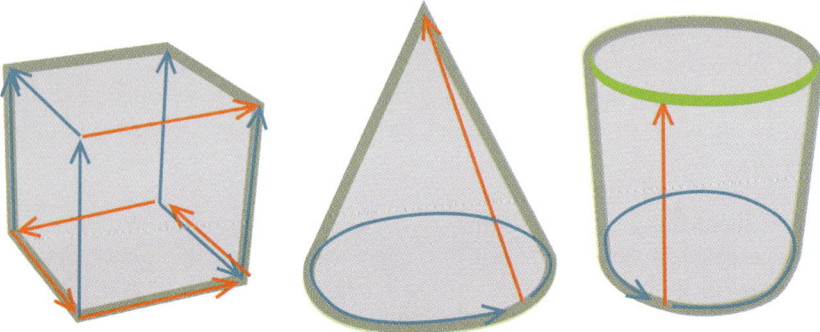

Fig 14.2
Four-sided primitive types

There are such a wide variety of shapes in the world that it can be hard to imagine all of them as four-sided patches. It can be done, but it requires an eye for topology. Look at something in your room and think of the folding carton exercise. How would that object pull apart and flatten out if it was a folding carton? Ask yourself if the object is made of one piece or more. If more than one, then each separate piece must be built of a minimum of one patch. Do the pieces have insets, holes, or projections? All of these things will require more patches. Practice draw-ing directly on objects, to find the best places to divide them into four-sided patches, and to give you a better idea what the curves should look like (Fig. 14.3).

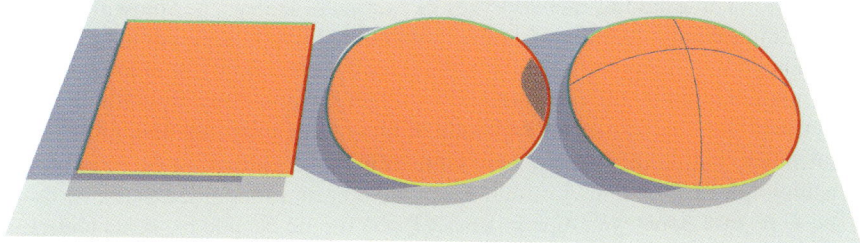

Fig 14.3
The deformability of nurbs surfaces is much greater than indicated in this illustration, but it does prove that even a square can be a circle, given the right amount of flexibility

Breaking an object into pieces is the first step to understanding four-sidedness. Unless you do this, you will have to imagine a square sheet of flexible material draped over your object and then sucked onto it, as if in a vacuum mold. Nurbs objects may be built this way, but can be extremely complicated to build because of the large number of isoparms required to hold the shape of every little detail in the target. If you break it into smaller pieces, it will be easier to spot pieces that can be made of four sides and those that need to be broken down further (Fig. 14.4).

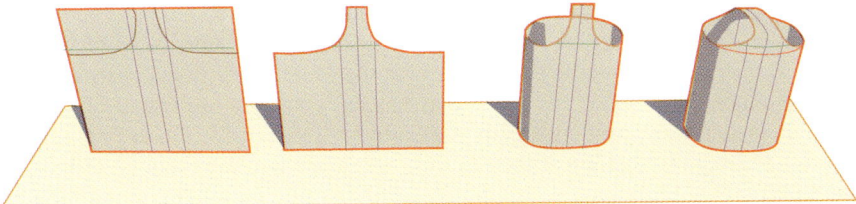

Fig 14.4
A three-holed primitive, like the Y-shaped intersection of two branches and the trunk of a tree

Topology/Schematic View of Things

In the movie *Terminator II: Judgment Day*, Arnold Schwarzenegger plays a cyborg from the future. In one scene, his character needs to find some clothes. To do this, he enters a bar and then analyzes its patrons to see which is most similar to his own dimensions. The filmmakers illustrated this with a series of shots where you see each bar patron from the cyborg's point of view (POV), with a wireframe mesh superimposed on different parts of the target persons' body. These highlights emphasized the basic dimensions of each of these body parts, but also provide an excellent illustration of a way to view subjects in the world around us. Each of the parts highlighted in the movie could easily have been a four-sided nurbs surface. In the same way, when you look at a model, you should be able to see its underlying topological characteristics, just as Schwarzenegger's character was able to size up bikers in a bar on a mission to steal clothes.

To build a complex CG object, it can be helpful if you first approach it schematically. Instead of worrying about specific shapes, you first determine the total number of parts and how they are attached to each other. This will allow you to understand the mechanical properties of your object better. It will also prevent mistakes that affect animation later in the art pipeline. After you have an idea how each part is related to the others, you can examine each part and try to understand the process that resulted in its final shape. When modeling with nurbs, this is not just a visualization exercise for students, but something you will do long into your career as a professional. It is not always obvious at first glance how an object was made, but it can be discovered if you pay attention.

The topological half of the carton project: balanced octahedral. In this illustration, one face of an octahedron, described by points *ABC*, is rotated out of position from pivot *A*. By looking at the octahedron's projected shadow, it is clear that edges *AB* and *AC* can only be coincident with the same edges of the parent object in three-dimensional space. In a two-dimensional construction, where all of the faces are planar, they must split apart at the seams. This is why, when mapping an object, CG artists typically tear their objects into *strips* when preventing distortion is a priority (Fig. 14.5).

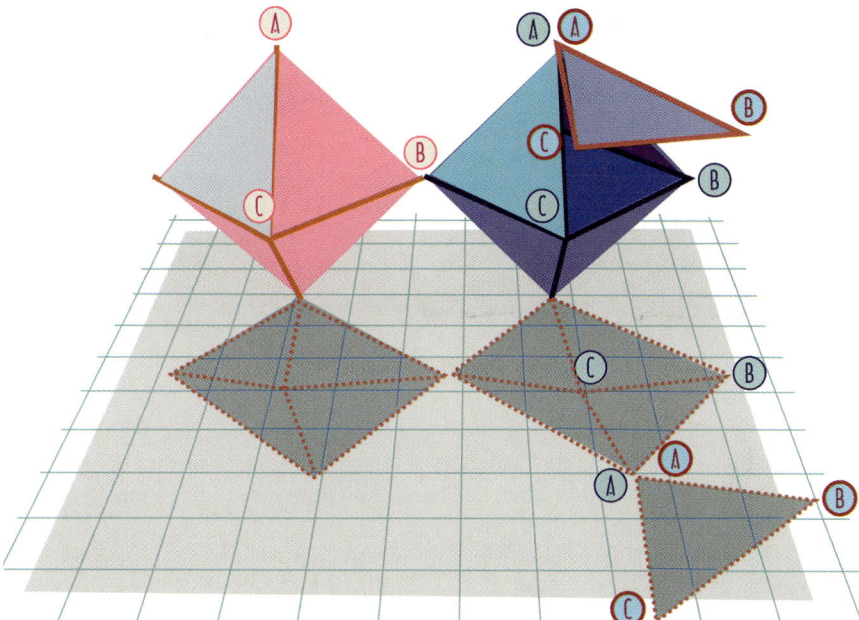

Fig 14.5
Topology of 3D space

The implications of this topological characteristic of polysets are huge. It is this simple fact that three-dimensional objects *require* three dimensions to retain their topological network intact that causes problems when this same 3D network must be turned into a 2D network for texturing purpose. The lost data from this lost dimension are visible in distorted coordinates and the number of seams in an object. This same problem is evident when a modeler attempts to build from drawings that fail to adequately describe the third dimension that must be absent from any drawing on a two-dimensional surface, whether a chalkboard or a piece of paper.

Here is a simple example of a lever made for the skewer of a bicycle hub. This object has some complex shapes combined with some simple ones, and none are well described using a primitive. In this case, each modification to the surface should be described with a curve (Fig. 14.6).

Fig 14.6
Complex curves become elegant surfaces

If you combine an object's schematic and topological properties, you will have a good idea how to build it, and which tools to use. With these factors known, you need only concentrate on your object's shape. You do not want to be puzzling over the shape of the object and topology or schematic hierarchy at the same time because these last two factors can affect your model so much that each time you see the topological structure breaking down a different way, the shape of all its parts will change as well.

Tool/Object Similarities

Sometimes, deciding which tool to use takes more time than any other single decision in the process of building a CG model. Just as you need to be aware of your object's topology, you should also be aware of the topological types your tools are capable of simulating. The more familiar you are with this characteristic of the tools at your disposal, the more efficient your workflow will be.

The first rule of surface tools is that the end product must have a U and a V direction. This means that either you will provide this information in a curve, or the tool will provide it for you by either default or modified values in its editable parameters. No matter what tool you use, these two values must be defined.

For a revolved surface, you define a profile curve, and the tool provides the other direction in the form of a formula described circle or circle arc. Whether you loft 2 or 20 curves from one to the next, each provides the U direction from the curves, and the V direction is calculated based on control points on the curves. In an extrude operation, you provide two curves, one for U, one for V, forming the topological equivalent of a cross shape.

For any nurbs surface, its interior is defined by the intersection of U and V isoparms that are defined by your curves or tool settings. These intersections create a grid network within your surface that may be used to further modify it. More importantly though, the intersection shape, two curves crossing at nearly right angles, is just as much a topological characteristic of a surface as the fact that it has four sides. This fact is important to keep in mind when selecting which tool to use. The boundary of the object is defined by the four-sided limit, but the shape of the object is defined by its internal grid intersections. Your tools generate this grid, and each tool does it in a slightly different way (e.g., revolve tool).

When the revolve tool generates a surface, it rotates a source curve around a pivot, generating a U surface based on the formula for a circle. A loft tool, on the other hand, connects the U direction of each of the source curves in a linear fashion, from one to the next, creating new V direction isoparms based on the position of control vertices on each of the source curves. A boundary patch tool will allow the user to define a surface by its border curves alone, or the border curves combined with out tangents of surfaces that lie upon those same curves. Extrusion defines a surface by its internal isoparms, and allows your application to create the boundary on its own, based on tool parameters and the shape of your source curves.

The number of options, as you may have noticed, is not that extensive. They are:

1. Boundary edges
2. Internal isoparms
3. One edge (U or V)
4. Combinations of the above

In addition to these surface generation types, surfaces may be modified through trimming and repositioning of control points. It can be confusing to see how many options most applications provide in their toolboxes, but if you can remember that all tools build surfaces with just the four basic options mentioned above, tool selection decisions should be easier to make. In polygons, the most important thing to remember is that your vertices need to be in the right place. With nurbs, it is your control points. No matter how many options you have, it always comes down to that. If you have to, you can always move the points using simple transform tools. In many cases, you will discover that is exactly what you want to do.

Shape Types

Here are some different shapes, as defined by the tools used to make them:

1. Basic primitive, parameter only adjustment
2. Basic primitive, manual manipulation of control points
3. Basic primitive, trimmed
4. Basic primitive, trimmed and combined with another surface
5. Basic primitive, trimmed, combined, made tangent with another surface

These shape types literally represent your range of options. Everything that looks like something else is just the same thing in a clever disguise. All nurbs objects are nurbs primitives; regardless how you created it, in the sense that they are all defined as a four-sided patch. Beyond the position of the points on your surface, it is the same as any other patch. Curve generation and projection are powerful tools for editing a surface, and as it so happens, the only other tools you have.

To achieve a likeness of your target is entirely dependent on your ability to put the points in the right place. You may be able to do it with a tool, but will probably have to manually manipulate the shape. If you understand your subject, have good reference, and know your tools, you will be able to model anything.

In other words, after all this technical discussion of nurbs curves and surfaces, your ability as a modeler is still totally dependent on your observation skills as an artist. Your observation skills will tell you if your tool did not produce the shape you need, and will tell you how to fix it. Do not allow your tools to direct your output, be an artist and direct the tools to do your bidding. If you don't get what you want, keep trying. There is always a way. Too many artists have poor observation skills and fail to recognize the difference between their goal and the results they get. Failure to recognize this is a key indicator that an artist is not paying close enough attention to either his subject, his work, or both. In these days of increased artistic and technological sophistication, don't be one of these artists. Learn to see (Fig. 14.7).

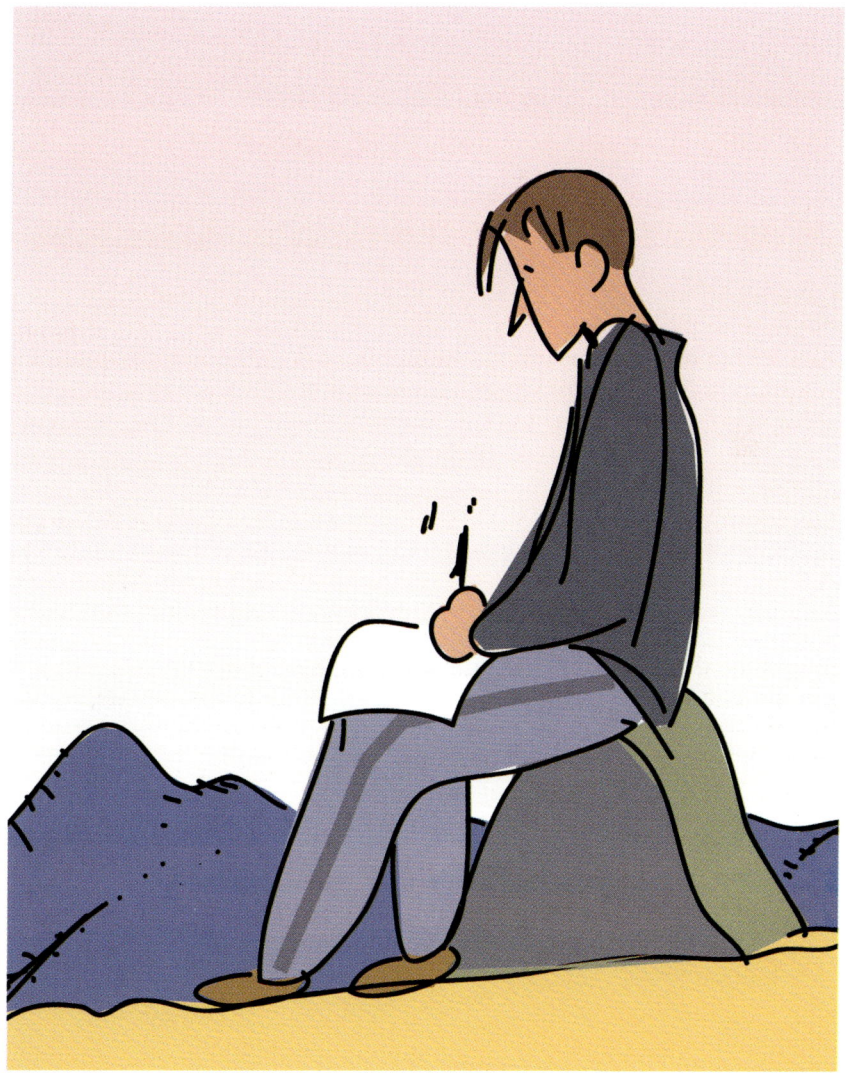

Fig 14.7
You, an artist

Chapter 15: Quality Standards

"Is it good enough?" is a question most people have asked at one time or another, for various reasons. It is a simple question that says quite a lot. Most importantly, it tells us that the person asking the question doesn't know what is, or is not, "good enough." It is a very important question to ask because it determines when a painting is finished, when a project is delivered, if a movie is released, or any one of many, many, other decisions are made. Even seasoned professionals aren't always sure when something is good enough, and will ask for multiple opinions before committing to a course of action.

Although standards vary, students of CG should have some idea what commonly accepted standards are in industries that use CG products. One of the most common mistakes students make, and almost all of them make this mistake, is that they tend to make their objects at such a high level of polygonal detail that they violate one of the most basic of standards: efficiency. It isn't done in opposition to the standard, but out of ignorance of it.

Here, then, are some basic standards you can keep in mind as you work, to measure whether the work you have done is "good enough."

Modeling standards. This book is about modeling, so the only standards under review are modeling standards. Where these standards intersect with other subjects, like lighting, texturing, or animation, this fact will be mentioned.

Clean geometry. Clean geometry, as described in Chap. 2, describes a model that is well organized and contains no overt technical flaws. This is a minimum standard. Any model that cannot credibly be described this way has failed the first test of professional quality.

Game-specific criteria. Geometry meant for use in the video game industry is held to a very high technical standard. On the other hand, it is not usually held to the highest artistic standard, except in triple-A titles. In addition to meeting the clean geometry standard, a successful game industry model will also be:

1. *Efficient.* It will have an absolute minimum amount of geometry and texture maps to define the structure and other attributes of the object.
2. *Cutting edge.* It will take advantage of the latest technological innovations in console hardware, specifically for the purpose of showcasing this technology, such as normal maps, as introduced in the first Xbox console.
3. *Obey engine limits.* Most video games use engines that have highly specific limitations or requirements. These vary from console to console, but these limits usually govern the size and bit-depth of texture maps (square,

power of two sizes is a common limitation), number of bones in an object for animation, file format types, and dimensions of interactive elements. Sometimes, the engine requires that an object be recognizable to the engine by a *flag*, or attribute, and the modeler will have to add these to the model. Whatever the requirements are, any model that fails to satisfy all of them will be insufficient.

4. *Art style.* There has been considerable latitude in this area with some games, but as games become more mainstream and more money is spent developing them, style standards are becoming more strictly enforced. When making a model for a client, you will demonstrate superior skill not by changing the style to suit your taste, but by matching exactly the style you are asked to work within. Violating style guides is considered bad manners at some companies.

5. *Art quality.* Although the "art" quality standard is rapidly being raised, video games still lag behind other industries in this area, probably because of console technology limitations that do not apply to prerendered graphics. Another limitation that affects this standard is that art directors in games generally have a different type of experience than their counterparts in film and design. Video game-specific experience is based on previous work, which only a few years ago was so limited by technology that it was impossible to take advantage of the abilities of extremely gifted artists. As that changes, the art standard is improving. At the moment, the area of greatest difference as far as models are concerned is in accurate environment dimensions. Although inaccurate dimensions distort an object, it is generally allowed in games, though this is changing.

6. *UVs.* Games have a very high standard for UV layouts, possibly higher than any other industry. The reason is that a good UV layout is not only just efficient for that object, but can also be reused to create numerous object modifications easily. A poor layout does not allow this kind of flexibility.

Film FX Criteria

Unlike games, the final output in an animation created for film is a rendered frame, a digital image file. The high game industry efficiency standard is not required in film for two reasons. First, the ability to edit the finished image itself allows artists some flexibility with their models. Secondly, film FX artists are not limited to the rendering power of a game console. Instead, they can, and frequently do, use dozens of high-speed processors working simultaneously on the same frame of animation. Another difference related to the output type is that film FX artists are not limited to working with polygons. Some studios use nurbs objects almost exclusively. Some use nurbs, polys, sub-ds, or custom geometry types. Whatever the mix is, it doesn't matter as long as it can be rendered into an image.

Film studios and film FX specialty studios usually pay top dollar for the best artists they can find. Studios have about a hundred years of experience finding and recruiting highly skilled art talent for the film industry. This has created a large pool of very talented artists in the Hollywood community, and this has in turn helped create a very high standard of aesthetic quality for the final product. In film, very little less than perfection is considered acceptable:

1. *Technical criteria.* The clean geometry rule applies to film work as well as games, though there are some differences. In film, texture maps are used much more heavily than in games, and at much higher resolutions. So, what is not acceptable in games for technical reasons may well be acceptable in a film, as long as the end result is a better image. The same is true of geometry. Whether it is nurbs, polys, sub-ds, or something else, the primary concern is that it is renderable. Therefore, although clean geometry is always appreciated, it is possible to be praised for work that contains numerous technical errors, as long as the errors do not affect the final render quality.

2. *Aesthetic standards.* There are artists who have literally spent months building simple objects like a tennis shoe for *Spider-Man*, or a naval vessel in *Contact*, or an alien spaceship in *Space Jam* because of the high aesthetic standard applied in film visual FX. Sometimes, the standard is "photo-real."

   (a) A photo-real standard implies that all dimensions are accurate, all colors are accurate, and all material properties are perfectly described. This is not usually possible to achieve, so the standard in practice is simply that the object in question is credible enough to be considered photo-real. To test this, objects are composited into background plates they are meant to be a part of, to see if they blend in well enough and are convincing. If not, they get sent back for more work.

   (b) It is possible to have numerous obvious mistakes and get away with them even when measured against a photo-real standard. The reason is that the *photo* in "photo-real" is a term that is most closely linked to lighting. If the lighting in a scene is photo-real, most objects in the scene will blend in regardless of errors. In *Spider-Man*, there are buildings where windows are literally cut in half and offset from their correct position, but this is almost impossible to spot because of motion blur in their scenes. In that example, the rendering "fixed" an error in the models.

3. Another standard is simply to match the style of the film. This is true of all films, but is most important for all-CG movies like *Cars* or *Shrek*. If your work, whatever it is, doesn't meet the style of the film, there is almost no chance at all that it will be used. There is a reason film studios pay five to ten thousand dollars a week for a good production designer, it is so that someone who knows how to design can save you a lot of time

by designing everything for you. It is true that production designers aren't perfect and will make mistakes, but it is still the job of the CG art staff to follow the style guides as closely as possible, within the limits of their medium.

These standards may seem generic, but they aren't much more complicated than this. There are many ways to violate these standards, but all violations fall under one of these two categories:

1. It contains technical problems.
2. It doesn't look right.

This book describes the majority of all technical errors you are likely to encounter. Because of changing technology, it can't ever be complete, but it is certainly enough to catch the majority of any errors you will make.

Problems related to whether your object looks right or not come down to your observation skills. This is literally the most valuable of any group of skills you may bring to a company. If your observation skills are poor, or you are lazy about fixing errors that you see, your work will always fail to completely satisfy this standard. If your observation skills are strong and you are diligent, you will excel.

Chapter 16: 3D2: Checklist and Projects

Clean geometry checklist; with additions for nurbs:

1. Surface direction must result in proper surface facing for rendering
2. Trim surfaces should not be used when they violate a renderer's definition of legal geometry
3. Triangular surfaces are to be avoided
4. Consideration of mapping requirements should be taken into account when designing a nurbs surface
5. Curves and surfaces should be made of minimum number of control points necessary
6. File naming convention must be followed, for example: lastname-firstnameProjectname.extension
7. File must be archive file to contain multiple files
8. All objects named
9. All objects grouped
10. All grouping hierarchies correct
11. All layers named
12. No unused layers
13. All shaders named
14. All construction geometry deleted
15. All null nodes deleted
16. Appropriate polycount (not too low to catch important detail, not too high for game engine)
17. No coincident vertices within the same polyset
18. No gaps in geometry, all objects are solid
19. No spikes
20. No bow-tie faces
21. No smoothing errors
22. No floating faces
23. No separated faces
24. Self-penetration not allowed

25. Object to object penetration not allowed
26. Object must be centered on 0, 0, 0, with its bottommost point at $Y = 0$
27. Pivots for all parts and groups should be positioned correctly
28. Nonplanar quads must be made planar or triangulated by hand
29. No n-gons
30. No distorted geometry
31. No distorted UVs
32. No wrong-way normals
33. No misaligned textures
34. No isolated vertices
35. Aspect ratio for all triangles and quads should be as close to 1.0 as possible. This does not mean that other aspect ratios are illegal, but that they are not ideal
36. Triangulation patterns should be well-ordered, neat, and follow shortest-edge rule wherever possible
37. Lamina faces are illegal
38. Coincident faces within the same polyset are illegal
39. Coincident faces between separate polysets are allowed
40. Nonparallel part-to-part intersections are allowed for the purpose of derezing only
41. Duplicate edges are illegal
42. Holes are illegal
43. All vertices must contribute to surface or texture border definition
44. Ragged edge shapes are not ideal. Borders must follow target border shape
45. Locked normals are illegal
46. Reference map path must refer to image in same directory as project file
47. Reference map must be correctly attached
48. Zero edge-length faces are illegal

Projects

3D2
Project 1
Airplane

Project type: Workshop
Time limit: One class period
Supplies/materials required:

   1.   Airplane reference

Instructions:

   1.   Select subject from examples provided and obtain reference
   2.   Open reference file
   3.   Trace reference images using nurbs primitives
   4.   Modify primitives as needed with component editing and transform tools
   5.   Deliver file. The file should contain:
      (a) Nurbs model of airplane

Criteria:

The finished 3D model should resemble source images very closely or exactly. The model file should be clean and free of obvious errors. The model should be as simple as possible. Excessively complex geometry, failure to match appearance of target, or quantities of geometry errors are grounds for failure.

3D2
Project 2
Boat Hull

Project type: Workshop
Time limit: One class period
Grading: Failure to deliver a satisfactory file by end of class will result in a half-point reduction to final grade

Supplies/materials required:

1. Boat hull reference

Instructions:

1. Select subject and obtain reference
2. Open reference file
3. Trace reference images using nurbs curves
4. Modify curves as needed with component editing and transform tools
5. Create surfaces from curves
   (a) Surface *may not* be edited as a surface. All errors in surface must be fixed by modification to its base curves
6. Deliver 3D file. The file should contain:
   (a) Curves on their own layer
   (b) Surfaces built from curves on their own layer

Criteria:

Surfaces built from curves should be distortion free. Curves should be made of the smallest number of CVs possible. File should contain a minimum of two surfaces that share an edge. Tangents at shared edge(s) must be correct.

3D2
Project 3
Motorcycle

Project type: Homework and workshop
Time limit: Five class periods
Supplies/materials required:

1. Drawing supplies

Instructions:

1. Select your subject
2. Create or acquire reference
3. Build nurbs model of motorcycle from reference

4. Build at 50:1 scale (1 m = 2 cm)
5. Convert model to polygons
6. Optimize polygonal model
7. Polygon limit: 5,000 triangles
8. Project and edit UVs
9. Create and assign texture map and shaders to all parts
10. Texture size limitation: all maps should be combined into one 1,024 × 1,024 map
11. Check model for errors against both polygon and nurbs checklists and fix all errors
12. Deliver an archived file containing the following:
    a. Two orthographic reference images, jpg format, no bigger than 800 × 600
    b. Nurbs model
    c. Polygon model
    d. Texture map

Criteria:

The finished model should resemble reference images closely, be free of obvious errors, technically sound, contain undistorted, well-packed UVs, and be in agreement with optimization goals. Violations of polygon *geometry checklist* will count against your grade at double their previous value.

Glossary

2D Two dimensional.

2D Projection The act of projecting three-dimensional objects onto a two-dimensional picture plane.

3D Three dimensional.

3D Paint A method for creating texture maps where the artist paints directly onto a 3D object.

3D Scanner A device that uses a laser to scan an object and capture coordinate data for its surfaces. These devices are most commonly used to capture or measure complex 3D objects.

3D Space Three-dimensional or virtual space.

Absolute Pertaining to a measurement of a definite fixed amount.

Acute Angle An angle of less than 90°.

Adjacent Immediately adjoining without intervening space; sharing a common border.

Aerial Perspective The effect of an accumulation of light reflected from minute airborne particles over great distances muting the color of distant objects.

Align To arrange according to a value derived from another object, especially position or normal. To arrange elements or objects so that they are parallel or straight.

Alignment The act of aligning to cause objects to be aligned.

Angle The measure of deviation of two points from a common location.

Anomaly In CG, an unexpected result for which there is no known cause.

Antialias A method to reduce contrast between adjacent pixels with different color values.

Application A computer program.

Arbitrary Axis An axis designated by the user, as opposed to the global axes of the global coordinate system.

Arc A curve in the shape of an incomplete circle or ellipse.

ASCII File A readable text-only file.

Aspect Ratio The height to width ratio of any given object. If an object's height is 3 and its width is 1.5, then it has an *aspect ratio* of 2. If it is the other way around, with a height of 1.5 and a width of 3, the AR = 0.5.

Assembly View A technical drawing of all parts of a given object, as they appear when joined to gether in their proper positions.

Attached Combined for the purpose of translation, but without losing individual identity.

Attribute A characteristic of any element in CG, usually governed by user-defined variables.

Averaged Normal The average of two or more normal values. Used to cause smooth shading at any given vertex or number of vertices.

Axis The line about which a rotating body turns.

Back-Facing Polygons Polygons whose normals point away from the desired direction, usually by 180°.

Bevel To cut at an inclination that forms an angle other than a right angle.

Boolean Operation When two or more objects intersect, the intersection boundary is calculated for the purpose of modifying one or more of the intersecting objects. In a *Union* operation, all polygons from all polygons that penetrate each other are subtracted, and the remaining polygons combined into a single polyset. In a *Subtraction* operation, the shape of one or more polysets is subtracted from the other. In an *Intersect* operation, all faces that do not exist within penetration boundaries are removed and the remainder made into a single polyset.

Boundary A line defining the limits of an area.

Bow-Tie Face An *n*-sided face (usually a quad) that has been twisted so that its normals, if triangulated, would be facing almost 180° away from each other.

CAD An acronym for computer-aided design.

CAM An acronym for computer-aided machining.

Card Geometry Usually one or two triangle planar polysets, combined with an opacity map to change the silhouette of the polyset. These are most often used to represent plants and trees.

Cascading Effect A series of actions that occurs in successive stages, each of which is dependent on the preceding one.

Center A point that is equidistant from the furthest bounding points of an object or collection of objects.

Checklist A list of items to be checked for compliance with project criteria or industry standards.

Child Node A dependent node.

Circle A planar curve where every point on its surface is equidistant from its center point.

Circumference The length of a circle.

Clean Geometry The contents of a 3D file when those contents are free of technical errors, well organized, and a good likeness of the subject.

Closed To join the endpoints of, and cause them to be inseparable.

Coincident Two or more vertices, edges, faces, or polysets that share exactly the same vertex coordinates.

Compatibility Capable of being used by more than one application without change.

Component A subordinate part of a geometric entity.

Component Editing The editing of a component.

Computer Graphics A group of technologies used to produce art with a computer. Although the term includes 2D graphics, its acronym, CG, is used almost exclusively to describe 3D graphics.

Construction Error An error that is the result of the construction process.

Control Point A point that lies off a nurbs curve and directly at either end, to define the curvature of the curve.

Converge When two or more things draw near to each other.

Convert When one geometry type is translated into another; especially when translating nurbs geometry into polygons or vice versa.

Convincing A CG representation that, whether or not it is perfectly accurate, is a credible representation of its target.

Coordinate The single-axis position of a given element. If plural, this can be a complete description of the location of a point of group of points.

CPU Acronym for central processing unit.

Credible Capable of being believed.

Cube A geometric primitive defined by eight equidistant points joined by straight edges that form three right angles at each point. In CG, a cube may be a solid or wire representation of this type of primitive.

Curvature Continuous Similar to *tangency*, but to a greater degree. Instead of tangency being held by one control vertex on either side of the respective endpoints of two curves, there will be a minimum of two control points with matching tangents on either side of the join.

Curve A collection of points whose coordinates are continuous functions of a single independent variable.

Curve Detail See *Curve Resolution*.

Curve on Surface A curve that has been projected onto a surface. Several methods are available to do this, their chief difference being that

some will project in a perfectly straight line and others project based on normals or other surface-specific values. Straight-line projection often changes the length of the projected curve, but surface-specific methods do not.

Curve Resolution The number of line segments used to define a curve. This is expressed as the length of the curve divided by the number of segments used to represent it.

Cylinder A geometric primitive defined by height and radius.

Cylindrical Projection A type of projection where UV coordinates are projected from a cylinder onto a usually cylindrical object.

Default A predefined value for a variable. Values of this type are used extensively in computer applications for two reasons: to have a value where the application requires one, prior to user input. To have a value that is understood to be common or standard.

Delete To permanently remove from the current scene or file.

Depth Axis The Z-axis.

De-rez To reduce the number of polygons or other elements in a given object.

Design The act of graphically communicating desired characteristics of an object or effect, and determining the appearance of it.

Design Choice To select between two or more options.

Diameter The length of a straight line that passes through the center of a circular object and terminates at either end where it intersects the surface of the object. This measurement type is not used in CG, but may be used to determine radius.

Dichromatic Distance An effect of aerial perspective where all colors are progressively eliminated until in the farthest distance only two remain: the primary light color and primary shadow color. A variety of tonal difference may exist, but will be shallow in extent.

Digitizer A device capable of recording coordinates based on the position of its base and the stylus-like pointer relative to its base. When used properly, the device can accurately recreate the surface of most three-dimensional objects.

Dimension The product of a measurement.

Direct Entry A method of modeling where the artist enters coordinates by typing them in instead of using the GUI or any tool to create them.

Directional Light A light that projects along parallel vectors only.

Distort To change the shape of something.

DPI Dots per inch. A ratio of the number of pixels to each unit of linear measurement. DPI is sometimes used to refer to non-English units of measurement.

Duplicate To copy every part of a given object's definition exactly.

Edge Straight-line segments that lie along the boundary of every polygon and serve to connect the vertices of one or more faces. This word has no meaning for nurbs geometry, where *curve* and *boundary* satisfy the same function.

Edge Layout The orientation of edges in a polyset. Because there is more than one way to connect vertices, the edge layout can have a strong effect on the appearance of a model.

Edge-Star Formation A group of five or more edges that share a common vertex.

Edit Point An element of a nurbs curve. It lies on the curve itself and defines position of a point along the curve, and tangents at the point.

Editing To modify.

Element A subordinate part of a larger geometry whole.

Elevation A drawing representing a view of an object that includes its height.

Ellipse A circle that has been modified so that it does not have a 1.0 aspect ratio.

Environmental Fog An effect in CG where colors become less distinct over distance. This imitates *aerial perspective*, but is usually a serious exaggeration of it that is used more to optimize renderings by eliminating detail than to achieve an imitation of a real-world effect.

Extraneous Unnecessary.

Extrude To project a face or group of selected faces along a chosen vector, and then create duplicates of the original faces at that location and connect them with new faces to the original selection of faces.

Eye–Hand Coordination The ability to coordinate visual information as observed through the eyes with movements of one's hand, especially when drawing or painting.

Often mistaken as the primary skill of an artist.

Face A polygonal plane defined by a minimum of three vertices and three edges.

False Gap When a polygon has a *reversed normal* and appears to be missing, but is not.

Flag A geometry element with an attached variable that is recognized by a render or game engine, but is invisible in a finished rendering.

Flicker When the renderer is forced to decide which of two coincident faces is in front of the other. Because they are *coincident*, it cannot determine that either is truly in front of the other. The renderer will then either try to draw both at the same time or it will switch from one to the other and back again. Either way, because the renderer alternates between two or more faces in the same space, the change from one polygon to the next will be noticeable as an alternating pattern.

Floating Face One or more faces that belong to a polyset but are not physically connected to the main body of the polyset.

Focal Length The distance between lenses in a camera. The greater the distance, the larger the lens elements and housing become, and the less distorted any image passing through the lens will be. A long focal length lens is called a *zoom lens*, and a short focal length is called a *macro* lens.

Fold Axis An axis around which a face or group of faces is rotated.

Four-Sidedness A CG object that has four sides, or, an object that is broken into pieces, each of which has four-sides. The ability to see how a real-world object may be broken down into four-sided CG objects without destroying its likeness.

Fractal A complex geometric pattern that repeats its larger details in successively smaller forms into infinity.

Fractal Complexity A quality of certain fragmented physical structures that, because they endlessly repeat at smaller scales, can be described as having dimensions that exceed their normal spatial dimensions.

Frame Rate The number of frames rendered in a real-time renderer per second. A common frame rate is 30 frames per second.

Game Engine Software designed to perform all functions necessary to allow a game to be interactively played.

Gap A condition where a polyset is missing one or more faces.

Geodesic Sphere A sphere built entirely of equilateral triangles. Spheres of this type can only have a certain number of triangles or they will not be complete.

Geometric Subdivision A method of measurement that relies on successive division of geometric primitives, like circles, squares, and triangles to derive measurements and position information.

Geometry An object defined by rules of mathematics that define the properties of points, lines, faces, surfaces, solids, and angles.

Global Axes The three major axes, *X*, *Y*, and *Z*, which intersect at global coordinate 0, 0, 0.

Global Coordinates A coordinate based on the location of 0 ,0 ,0.

Global Operation An operation that affects all things in a scene equally.

Global Origin The coordinate 0, 0, 0.

Graphic Communication The act or the product of communication with images.

Grid An arrangement of horizontal and vertical lines, spaced at equal intervals from each other.

Grouping An operation that combines objects under a common node.

GUI Acronym for graphical user interface.

Hard Edge An edge that, at either end, has a minimum of two normals with different values. Because the normals are different, any light calculation will result in greater contrast along an edge defined in this way.

Helix A spiral.

Hierarchy A nested arrangement of subordinates and superiors.

Highlight The brightest portion of reflected light on any given surface.

Hole A polygon with two or more complete borders, one inner and one outer, made of adjacent edges that form two or more unbroken loops.

Homotopic Topologically identical.

Horizon Line An imaginary horizontal line located at the center of a lens that can be used as an aid when drawing in perspective.

Hull An element of nurbs geometry that links control points with straight-line segments.

ID Acronym for industrial design.

Illegal UV Space Any coordinates either smaller than zero or greater than one.

Inaccurate Not correct, not exact.

Incised Detail A polyset or surface with an internal boundary defined by edges or curves, where all parts of the boundary are coplanar with their parent object.

Industrial Design A branch of design that specializes in the conceptualization of objects intended for mass manufacture.

Instance A data node that represents another object, for rendering purposes. An instance contains no geometry, but only translation information and the name of the object represented.

Interactive The quality of responding nearly instantaneously to input.

Interface The method by which a computer user interacts with a computer program.

Intrinsic Color An object's absolute, unchanging color value, regardless of lighting conditions.

Invoke To call up a command in a computer program, usually meant to cause the command to be carried out.

Isolated Vertex Any vertex that is connected to no more than two other vertices by edges.

Isoparm An interior curve of a surface, as defined by identical positions on either end of two nonadjacent surface borders.

Knot A component of a nurbs curve used to define and regulate how a curve flows through a given control point. The more knots are present, the sharper the flow becomes.

Lamina Two or more faces that share all of their vertices.

Layer A method for treating objects differently within an interface, usually by allowing items on different layers to be displayed differently, to more easily navigate what would otherwise be an excessively complicated image.

Left-Hand Rule A rule to define orientation of the three global axes. To visualize this rule, extend the left index finger straight up, the middle finger toward your right, and your thumb straight toward your chest. In this configuration, your middle finger is the *X*-axis, the index finger is the *Y*-axis, and your thumb is the *Z*-axis.

Legal UV Space All coordinates between the numbers 0, 0 and 1, 1.

Lens Curvature A quality of lenses that affects how reflected light is received. The greater the degree of curvature, the greater the degree of distortion, but also the more detail is received.

Light A virtual entity used to calculate the effect of casting photons of given attributes from a given location.

Linear Measurement A dimension derived from two points only.

Linear Perspective A method for projecting the image of three-dimensional subjects onto a two-dimensional plane.

Local Axis An axis defined within an object's attributes.

Local Origin The origin of a given object.

Locked Normals A condition where the normals of a polyset no longer react to lights in a scene because a lighting calculation already performed on it, usually in another application, has been baked into the object, preventing it from responding to new lighting conditions.

LOD Acronym for level of detail.

Loft To create polygons or surfaces by extension of existing faces or curves, usually by a specified distance or from one curve to any number of other curves arranged in sequence.

Manifold Geometry that may be unfolded flat without any overlapping part.

Mapping The process of creating matching topologies between different elements, usually used to describe attaching UVs to polysets.

Margin of Error An amount of deviation from a target that is considered acceptable, or as if no deviation was made.

Master Design Document A document intended to contain all information pertinent to the design of a particular thing or group of things.

Material A definition intended to simulate the appearance of different substances.

Material Schedule A description, in table form, of substances and the objects to be made from them.

Measurement A measured dimension.

Mechanical A type of object that is human-made and usually built of numerous moving parts.

Memory A physical repository for storing computer-generated data.

Mercator Mapping A UV layout that imitates the projection type used for globes that have been cut into elliptical strips joined at the equator. This is known as *Mercator projection* after the cartographer Mercator, who first used it.

Merge To fuse two or more things into one.

Misaligned A condition where objects that are meant to be oriented relative to each other or a common reference are not so oriented.

Möbius Strip A type of surface that, as a mathematical construct, has only one side and cannot be filled with properly oriented triangles.

Naming To name a node.

***n*-gon** A polygon with more than four sides.

Node A data flag that may contain information about any element or group of elements in a CG file. Usually used to store grouping, hierarchical, and connectivity data.

Nonmanifold Geometry that may not be unfolded flat without overlap.

Nonplanar A condition where at least one point of a minimum of four points does not lie within a plane as defined by any other three points.

Normal A perpendicular vector used to define the orientation of a geometry element.

Normal Map A texture map containing normal information from one object, as projected onto another object's UV set. This type of map is used in some renderers to represent high-resolution 3D information on low-resolution models.

Null Node A node with no attached data.

Nurbs Acronym for nonuniform rational Bezier splines.

Object The top node of a data entity.

Observation Skill The ability to see, understand, and communicate what one has seen.

Obtuse Angle An angle greater than 90°, but less than 180°.

Occlude To progressively block the passage of light.

Offset To translate from a specific point, group of points, or vectors.

One-Sided An object that has been flagged to the renderer as one which should be rendered on one side only, usually the side that defines the positive direction of its normals.

Opacity Map A texture that defines the degree of transparency of an object. These are typically grayscale images, where each gradient value corresponds to a certain percentile of transparency. Also called *transparency map.*

Open A curve or surface whose endpoints, whether they meet or not, are not curvature continuous and fused together.

Optimization The act of making a file more efficient, usually by removal of unneeded elements.

Organic A natural object, grown, not made.

Organization The orderly arrangement of data.

Organization Error Disordered organization.

Orientation The constant outward direction of any given point, group of points, or any other element.

Orthographic Aligned at 90° to the picture plane.

Overlapping UVs UV coordinates that belong to faces that are covered, partially or completely, by UV sets belonging to other faces.

Padded Numbers Numbers used as suffixes at the end of an object name. The *padding* consists of leading zeroes at the beginning of the number. These cause the numbers to sort properly in a computer. Failing to do this will result in the number "2" coming after the number "002" or "19".

Pan Moves the camera within a camera plane as defined by the current viewport.

Parallel Never convergent, always equidistant alignment of two or more linear things, like edges or curves (whether straight or not).

Parameter A variable that defines a specific value within a fixed formula.

Parent Node The top node of a hierarchy.

Periodic Curve A curve without beginning or end. To define a periodic curve, the endpoints must cross with at least two overlapping CVs on either side of the join, for a total of five CVs. These must all have the same tangent. If these conditions are satisfied, *and* the curve is identified to your software as "periodic," then it will be periodic.

Perpendicular Meeting at a 90° angle with a given location.

Perspective A system used for projecting a three-dimensional scene onto a two-dimensional surface.

Photon A virtual light unit consisting of various properties in common with a *ray* but with the added property that it can continue bouncing until all of its light energy is expended, causing a more accurate lighting simulation than ray tracing.

Pivot A coordinate around which a translation operation may take place.

Pixel The smallest visible unit used in computer-based raster graphics.

Planar A condition where all points in question lie within the same plane.

Planar Projection To project texture coordinates based on the normal direction of a single plane.

Plane A flat surface of determinate extent.

Point A dimensionless object with no properties other than location. In CG, flags and other properties may be attached to a point without changing the character of the point.

Pointillism A style of painting popularized by the work of Georges Seurat, inspired by the work of the Impressionist painters, including that of Claude Monet and Pierre Auguste Dominique Renoir.

Point Light A light source that casts light in all directions from its location.

Poly Budget The number of triangles, or polygons, allocated for a given use.

Polycount The number of triangles or polygons contained in a given polyset.

Polygon A geometric primitive containing a minimum of three vertices, three edges, and a face. It can have only one face, but any number of vertices and edges above the minimum.

Polyset A group of polygons, whether or not they are topologically contiguous, that are treated as a single object-level entity.

Prerendered Graphics Used to define the difference between using a sequence of image files as an end product from 3D objects that are rendered directly to screen, or *real-time graphics*.

Primitive A polyset defined by a parametric formula.

Production Design A trade specialty of designing the look or style of a given production. Production designers are most often employed in film, television, and theatre, but are increasingly working in the video game industry as well.

Project To push forward, usually in a perfectly straight line, either along a constant axis or a variety of normals, for the purpose of calculating intersections with geometric objects or elements.

Projection Plane The plane from which a projection is made, based on its normal direction.

Proportionate Similar to *aspect ratio*, the relative measure of related objects, or internal ratio of different dimensions within the same object.

Quadrilateral Four-sided, regardless of parallel or perpendicular edges.

Radius The distance from the center of a circle to any point on the circle. This is the most common method of describing a circle in computer graphics.

Real Time Something that is rendered immediately to screen, without noticeable intermission for the rendering process to complete.

Reference Source material used for the purpose of ascertaining information about target objects.

Reference Cube A construction object used to define an area of cubic space for the purpose of ensuring that all UVs projected with it as a part will be projected at the same scale.

Reference Map A texture designed to test an object's mapping coordinates for distortion, alignment, and orientation.

Relative Something dependent on external conditions for its specific size, scale, rotation, etc.

Render An image file created as an end product of calculations made in a CG application where three-dimensional objects are projected onto a two-dimensional picture plane, and then other calculations are made to determine the color of each pixel in the image, usually with a highly realistic image as a goal.

Renderer A software application that renders.

Rendering The process of creating a render.

Resolution In pixel graphics, this is the number of pixels in an image, usually represented by the number of pixels in X and Y, or horizontal and vertical. In polygonal models, resolution refers to polycount and curve detail.

Resolution Contrast A condition where two or more objects of differing resolution are either adjacent or near enough that their different resolutions are easily noted.

Resolution Limit The maximum allowed polycount or image size.

Reversed Normal A polygonal face where the normal vector is pointing 180° away from the front of the object.

Revolve To loft around a circular axis.

Right-Hand Rule The opposite of the left-hand rule.

Rotate To turn around an axis.

Rounding Error When a number is averaged to the next highest or next lowest whole number, its accuracy is reduced, or made errant.

Scale To change the size of.

Scan To import by the use of either a 2D or 3D scanner.

Schematic A way of looking at things that is more topological than object-specific.

Schematic View Drawings of an object in one or more orthographic views, drawn primarily as outlines. Also known as *plan view*.

Seam Used most often to define a break in a UV set between faces that have a common edge, but do not share UVs along the shared edge.

Selection Set An arbitrary group of components or objects, identified as belonging together by pick-based selection. These may be named, but this is not always true.

Self-Penetration When a part of an object intersects another part of the same object.

Shaded Display A graphic representation of a three-dimensional object where the object is drawn with filled colors based on the position and orientation of a light source in combination with the shape and normals of the object represented on screen.

Shading Anomaly A condition where the shading on an object has no apparent motivation.

Shape An object's combined attributes of boundary, surface orientation, and location of all points relevant to description of its every surface deviation.

Shortest Edge-Length Rule A method designed to help organize edge patterns by flipping them so that all edges are as short as possible.

Simulation An interactive software product with the goal of accurately predicting the outcome of user behavior in a given scenario.

Skeleton A topological representation of a skeletal system, where each joint connection is a transformation matrix, for the purpose of animating an attached model.

Smoothing A rendering effect dependent on averaged normals at shared edges between faces. The result is a smooth gradient from light to dark across affected edges, instead of a sharp line of contrast along the edge.

Snaps A tool that allows a user more exact control when positioning objects or elements in a scene. The tool allows a user to skip from one predefined unit to the next, effectively eliminating slight errors due to uncertain mouse movement.

Soft Edge A designation for an edge that has averaged normals at every vertex.

Sphere A geometry primitive whose points are all equidistant from its center. Created by revolving a semicircle around its full diameter.

Spherical Projection A UV projection along the normals of each face of a sphere.

Spike An out of position vertex, usually with very long trailing edges.

Spline A type of curve built from weighted control points.

Split Normal Two or more normals attached to a single vertex. The result of this condition is a hard edge when rendered.

Spotlight A light containing a minimum of the following parameters: light location, target location, and penumbra.

Station Point A location from which another thing is measured.

Stretched Coordinates A condition where the shape formed by UVs does not match exactly the shape of the vertices they are mapped to. The result is that any texture map applied to an affected polyset will be distorted. Most often, this term is applied to UVs that have either an identical *U* or *V* value. This happens when UVs are projected from a parallel, instead of perpendicular axis.

Structural Detail Vertices or control vertices that define a change in the shape of the object they belong to.

Structure The manner by which a thing is built, or the representation of objects that define the shape of an object or collection of objects.

Subdivide To divide a face into smaller faces, either by dividing from existing vertices or by adding new vertices at the center of all edges.

Subject An object designated as an absolute standard against which the likeness of a CG model may be measured.

Subordinate Node Any node that is below another in a node hierarchy.

Superior Node Any node that is above another in a node hierarchy.

Surface A flexible nurbs plane, capable of extreme deformation into nonplanar shapes, such as a sphere.

Surface Curvature The angle of inclination of a tangent at a location on a surface combined with arc length.

Surface Tension The degree of pressure at any given point on a surface, or lack of it.

Tangency When a curve's *out tangent* is equal to another curve's *in tangent* at a common point.

Tangent A line that is in contact with a curve at a given point and is pointing in exactly the same direction as the curve is moving at that point.

Tangent Break A condition where coincident endpoints of two or more curves are not tangent.

Taper To become narrow at one end.

Target A fixed standard against which the likeness of a CG model is compared.

Technical Error A mistake of a technical, rather than aesthetic, nature.

Texture An image file that is rendered onto any number of faces or surfaces for the purpose of describing the color of that object.

Texture Border An edge or group of edges within a polyset that have two or more UVs for every vertex.

Texture Coordinates Coordinate locators attached to polyset vertices and that have affixed UV position value in texture space.

Throughput The amount of data processed through a renderer by the CPU.

Tile A single image or object, to be repeated according to a formula.

Tiling Repetition of images or geometry as defined by a formula. The resulting pattern may be regular or irregular.

Tolerance An acceptable range.

Topology The study of shape-related networks, particularly the distinction between homotopic (similar) and nonhomotopic (dissimilar) shape types.

Torus A surface that is periodic in *U* and *V* and built as a full revolution of a circle around a center point that lies off the circle.

Transform To change the position of, usually by linear movement, but also by rotation or scaling.

Transformation Matrix A table of numbers that represent transformation values for all three global axes and all three transformation types; move, rotate, and scale.

Triangle A geometric body made of a face defined by exactly three points.

Triangulate To modify a polyset so that all of its constituent polygons are reduced to triangles by successively splitting all *n*-gons and quadrilaterals.

Triangulation Pattern The arrangement of triangles within a polyset, specifically, the ordering of triangle edges and how this affects the object's surface structure and its readability in wireframe.

Trim A section of a surface defined by either a closed *projected curve* or a group of open projected curves that together completely enclose an area. The area within the defined region may be defined as either *cut away* or *remaining*.

Tumble Rotate the camera in three axes around a fixed point, usually a selected object or component (your choice).

Two-Sided An object where the renderer has been instructed to render both sides of every face. This is not used for objects that will never be seen from both sides because it increases render time for the object. It is sometimes used to *save* render time, because a two-sided polygon can be used in place of a larger polyset, required to define the depth of an object correctly.

Up-Axis The axis that points in an upward direction. Also known as an *up-vector*. Most CG applications use *Y* as the up-vector, some use *Z*.

UV [1]Designates two axis directions within geometric parameter space for nurbs objects. [2]An alternate name for a texture coordinate.

UV Layout The pattern created by projected texture coordinates, whether or not they have been edited.

UV Packing A technique for compressing the amount of space required by texture coordinates, to eliminate the largest amount of wasted pixels in a texture map.

UV Projection The act of causing texture coordinates to come into being and be attached to vertices.

Vanishing Point The point at which all vectors converge. An element of linear perspective.

Vector A direction, as defined by the coordinates of a point and the world origin.

Vector Graphics Images based on curves, as opposed to pixels.

Vertex A coordinate in 3D space, used as a boundary for polygonal faces in quantities greater than 2.

Weld To fuse two or more geometry elements into one.

Wireframe A method of displaying vertex and edge geometry on screen without shading to describe faces.

World Origin The coordinate 0, 0, 0.

World Space The coordinate system used to contain all things in a CG environment, home to the world origin.

Wrong-Way Normal A polygonal face where the normal vector is pointing 180° away from the front of the object.

Zero Edge-Length Face A face whose edges are each zero units in length.

Zoom Moves the camera closer or farther away from an object, following a vector perpendicular to the viewport.

Sources

http://www.dictionary.com; results from dictionary.com are based on several different dictionaries, including the following:

- *Random House Unabridged Dictionary*, © 2006, Random House
- *Webster's New Millennium Dictionary of English, Preview Edition*, © 2007, Lexico Publishing Group
- *American Heritage Science Dictionary*, © 2002, Houghton Mifflin Company

http://www.wolfram.com; an excellent resource for anyone interested in Math. Used primarily for the chapters on curves and nurbs surfaces

http://www.wikipedia.org; principally for articles on concepts related to topology

Index

Printed in the United States